# Modernism's Print Cultures

# NEW MODERNISMS SERIES

Bloomsbury's *New Modernisms* series introduces, explores and extends the major topics and debates at the forefront of contemporary Modernist Studies.

Surveying new engagements with such topics as race, sexuality, technology and material culture, and supported with authoritative further reading guides to the key works in contemporary scholarship, these books are essential guides for serious students and scholars of Modernism.

## Published Titles

*Modernism: Evolution of an Idea*
Sean Latham and Gayle Rogers

*Modernism in a Global Context*
Peter J. Kalliney

## Forthcoming Titles

*Modernism, War, and Violence*
Marina MacKay

*Modernism, Science, and Technology*
Mark S. Morrisson

*Modernism and the Law*
Robert Spoo

*The Environments of Modernism*
Alison Lacivita

# Modernism's Print Cultures

*Faye Hammill and Mark Hussey*

Bloomsbury Academic
An imprint of Bloomsbury Publishing Plc

B L O O M S B U R Y
LONDON • OXFORD • NEW YORK • NEW DELHI • SYDNEY

**Bloomsbury Academic**

An imprint of Bloomsbury Publishing Plc

50 Bedford Square
London
WC1B 3DP
UK

1385 Broadway
New York
NY 10018
USA

www.bloomsbury.com

**BLOOMSBURY and the Diana logo are trademarks of Bloomsbury Publishing Plc**

First published 2016

© Faye Hammill and Mark Hussey, 2016

Faye Hammill and Mark Hussey have asserted their rights under the Copyright, Designs and Patents Act, 1988, to be identified as Authors of this work.

All rights reserved. No part of this publication may be reproduced or transmitted in any form or by any means, electronic or mechanical, including photocopying, recording, or any information storage or retrieval system, without prior permission in writing from the publishers.

No responsibility for loss caused to any individual or organization acting on or refraining from action as a result of the material in this publication can be accepted by Bloomsbury or the authors.

**British Library Cataloguing-in-Publication Data**
A catalogue record for this book is available from the British Library.

ISBN: HB: 978-1-4725-7326-1
PB: 978-1-4725-7325-4
ePDF: 978-1-4725-7328-5
ePub: 978-1-4725-7327-8

**Library of Congress Cataloging-in-Publication Data**
A catalog record for this book is available from the Library of Congress.

Series: New Modernisms

Cover design: Daniel Benneworth-Grey
Cover image © Flickr

Typeset by Newgen Knowledge Works (P) Ltd., Chennai, India

# CONTENTS

*Acknowledgements* vi
*List of illustrations* vii

Introduction 1
Types of modernist print 11
Print culture and the history of modernist studies 24

1 Sensuous print 37
   Bibliographic codes and the study of the page 44
   Art and the book 53
   Design, image and typeface 68

2 Print in circulation 87
   Networks 92
   Sites of circulation 104
   Finance, marketplace, celebrity 116

3 Purposeful print 131
   Educational print and the middlebrow 138
   Political print 150
   Copyright and censorship 162

Conclusion 171

*Notes* 177
*Toolbox* 179
*Works cited* 187
*Index* 209

# ACKNOWLEDGEMENTS

We would like to thank the series editors, Gayle Rogers and Sean Latham, for their most helpful initial ideas and suggestions, and for their valuable feedback on our manuscript. The anonymous reader of our book proposal also provided important advice. Many thanks go to David Avital and Mark Richardson at Bloomsbury for excellent support through the process of preparing the book. For help with research queries, we are grateful to Claire Battershill, Mark Gaipa, Lise Jaillant, Huw Osborne, Jennifer Sorensen, Helen Southworth, Alice Staveley, Nicola Wilson and Elizabeth Willson-Gordon.

# LIST OF ILLUSTRATIONS

I.1 *Wheels* Series 1. Courtesy of the Modernist Journals Project (searchable database); Brown and Tulsa Universities, http://www.modjourn.org 15
1.1 Claude McKay, *Home to Harlem* (1928), cover design by Aaron Douglas. © Heirs of Aaron Douglas/VAGA, NY/DACS, London 2014. 57
1.2 Vanessa Bell. Woodcut illustration for 'A Society' by Virginia Woolf. *Monday or Tuesday*. London: Hogarth Press, 1922. Courtesy of Manuscripts, Archives and Special Collections, Washington State University Libraries. 65
1.3 E. McKnight Kauffer, *Words and Poetry* by George Rylands. London: Hogarth Press, 1928. Image courtesy of the Bruce Peel Special Collections Library, University of Alberta, and the Modernist Archives Publishing Project (MAPP). © Simon Rendall. 69
1.4 Guillaume Apollinaire, 'Il pleut' from *Selected Poems* by Guillaume Apollinaire, translated and introduced by Oliver Bernard, Anvil Press Poetry, 2004. 74
1.5 Ilia Mikhailovich Zdanevich, 'Soirée du Coeur à Barbe'. Courtesy of the Merrill C. Berman Collection. 75
1.6 Margaret Thomson, 'Rajputana Village'. *Rhythm* 5.1 (1912): 5. Courtesy of the Modernist Journals Project (searchable database); Brown and Tulsa Universities, http://www.modjourn.org 80
2.1 Frank Shay and his travelling bookshop. 107
2.2 Café des Westens, Berlin, 1905. Photograph from *Kurfürstendamm: Berlins Prachtboulevard* by Peter-Alexander Bösel. Erfurt: Sutton, 2008. 112

2.3 *The Smart Set* May 1915 Contents. Courtesy of the Modernist Journals Project (searchable database); Brown and Tulsa Universities, http://www.modjourn.org 124

# Introduction

And here are posters in red in green all colors like my past in a word yellow
Yellow the proud color of the novels of France
In big cities I like to rub elbows with the buses as they go by
Those of the Saint-Germain – Montmartre line that carry me to the assault of the Butte
The motors bellow like golden bulls
The cows of dusk graze on Sacré-Cœur
O Paris
Main station where desires arrive at the crossroads of restlessness
Now only the paint store has a little light on its door
The International Pullman and Great European Express Company has sent me its brochure
      – *La prose du Transsibérien et de la Petite Jehanne de France* (Cendrars 28)

*La prose du Transsibérien et de la Petite Jehanne de France* (1913) hangs upon the walls of museums, yet is often described as a book. It can be folded into an envelope roughly the size of a modern paperback. It incorporates a long prose poem by Blaise Cendrars on the right hand side, and an abstract composition in watercolour by Sonia Delaunay-Terk on the left, the colours of which interpenetrate the spaces between Cendrars's words. There is also a Michelin route map of the Trans-Siberian Railway in the top corner. Delaunay-Terk and Cendrars described it as the first 'simultaneous book', a gesture towards the Simultanism that was exciting the Parisian avant-garde. Simultanism refers to the synthesis of fragmentary impressions from different places or times into a single image. Both Cendrars's poem and Delaunay-Terk's visual work end with references to the Eiffel Tower and the Ferris Wheel, two modern marvels which were associated with the urban experience of simultaneity because of the perspectives they offered on the kaleidoscopic phenomenon of the Parisian scene. Were all the copies of *La prose du Transsibérien* to be unfolded and pasted together, Cendrars maintained, they would rise to the height of the Eiffel Tower (Rabaté 60–61).

Although of course not every modernist work presents such challenges to genre categorization and disciplinary point of view, the blurring of boundaries in *La prose du Transsibérien* speaks to a widespread fascination within European and American artistic movements of the early twentieth century with disrupting the distinctions among poetry, painting, music and prose. Print itself began to escape the confines of the periodical's or book's page and to migrate across generic boundaries, concurrently with the modernists' creation of hybrid literary, visual and auditory art forms. Stephane Mallarmé's poem *Un coup de dés jamais n'abolira le hasard*, published in the international magazine *Cosmopolis* in 1897, exploited the technology of print, its words printed in different fonts and sizes, and the white space of the page intended as an aspect of the poem's meaning. Inspired by this poem, the painters Picasso and Braque both began to introduce words into their paintings in 1911. Vanessa Bell, a few months after being taken by Gertrude Stein to visit Picasso's Paris studio in early 1914, incorporated a bank cheque, railway timetable and commercial advertisements in her painting *Triple Alliance*. The ubiquity of print on Paris streets itself might have influenced Bell; as Jack Flam points out: 'Posters, signs, newspapers, handbills, advertisements, branded packages, and other accumulations of words covered the surfaces of walls and kiosks all over Paris, as can be seen in early twentieth-century photographs of the city' (136). Modernist printed texts frequently announced themselves through visual display, such as the 'rather unusual, gay Japanese paper' that Leonard Woolf went to 'a good deal of trouble' to find for the covers of early Hogarth Press publications (*Autobiography* 171), which were often issued in a variety of colours and patterns, disrupting the notion of an edition's uniformity.

Print was on the move throughout the modernist period; many artists viewed 'the book' no longer as merely a vehicle for the printed expression of ideas but as a material object to be manipulated as part of the experimentalism by which modernism was initially defined. The forms of modernist print multiply across books and their covers, across periodicals in which stories and poems nestle alongside advertisements for household appliances and clothes, into paintings where the pigment is not bounded by the frame, and onto walls where posters and handbills announce performances of startling new ballets or extraordinary operas. The works of modernism move from pamphlet to book to anthology, from deluxe limited edition, published privately, to cheap paperback sold at a railway bookstall, from obscenity to set text.

During the nineteenth century, as Jennifer Wicke has observed, advertising emerged as 'a radically new discursive practice' (1) which was initially dependent on the book and, later, the newspaper and magazine trades. 'The technology of print', writes Wicke, 'opened a space for the creation of advertisement' (3). By the end of the century, a series of innovations in printing technology, together with the introduction of wood-based (rather than rag-based) paper, had made the production of printed materials a far easier and quicker process. This at once served and further stimulated the desires of a greatly expanded reading public who became, in turn, the audience for the advertisements on which nearly all publishers soon came to depend. The explosion of commercially oriented printed forms in the 1880s and 1890s has received a great deal of scholarly attention, and has been identified as the matrix from which both mass culture and modernist print culture arose, in an often antagonistic relationship. By 1901, five thousand periodicals were being published in Britain alone (Eliot, *Some* 148), but by 1922, this figure was fifty thousand (Ardis and Collier 1). Among these fifty thousand were the little magazines which often defined themselves through resistance to the increasingly consumerist culture surrounding them.

In recent decades, the material forms of modernism have attracted increasing attention from critics. Landmark studies such as Lawrence Rainey's *Institutions of Modernism: Literary Elites and Public Culture* (1998) and George Bornstein's *Material Modernism: The Politics of the Page* (2001) have inspired and informed a wealth of subsequent research projects. This development should be understood in terms of two larger movements in literary studies: the development of 'book history' in the 1980s, and its gradual expansion into a broader notion of 'book studies' or, more commonly, 'print culture studies' over the following decades. In 2003 Jonathan Rose, one of the leading figures in the establishment of book history, published an article surveying developments in this interdisciplinary academic field. He began:

> Historians have always used documents to reconstruct the past, but only in the closing years of the twentieth century did they come to understand that documents themselves have histories. They had not truly appreciated that earlier, no more than a fish appreciates the water. But certainly after Elizabeth Eisenstein's *The Printing Press as an Agent of Change* (1979) historians began to ask, in a methodical way, how the vast mountains of paper called into existence by all literate societies were created, reproduced, disseminated, read, stored and (in some cases) destroyed.
> 'Book history' is the best (or least inadequate) name for this new academic frontier, as long as it defines 'book' broadly to take in periodicals, manuscripts, letters, ephemera, and even websites, as well as books per se. (11)

The traditional methods of textual scholarship and bibliography have been transformed through the insights of book history, with its theories about textuality, about the influence of the material form of a text on the way that it is read and interpreted, about the institutions of literary culture, and about the lifecycle of the text and its transmission from author to reader. In turn, the expanding range of research in the field has led scholars to seek a new name to describe it. Rose's 2003 article was boldly titled 'The Horizon of a New Discipline: Inventing Book Studies', and proposed that 'Book Studies' was a better label than 'Book History', since it could name a new interdisciplinary academic project designed 'to explore the past, present, and future of all forms of written and printed communications' (12). 'Book Studies' did not catch on very well, but the expansion of the field, in its disciplinary and conceptual aspects, was recognized, and has resulted in a widespread adoption of the alternative description 'print culture'.

This term, which has the advantage of not naming one specific form of printed matter, brings books into relationship with periodicals and other, more ephemeral forms such as pamphlets, chapbooks, posters and postcards. As Leslie Howsam writes in

*Old Books and New Histories: An Orientation to Studies in Book and Print Culture* (2006), 'for those whose interest focuses on post-Gutenberg periods in the west the compelling term is *print culture*, which encapsulates the material nature of the printed word as well as its cultural context. It privileges such ephemeral forms as newspapers and periodicals equally with the apparent solidity of bound volumes and accords advertisements as much attention as canonical texts' (5). The term 'print culture' brings its own complications and risks (see Dane, *Myth*), and might be used differently in different areas of study (Dane, *Blind Impressions*), yet it has become the preferred term, especially for those working on the history of twentieth-century authorship, reading and publishing. We are persuaded by Ann Ardis and Patrick Collier's justification of their own choice of term, for the title of their collection *Transatlantic Print Culture, 1880–1940: Emerging Media, Emerging Modernisms* (2008). They argue that: ' "print culture" defines a more inclusive field of study than either "print media" or "book history" ', and point out the relevance of Raymond Williams's use of 'culture' as a key word for mapping ways of life, patterns of ordinary behaviour and the meanings of institutions in particular periods ('Introduction' 3–4). In this evolving area of print culture studies, the emphases are on the collaborative editing and production of printed materials, their material and visual aspects, their physical condition, their circulation in the marketplace, and the ideological dimensions of these processes.

In the specific context of modernist studies, recent research has responded to this burgeoning interest in print culture by focusing on the original publication contexts of canonical figures, transforming our understanding of them by exploring their professional networks and their involvement in editing, publishing and marketing. As we will discuss in Chapter 2, the 1890s and the decades following saw the development of the small press movement and, alongside this, the rise of little magazines. Small presses – such as the Hogarth Press or Contact – and magazines – such as *The Little Review* or *Rhythm* – fostered new forms of collaboration among authors, editors, publishers and artists, and offered crucial publication opportunities to unknown writers. They are central to current research on modernism's print cultures. Yet many of the more surprising insights generated in this field of study relate to the commercial side of print enterprises: the vigorous activity of modernist authors and artists in promoting sales of their work; the showcasing of modernist texts and images in 'glossy' periodicals such as *Vanity Fair* (1913–1936) which were financed increasingly by advertising; the republication of modernist novels in cheap paperback editions (such as Penguin Signet's 1948 edition of *A Portrait of the Artist as a Young Man*); or the discussion of colourful figures such as Gertrude Stein in the daily press. All these things contradict the notion of modernism as an artistic practice wholly committed to aesthetic values and maintaining, as the American writer Hamlin Garland put it in 1896, 'an attitude of superb indifference to the Board of Trade and department stores' (Bergel 157).

In accordance with the aim of the 'New Modernisms' book series, this volume will explore scholarship on print culture as an aspect of modernist studies that has expanded and gathered force since the early 1990s. At the same time, we show that print culture has been part of modernist studies since its inception. In the modernist era itself, many writers, artists and critics took a great interest in developments in printing, book design and journalism, while the earliest academic bibliographies of modernist publishing appeared in the 1930s and 1940s. Some of the most prominent modernist writers – for example, Virginia Woolf, Ezra Pound and T. S. Eliot – were profoundly aware of the complexities of the media ecology of their time and also, as our book will show, wrote frequently about print culture. In more recent decades, groundbreaking books and articles on the material, commercial and political dimensions of modernist book and magazine publishing have changed the way that we think about the relationships between art and commerce. Concurrently, digitization projects have made periodicals and material from publishers' archives available online, greatly expanding the scope for research.

There has, as yet, been no attempt to survey this field as a whole, or to account for the conceptual shifts which have caused this explosion of interest in modernist print cultures. The task does seem almost impossible because the variety of work done is so great. But by providing a guide to the most influential trends in this very active area of scholarship, we can at least suggest ways into the field for researchers and students who are new to it. This book is a guide to critical directions in the study of modernism's print cultures, and therefore, its 'primary' materials are, in effect, secondary texts. We focus for the most part on criticism published since the 1990s, examining the emerging discourse of print culture studies within the larger context of the New Modernist Studies. Yet, as the third section of this introductory chapter will demonstrate, the study of modernist print has a long history. Throughout the book, therefore, we acknowledge the earlier scholarship in the areas of textual scholarship, book and publishing history, and periodical studies on which newer research on modern print culture builds. The era of literary history covered by this volume, and by the critical materials it discusses, ranges from about 1890 until 1945. This includes the period (from the 1910s to the 1930s) that is most closely associated with high modernism, at least in a metropolitan context. Extending forwards into the Second World War years enables us to include recent scholarship on late modernisms and colonial modernisms. Extending backwards into the 1890s allows for discussion of the little magazines of that decade and the influence of Victorian fine printing, as well as for consideration of nineteenth-century periodical studies, which gathered force in the 1970s and 1980s – rather earlier than modernist periodical studies.

The 1890s, as well as being the decade when several of the aesthetic movements which coalesced into 'modernism' began, was also a turning point in the history of print culture. Ann Ardis neatly explains why:

> Although the circulating libraries still monopolized the literary marketplace in England in 1890, the next five years brought many changes in the publishing industry. Changes in international copyright law; the increasing effectiveness of literary agents in brokering contracts; attempts to expand the influence of the Society of Authors (a professional union for writers); publishers' increased use of advertising; changes in the format of the popular press; and the establishment of new venues for publication (both journals and publishing firms): these innovations in the publishing industry altered considerably the relations among authors, readers, and publishers. (*Modernism* 53)

Ardis focuses on England, but in other national contexts, similar changes were happening, often as a result of the export of industrialized book-trade models from France, Germany and other European contexts. Over the decades covered by our study, many further changes happened in the areas mentioned by Ardis. But the next really major shift coincided, roughly speaking, with the end of the era which we now tend to designate as the 'modernist'. The Second World War had major effects on all types of publishing enterprise, though these varied from one country to another. In *Under Siege: Literary Life in London 1939–1945* (1977), Robert Hewison describes the 'grand slaughter of magazines' (11) that occurred in Britain during 1939 and 1940, partly as a result of wartime paper rationing and a climate of uncertainty, but also because of competition from other media. Magazines which ended as the war began include *The Criterion*, *The London Mercury*, *New Verse* and *New Writing*. Hewison also points to the demise of many small presses at a similar period, and emphasizes the increased importance, to readerships at the time and to literary historians in later eras, of those magazines and presses which did survive. The effects of the war on North American publishing were less stark, but the postwar decade saw enormous changes, on both sides of the Atlantic, in the industrial and economic structures of publishing. As Richard Ohmann observes: 'Publishing was the last culture industry to attain modernity. Not until after World War II did it become part of the large corporate sector, and adopt the practices of the publicity and marketing characteristic of monopoly capital' (22). Perhaps as a form of resistance to this corporate publishing industry, a new generation of independent presses and small magazines arose in several countries during the postwar decades, although many of those involved retained a conviction, as Elliott Anderson and Mary Kinzie put it in *The Little Magazine in America: A Modern Documentary History* (1978), 'that the advances in publishing technologies and the conglomerations of their economies militate against the cultural coherence of the past' (4).

In geographical terms, the primary focus of this book will be on anglophone print cultures in Europe and the Atlantic world, since this is where the bulk of recent research has been concentrated. However, modernism was an international movement, and there is important current work on Russian, French, German and other avant-gardes. Print marketplaces do not, of course, necessarily coincide with nation states, even though national frameworks often determine aspects such as copyright regulation, pricing regimes, or postal and import regulations. Marketplaces can operate at a sub-national or regional level, or be based on minority languages – examples can be found in Wales, Quebec, the American mid-west and many other locations. Literary marketplaces can also operate at a transnational level, as in the book market in the British empire over the nineteenth and early twentieth centuries. Furthermore, exchanges between nation states are often mediated through print culture, as the essays in Robert Fraser and Mary Hammond's major collection *Books Without Borders: The Cross-National Dimension in Print Culture* (2008) so well demonstrate.

Andrew Thacker points out that 'an earlier generation of critics tended to talk about the international nature of the "little magazine" spawned by modernism, as if one type fitted all manifestations of the genre' (1–2). In this book, we will be drawing on some of those earlier studies, which constructed modernist print forms as cosmopolitan and border-crossing, arguing that these remain relevant since even the most locally anchored small presses and magazines usually shared the vision of modernism as an international artistic community. At the same time, we will take account of recent research focusing on the role of print and book culture in constructing specifically regional or national cultural paradigms: examples include Sascha Bru's work on Dutch avant-garde periodicals, Dean Irvine's research on Canadian modernist publishing, David Carter's book on Australian print cultures and modernity, and Tom Lutz's account of American regionalism.

The study of print culture often begins with a focus on aspects of design, such as illustration, typography and cover art, as well as on material dimensions such as paper, printing processes, pricing and distribution. It encompasses, as well, attention to the literary marketplace, and to networks of editors, publishers, reviewers and agents. And it also extends into considerations of audience, as researchers explore the kinds of readership addressed and constituted by different types of printed materials, and seek to recover information about readers' interactions with modernist publications. The structure of this book follows this three-part process, concentrating, in Chapter 1, on the physical and visual aspects of modernist printed objects; in Chapter 2, on the circulation of those objects in the marketplace; and in Chapter 3, on the political and educational dimensions of print enterprises. These chapters are framed by the opening accounts offered in the remaining two sections of this Introduction. The first, 'Types of modernist print', explores the diverse forms of printed material which constitute the archive of modernist publishing, and examines the ways that these forms have been categorized and catalogued, as well as the meanings that critics have ascribed to them. The second section, 'Print culture and the history of modernist studies', explores print culture as an aspect of the intellectual and disciplinary history of the field.

Each of the three main chapters has an introduction and three topic-based sections. Chapter 1, 'Sensuous print', is about the material dimensions of modernist print and the changing ways in which they have been analysed by critics. The first section discusses critical methods for studying 'the page', the book as object, and the serial, including commentary on Jerome McGann's notion of the 'bibliographic code' and related concepts. The second section explores book art, recent research on collaborations between artists and writers, and the renaissance of fine printing which happened partly in reaction to the move towards mass-production of books in this era. In a third section we consider aspects of design, noting the influence of changing print and photographic technologies, and exploring research on typographical experiment as well as on dust jacket advertising.

Chapter 2, 'Print in circulation', concentrates on the commercial and collaborative aspects of print culture. The first section examines the current critical emphasis on the networks of authors, editors, designers, agents, publishers and reviewers which sustained modernist literary production, and also points to the developing critical interest in modernist small presses. This interest has, to date, focused almost entirely on the Hogarth Press, but other presses, including Hours, Contact, and Cuala, are beginning to attract attention. In a related area of research, archival explorations of editorial intervention and revision have uncovered practices of both collaboration and control in modernist literary production, and have considered the effects of these on the status and reception of works such as Eliot's *The Waste Land* or Djuna Barnes's *Nightwood*. In the second part of the chapter we turn to sites of circulation, ranging across bookshops, libraries, cafes and performance venues. This section also considers the developing scholarly interest in geographies of modernist print: that is, the circulation of print artefacts through regional, national and transnational marketplaces. Lastly, we move to the topic of financing modernist publication, exploring recent interpretations of attitudes to advertising, the subsidy of art publications through mass-market print ventures and modernist promotional activity in the mainstream press and broadcast media.

Chapter 3, 'Purposeful print', explores print initiatives which had a clear agenda, and the critical strategies which are being used to interpret these. A section on educational print encompasses commercial and philanthropic appeals to aspiration, as evident in projects such as paperback publishing, reprint series and book clubs. These initiatives have been the focus of some of the work in the rapidly expanding field of middlebrow studies. The next part of the chapter is on political print, and discusses publications centred on protest and/or addressed to minority audiences, including the black press, the suffrage press, and radical print. These types of publication are at the centre of current research on print networks and print activism. A shorter final section examines the legal context to modernist publishing, referring to new work on copyright and censorship.

## Types of modernist print

'Print culture', in an early twentieth-century context, encompasses many types of printed product, including journals, newspapers, pamphlets, artists' books, chapbooks, posters, postcards and other ephemera, as well as conventional books, which themselves come in a range of formats, and may be published in series or in multiple editions. There are various ways of categorizing these different types of publication, although none of the possible categories is very stable, and there is a good deal of messiness at the boundaries. It is crucial, nevertheless, to look at how different critics, and different projects, have set out categories for analysing print media, and to explore the challenges they face in doing this.

The most obvious distinction is between book and serial publications. In his work on what he terms 'periodical time', James Mussell defines serials as being

> established through the interplay of sameness and difference, where changing content is presented through a set of features that recur, issue after issue. No article is encountered in

isolation, but sits alongside others on the page, in the issue, and in the issues that have appeared previously; equally, each issue reminds readers of those that have come before and promises more to follow. ('Matter' 1)

In broad terms, this difference between the serial as a repeating print event and the book as a one-off print event, corresponds to the difference between two academic specialisms: book history and periodical studies. But these two areas of study have many points in common, and our volume has been designed to overcome the division by considering books and serials together, as part of a larger modern print ecology.

We have just used the term 'periodical studies' rather than 'serial studies'. In this, we are following current academic practice, but it is important to note that the terms 'periodical' and 'serial' are not quite interchangeable. The category of 'serials' is often used in a more inclusive sense, encompassing newspapers as well as magazines, together with newsletters and books issued in parts. 'Periodicals', in the context of literary studies, usually refers to magazines. As Laurel Brake notes in her discussion of Victorian print culture studies, in the scholarship of the middle decades of the twentieth century, 'the use of the term "periodicals" . . . was a means by which the newspaper press was initially and apparently excluded. While the overlap of high culture periodicals with books was acknowledgeable, that of newspapers and books was not' ('On Print Culture' 129). In recent years, the analysis of newspapers has become well established in Victorianist literary scholarship (Altick; Hewitt; Price, *How*; Rubery), and the interdependence of the serial press and the book trade have been more fully acknowledged. In her book *Print in Transition, 1850–1910: Studies in Media and Book History* (2001), Brake summarizes the change:

> Where once I saw 'periodicals', I now see the wider and deeper category of serials, which includes newspapers and part-issues. Where I saw a contained historical archive, I now see a continuum of journalism and media, all of which are historical. And where I saw a disjunction between periodicals and books in the nineteenth century, I now view series and books as part of the same economy, both culturally and specifically within the period's publishing industry. (xiii)

Brake's comment draws attention to the need for interdisciplinary approaches to the study of newspapers. Recent work on twentieth-century popular print combines approaches derived from cultural and media history with formal and discourse analysis. For example, Adrian Bingham has done important research on the interwar and mid-century popular press, exploring in particular the mediation of discourses of gender and sexuality in British dailies (*Gender*; *Family*) and the ways in which ideas about reading practices shaped the layout and content of newspapers ('Putting').

From the perspective of literary studies, the major contribution in this area is Patrick Collier's *Modernism on Fleet Street* (2006). Collier points out that 'the troubling cultural centrality of newspaper journalism is hard to miss, as it is a significant motif in the works of canonical modernist authors', adding that, 'the narrative of anxiety about journalism has long been part of our understanding of modernism, which was seen for years as a rejection of mass culture in all its forms' (2). At the same time, he notes, few previous studies have actually foregrounded the relationship between modernism and journalism. This has now become a lively area of scholarly activity. Recent research has revealed the level of attention to modernists in the US daily press (Leick), analysed the role of papers such as the *Daily Mail* in creating a masculine readership for modern British novels around the turn of the century (Wild, 'Watching'), discussed the publication of proto-modernist American works by authors such as Stephen Crane and Henry James in instalments via newspaper syndication (Lutes) and explored the newspaper work undertaken by major modernist authors such as Djuna Barnes and the way it influenced their literary writing (Warren). Space does not allow us to consider newspapers in depth, but as they are often very relevant to discussions of the reception of modernism, as well as to more theoretical considerations of periodical time, they will be brought into this volume occasionally.

Brake argues that in the nineteenth century, many periodicals 'were contingent on the book trade' – for instance, quarterly reviews, whose primary subject matter was new books – while 'authors and publishers came to view the periodical press as an extension of their sphere' (*Print* 3). This interdependence continued, of course, into the twentieth century. Modernist books and journals were often designed by the same artists, produced on the same presses, sold in the same bookshops and read by the same people. And in generic terms, the distinction between the two forms becomes unclear when we come across a publication that will not fit easily into either category. For example, anthology series such as Amy Lowell's *Some Imagist Poets* (1915–1917) and Edith Sitwell's *Wheels* (1916–1921) are included in the online *Modernist Journals Project* (MJP) (Figure I.1). This suggests a notion of them as 'annuals', yet they might equally be understood as book series. Or what about a single-issue journal, such as *New York Dada* (1921) or *Fire!!* (1926)? And do Wyndham Lewis's journals *Blast* (1914–1915) and *The Tyro* (1921–1922) really constitute serials, when they had only two instalments? Even newspapers, apparently the most ephemeral of serial forms, could blur the boundary between book and serial. James Berkey, as part of his research on soldier newspapers of the Spanish-American War, has identified one paper, the *Co. F. Enterprise*, which published only one 'small souvenir edition', chronicling the adventures of the Thirty-Third Michigan Volunteers (161). Finally, what do we do with serial publications with 'book' in their title, such as *The Yellow Book* (1894–1897), each issue of which appeared as a bound volume, or *The Chap-Book* (1894–1898)?

The title *The Chap-Book* evokes the earlier genre of the miscellaneous small book or pamphlet, published in the hand-press period (from the fifteenth- to the mid-nineteenth century) and sold by a travelling 'chapman' or pedlar. The contents were generally somewhat ephemeral texts such as political or pious tracts, nursery rhymes, ballads, verse, folk tales or almanacs. In his chapter on *The Chap-Book* in the North American volume of *The Oxford Critical and Cultural History of Modernist Magazines*, Giles Bergel observes:

> Although formal and thematic unity is more often found in monographs than in periodicals, this does not mean that the only possible history of the magazine is the magazine itself, or a bibliography of its contents. *The Chap-Book* had forerunners and imitators; relations with other authors, other publishers, and readers; and commercial and cultural priorities peculiar to itself. The methodology of this chapter is derived from book history, and the situation of that history within the regional, national, and international milieux in which the magazine circulated. (155)

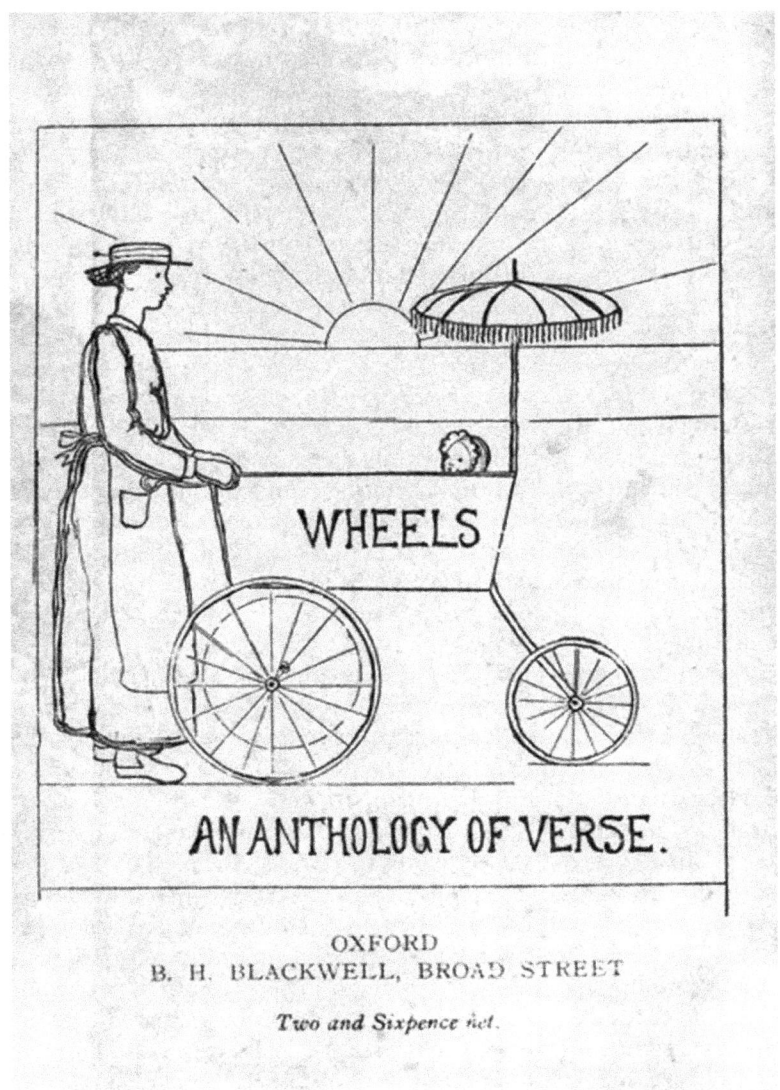

FIGURE I.1 Wheels *Series 1. Courtesy of the Modernist Journals Project (searchable database); Brown and Tulsa Universities, http://www.modjourn.org*

*The Chap-Book* was established by Herbert Stone and Hannibal Kimball, who had also set up a publishing firm in Chicago. It often printed short works by authors whose books were published by Stone & Kimball, as well as notices of the firm's forthcoming publications. Stone wrote in an 1894 letter: 'To speak plainly *The Chap-Book* is no more nor less than a semi-monthly advertisement and regular prospectus for Stone & Kimball' (Bergel 157). Like the mass-market consumer magazines of its day, *The Chap-Book* somewhat resembled a commercial catalogue. At the same time, its innovative and decorative design features, as well as the binding service for complete volumes which it offered to readers, meant that it soon became a collector's item.

*New York Dada* was a journal that questioned the division between book and serial in quite a different way. Emily Hage argues that it should be understood as a readymade: that is, a found object presented as a work of art. She points out that the editors 'clearly recognized that they could manipulate the expectations of their readers by adopting the material markers of American commercial print media. The price and the dimensions are comparable, and the magazine also parodies ads found in women's and culture magazines and . . . imitates the types of content usually found in such publications' (178–79). She gives the example of 'Pug Debs Make Society Bow', a spoof on a coming-out party announcement, describing the supposed 'debut' of Marsden Hartley, one of the New York dadaists: 'Marsden Hartley will be attired in a neat but not gaudy set of tight-fitting gloves and will have a V-back in front and on both sides. . . . He may or may not wear socks' (Hage 179). The Dada journal here appropriates the whole genre of the mass-market magazine, even though that genre is marked by repetition and continuity, while *New York Dada* is, in chronological terms, a one-off. It was, however, printed in multiple copies, sold in a bookshop and distributed through the post, so that – far from claiming the status of a unique 'original' – it participated fully in the systems of commercial exchange that defined the print marketplace in this era.

Some of the small presses of the early twentieth century issued series of pamphlets or small books that, once again, bring the division between book and serial into question. Leonard and Virginia Woolf's Hogarth Press, for example, published several such series, including the Hogarth Essays, the Hogarth Sixpenny Pamphlets, the Hogarth Letters and Day-to-Day Pamphlets. As the press's catalogue for 1925 puts it in its entry for the Hogarth Essays: 'This series was started a year ago to give writers a chance of expressing themselves upon any subject under the sun at greater length than in a magazine article, but more briefly than in a book.' The pamphlets were disruptive in terms of genre, just as their content was politically and intellectually disruptive (see Snaith, 'Hogarth'). Among the earliest Hogarth Essays were a contribution by Willa Muir, described in the catalogue as 'one of the few essays upon the relation between the sexes which can be read with interest and without loss of temper', and one by John Maynard Keynes on Russia, which explores the history of Laissez-Faire and 'the present position of the doctrine in relation to Socialism and Capitalism'. These were provocative topics. The Essays could be brought out on a relatively short timescale, meaning they could address topical issues, but they were also long enough to allow for in-depth exploration of a subject, and substantial enough to generate discussion via reviews in the literary periodicals.

To some extent, pamphlets such as those produced by the Hogarth Press allow for what Mark Turner, in his work on periodical time, has called the 'reflective pause' (194). He explores the anxieties generated by the accelerated publication schedules of the nineteenth century – especially the move from quarterlies and monthlies towards weeklies and dailies, which meant that 'there seemed to be less time for extended reflection than ever before' (194). 'The creation and circulation of news is all about speed', Turner observes, yet 'the understanding of that news requires a gap and a pause' (194). Another aspect of the modern obsession with news, which gathered force with the technological innovations of the twentieth century, was the rapidity with which things went out of date. One of the primary insights of print culture studies is that the artwork has a different meaning, and is valued differently, according to its publication context. The lowest value would be assigned to the most ephemeral print forms – in the early twentieth-century context, examples might include verses appearing on a labour movement poem card (see Nelson, 'Politics') or in a greeting card (see Rifkind). Serial publications were valued more highly, and were much more likely to be preserved in libraries, but they could not give an artwork the kind of status and solidity which was conferred by publication in the more permanent and 'bounded' form of a book. And once a text had been published in book form it could, of course, appear in a succession of different editions which might accrue varying amounts of cultural capital. Many modernist works appeared first in limited editions, often hand-printed on small presses, and sometimes expensively illustrated with wood-engravings or original paintings. These publications were influenced by a tradition of fine printing which extended back into the nineteenth century, and represented a form of resistance to mass-market publishing. Yet, as important research by David Earle and Paula Rabinowitz demonstrates, the 1940s and 1950s saw many of the major works of modernist fiction republished in cheap paperback formats, often with racy cover designs. This, in effect, marked the entry of these texts into popular culture.

According to Sean Latham, '[p]art of what energizes the current interest in magazine culture is its ability to disrupt our traditional conceptions of modernist practice, extracting familiar texts from anthologies and critical editions and resituating them in a strange and often productively alienating context' ('New Age' 412). Indeed, interest in the original publication context of canonical literary works has motivated much of the research in modernist print culture studies. As early as 1978, Lewis P. Simpson, in a passage that is now often quoted, observed:

> Today when we pick up, say, a forty-five-year-old number of an American literary quarterly (often a hybrid form, a mingling of the critical quarterly and the general literary magazine, containing not only essays and reviews but stories and poems), we may find in it a poem, a story, or an essay that we have long regarded as speaking with its own luminous autonomy. We are slightly shocked to see it in a magazine. Marked by periodicity, it seems to bear the aspect of mortality. It assumes the appearance of an artifact of literary history; and we are averse to relics. (79–80)

This essay appeared in *The Little Magazine in America: A Modern Documentary History*, edited by Elliott Anderson and Mary Kinzie, which was intended as a companion to Hoffman, Allen and Ulrich's pioneering 1946 volume, *The Little Magazine: A History and a Bibliography* (discussed in our next section). Anderson and Kinzie wished to supplement the coherent history of the motivations and themes of the little magazines that had been provided in the earlier volume by adding 'a sense of the living reality of the publications' (Prefatory 3) and the continuation of the genre into the later twentieth century. Their definition of little magazines, in their Prefatory Note, remains resonant:

> Little magazines generally put experiment before ease, and art before comment. They can afford to do so because they can barely 'afford' to do anything; in other words, as a rule they do not, and cannot, expect to make money. Consequently, the ways in which they appeal to their readers need not be coercive, stylistically uniform, or categorically topical, as the ways of commercial presses must be.
> There is something edgy, something peculiar and asocial, about a great many little magazines. Those who write for them are in some sense the disadvantaged, at least by commercial standards: people who have a bone to pick, people who are writing against the grain, but who nevertheless want recognition. Not content to wait until the new sensibility of which they may be the harbingers has proven itself in time, they insist upon a revolution in taste now. (3–4)

This passage successfully captures the appeal of twentieth-century little magazines, both to their contemporary audiences and to scholars in later decades. Yet it presents a reductive view of commercial magazines, which are by no means always 'uniform' or 'categorically topical'. Indeed, as we will discuss in our later chapters, much recent scholarship on modern consumer-oriented magazines emphasizes their visual and stylistic diversity, generic openness and ability to hold conflicting views in a productive tension (among recent examples are Aynsley and Forde's 2007 collection *Design and the Modern Magazine*; work on British *Vogue* by Jane Garrity, Christopher Reed and others; and Fiona Green's 2015 collection on *The New Yorker*). It is therefore important to include 'smart magazines', women's titles and fashion magazines in the conversation about modernist print, even though they are rarely assimilable to conventional definitions of 'modernism', and are in no sense 'little'.

Clearly, the dividing line between 'little' and other magazines is not nearly as distinct as Anderson and Kinzie imply. Good discussions of the problems of defining 'littleness' can be found in the introductions to the volumes in *The Oxford Critical and Cultural History of Modernist Magazines*. Peter Brooker and Andrew Thacker, introducing the first volume, on Britain and Ireland, comment:

> Most of the magazines discussed in this and future volumes are devoted to a conception of the new . . . they struggle financially, and are, at their most successful, advocates of an adversarial minority cultural position who find a supportive, independently minded readership. At the same time, however, many key magazines like *The New Age, The Athenaeum,* and *Criterion* do not conform to the type delineated above. Some claim, or are given, different identities by the more neutral sounding 'periodical' or 'journal', some take on the more traditional subhead of 'quarterly' or 'weekly', and some present themselves as more popular 'papers' or as more highbrow and academic, 'literary' or 'critical reviews'. Even as 'little magazines' a number are on occasion, by instinct, or on principle, more conservative in form and content (*New Numbers*); some have more stable subscription lists (*Century Guild Hobby Horse*) or large readerships (*New Writing*); others acquire the sponsorship of individuals, publishers, or institutions (*Egoist, Criterion, Close Up, Tyro*); many welcomed commercial advertising (*Life and Letters; Adelphi*) and some survived for a longer period than the stereotypical fugitive magazine (*The New Age, The Mask*). (13–14)

The repeated use of the word 'more' in this quotation reveals the necessity of constructing a continuum, rather than a set of distinct categories, in order to distinguish these periodicals from one another. Introducing the second volume in the series, on North American magazines, Andrew Thacker notes that they 'might be sorted into many different categories (pulps, slicks, highbrow, quality, avant-garde, little, mass, radical, bibelot, middlebrow, etc.) and, following Bourdieu's model of the cultural field, we might construct a *periodical field* upon which they are placed in different locations.' The field, he suggests, might be structured in terms of content, or intended reader, or sales figures. Yet, he goes on, such an exercise would 'ultimately raise more questions than it answers' (19), because of the diversity of content which is often mixed together in one magazine, because of the tendency of periodicals to change over time, and also because 'the dominant feature of the periodical field of American magazines in 1920 is that of a "cross-fertilization", shown in the multiple networks of connection between and across supposedly distinct categories of publication' (20). Nevertheless, most books offering histories of periodical culture in particular countries or periods, as well as most magazine digitization projects, have necessarily adopted some form of categorization. Even studies restricting themselves to an apparently intelligible genre, such as the 'modernist' magazine, have found a set of sub-categories essential. For example, Robert Scholes and Clifford Wulfman in *Modernism in the Magazines: An Introduction* (2010) offer a list of types of modernist magazine, including poetry, leftist, regional, experimental, critical and eclectic, and they also consider 'ethnic' as a possible descriptor. Yet, as they note, these categories 'do not connect; they do not even stay on the same level' (55). Another example is provided by the *Modernist Journals Project* at Brown University and the University of Tulsa, which categorizes the titles listed in its online Periodical Directory. After an intense debate within the modernist studies community, the labels settled on were 'little', 'mixed' and 'popular', as well as 'bibelot', for very small magazines, and 'intermediate', for generalist titles established before the modernist era but still publishing during that time. Their need to include 'mixed' points to the underlying difficulty with producing a typology of magazines. The appeal of most periodicals is based on the varied selection of content which they offer, and this means that they can literally transmit 'mixed messages', in ideological terms as well as in terms of cultural or class level.

A further complication is that the label 'little magazine', while clearly indicating a restricted circulation, does not necessarily imply that the magazine is 'modernist' in any straightforward sense. As Ann Ardis points out in *Modernism and Cultural Conflict*, the MJP's choice of *The New Age* (1907–1922) as its first journal to digitize should give us pause. The impression of *The New Age* as a modernist journal arises, Ardis notes, from 'all the famous modernist manifestos redacted from its pages and published subsequently elsewhere under separate, and more prestigious, cover'. But every 'sample of modernist writing or art that is featured in its pages is counterbalanced by a parody or critique or countermanifesto'

(144). Ardis's reading of *The New Age* foregrounds its 'political and aesthetic commitments to Guild Socialism, a radical fringe socialist movement' (145), and emphasizes the 'crucial distinction between the journal's modernist *style* of presentation and its socialist politics, which are insistently and consistently differentiated from modernism's by the editors' (146). Indeed, a large majority of critical discussion of early twentieth-century print culture is arranged around the concept of modernism, and this can occlude many important cultural developments, or lead to interpretations which are too narrow. In their contribution to Ardis and Collier's *Transatlantic Print Culture, 1880–1940*, Lucy Delap and Maria DiCenzo argue forcefully that 'modernism' is 'too selective and distorting a framework' through which to try to understand the material history of publishing and print media in the late nineteenth and early twentieth centuries. The focus of their chapter is on the Anglo-American feminist press, and they point to the 'problem of establishing categories for analyzing print media', explaining that the 'feminist press does not adhere in obvious ways to conventional categories', such as distinctions between 'popular' and 'avant-garde' (54). For instance, the British feminist weekly *Time and Tide*, which has been the focus of important recent research by Catherine Clay, is sometimes categorized as 'literary', sometimes as 'political' and sometimes simply as 'highbrow', yet it ran extensive advertising for consumer goods as well as for cultural products.

In general terms, then, there are many different ways of constructing typologies in the print marketplace. Categories of periodical may be established on the basis of circulation, of format, of content, of editorial orientation and so forth. For book publishing, a spectrum of value, based on production standards, might extend from the luxury edition to the sixpenny paperback, while alternative systems of classifying books or publishing houses might be based on sales figures, or print runs, or the status of the authors on a given publisher's list. The resulting hierarchies will not always coincide with one another, and recent scholarship has repeatedly proved that the different strata of the literary marketplace always turn out to be interrelated and interdependent. And, of course, the terminology used is value-laden. The supposed opposition between the 'small press' and the trade publisher, or between 'little' and 'mass-market' magazines, is ostensibly a measure of audience size, yet the critical use of these terms actually implies quite a lot about aspects of design, and of taste. A student newspaper or community publishing project might be 'little' in terms of number of readers, but such publications usually seek to be inclusive, appealing to all members of the local community rather than just to an elite. They are also likely to be rather plain and basic in design terms. The modernist small press edition or small magazine, by contrast, is generally understood as a coterie publication, with an exclusiveness in its audience address, and an acute consciousness of itself as a designed object.

In his 1989 book *Repression and Recovery: Modern American Poetry and the Politics of Cultural Memory, 1910–1945*, Cary Nelson issued a challenge to scholars of modernism to reread the periodicals of the earlier twentieth century 'as if they were themselves coherent and mixed genres, as if they were books like *Cane* or *Spring and All* that meld and juxtapose traditional genres' (219). This, along with other exhortations from similarly influential critics, has stimulated a very serious, sustained engagement with the archive of modernist periodicals. The new modernist studies encourages an understanding of serials as both 'autonomous objects of study' (Latham and Scholes 518) – that is, as belonging to a genre of their own, rather than being assemblages of work in other genres – and as material objects circulating in a marketplace. But Sean Latham, commenting in a 2004 article on the passage from Cary Nelson, contends that 'Nelson's attempt to reread modernism's little magazines through the lenses of narrative and genre fixes the archive in an unnecessarily constrained and linear form.' He adds that for twenty-first-century scholars, it is easier to break away from the linear forms of archival reading which are necessary when using bound or microfilmed periodical volumes because digital technologies 'alter fundamentally our conception of early twentieth-century journals and their place in our critical practices by lifting the sometimes severe constraints imposed by the materiality of the printed text' ('New Age' 412). Indeed, this applies equally to digital editions of modernist books. They, too, can be read, searched and explored in new ways, using tools which weren't available either to readers in the 1920s and 1930s or to scholars in the 1970s and 1980s. Digital texts are, in some senses, a new 'type' of modernist print: remediated for our own era, and deprived of some of the material dimensions of their paper-based precursors, yet able to bring out aspects of early twentieth-century print culture that were previously invisible to scholars. They pose new challenges to critics seeking to categorize modernist print forms and to analyse the ways that these forms impact on the meanings of texts. As this section has shown, this type of critical method is fundamental to print culture studies. The early bibliographical work we described was a necessary first step, and researchers continue to construct new bibliographies and taxonomies in order to account for changing notions of what should be included within the categories of 'modernist' and of 'print culture'. Concurrently, other scholars take a more theoretical approach, considering printed matter in relation to conceptions of time and speed, or ephemerality and permanence. Still others concentrate on the political implications of the material text in its different forms.

# Print culture and the history of modernist studies

The materialist turn in modernist studies that has focused attention on the periodicals in which so many writers of the period were first published, and has also repositioned the book as an object of study in itself, draws upon the print culture scholarship devoted to the long nineteenth century as well as upon the methodologies of book history. But the modernists themselves are the precursors of this turn. Although the new modernist studies evinces a preoccupation with the material forms of modernist production, it is possible to trace an almost continuous attention to the issues and questions addressed by the term 'print culture' from the late nineteenth century – a moment characterized by Kirsten MacLeod as 'a revolution in print' (*American* 6) – to now. Modernist writers were profoundly concerned with and interested in the literary marketplace, many of them playing multiple roles in what Robert Darnton describes as the 'communication circuit' that 'runs from the author to the publisher . . . the printer, the shipper, the bookseller, and the reader' (111). Thus, T. S. Eliot deployed multiple strategies as critic, poet, journalist, editor and publisher in his decades-long efforts to institutionalize modernist literature, contributing to more than

160 periodicals and concerning himself not only with the content of those he edited but also their visual style (P. White 101; and see Harding, *Criterion*). Also, Leonard and Virginia Woolf used their Hogarth Press not only to promote (and to profit by) the work of avant-garde writers but also to intervene in debates about the inter-relations of commerce and culture; visual artists submitted their work to periodicals and created advertisements that ran in those same periodicals.

Robert Scholes and Clifford Wulfman claim that we are still learning to be Ezra Pound's contemporaries because in a sense he 'founded modern periodical studies' in his 1917–1918 series for the *New Age*, 'Studies in Contemporary Mentality' (Scholes and Wulfman 2–3; 14). This extraordinary series of columns is regarded by Scholes and Wulfman as 'inaugurating the serious study of periodicals as a way into modern culture' (14). Published in *The New Age* between August 1917 and January 1918, they cast 'a withering eye on the magazines of the day' (Moody 336), with Pound adopting the persona of a 'simple-hearted anthropologist' ('The Sphere'). Pound's 'Studies' were by no means disinterested, and the cultural politics that motivated him have been widely explored by scholars. In his detailed survey of over twenty periodicals, Pound maps a territory he sees as ripe for usurpation by the new, carefully accounting for types of content and the intellectual standards produced and sustained by that content. It is his attention to aspects of those periodicals that have become familiar topics of contemporary scholarly interest, however, that prompts Scholes and Wulfman's claim. For example, the thorny question of taxonomy that we discussed in the previous section is introduced by Pound in the sixth instalment of the series, ' "The Sphere" and Reflections on Letter Press'. With characteristic humour, he proposes a fanciful set of categories by which to organize the periodicals he examines, anticipating how the boundaries that delimit different types would be difficult to fix. As well as 'trade journals' and 'crank papers' (a category which includes 'religious periodicals'), he proposes categories for periodicals 'designed to keep thought in safe channels; to prevent acrimonious discussion in old gentlemen's clubs', or for 'periodicals designed to inculcate useful and mercantile virtues in the middle and lower middle classes'. His last category is for 'Papers and parts of papers designed to stop thought altogether' ('The Sphere').

Fifteen years later, Q. D. Leavis undertook another mapping of the print marketplace in *Fiction and the Reading Public* (1932). Andrew Nash has recently described this as 'something of a lost landmark' in book history (323), noting that although 'it has proved easy to challenge the historical aspects of her study and disagree with nearly all of her conclusions' (323), the categories of her analysis continue to be productive. Leavis describes the objects of her survey as: 'daily and weekly newspapers in great variety'; 'cultural weeklies of different levels'; 'weekly humorous papers'; 'luxurious shilling illustrated news magazines with a *Punch* orientation'; 'literary periodicals'; 'substantial story magazines'; 'women's magazines'; 'film magazines'; '2d weekly papers in magazine form'; '6d., 9d., and 1s. paper novels'; 'light educational pamphlets'; inexpensive poetry collections; some 'Classics'; 'children's books, dictionaries and cookery books'; 'sixpenny novels published by the Readers' Library and the Novel Library' (10–12). What Patrick Collier ('Woolf Studies' 156) and others have described as a 'segmented' print culture was the object of intense awareness and controversy from at least the turn of the twentieth century. From issues such as the opportunities offered by new technologies of print to the intersections of commerce and art, from legislation governing the selling of books to debates about how to teach reading, writers, publishers, patrons and readers engaged in an animated public discourse about the modes of communication that carried that discourse, just as today debate about the consequences of the digital revolution is conducted via digital media.

In *The Mechanic Muse* (1987), Hugh Kenner argued that the absent narrators of modernist fiction can be related to a new consciousness about the technology of print in the machine age. Victorian novelists, he remarked, 'got into the way of exploiting printed pages' (for example, by representing dialect by misspelled words), but it is Joyce among English-speaking writers who Kenner believes 'alone seems to have understood from the first what it can mean to be writing for print' (70). When in *Ulysses* Martha Clifford mistakes 'wrote' for 'write' in her letter to Leopold Bloom, 'Joyce means us to notice it too, and to reflect not that Martha is illiterate but that "I" and "O" are adjacent keys on a typewriter' (Kenner 73). Kenner's treatment of Joyce as unique has cast a long shadow over modernist studies: Rainey, for example, refers to 'assumptions about the publication of *Ulysses*, and *hence* about literary modernism', seeming to equate one with the other (42, emphasis added). As a significant component of the 'expansion' characteristic of the new modernist studies (Mao and Walkowitz 737–38), print culture scholarship has made more visible the way in which canons and reputations were created in the first half of the twentieth century, dislodging the exemplary status of writers such as Joyce for the sake of a more dynamic and complex description of the way in which works came into print. Furthermore, it has given new impetus to the recovery work that began in the late 1960s as the research on modernist print cultures puts well-known works back into their original publication contexts where they can again be read in dialogue with works that dominant academic and critical discourses had eclipsed. As we will see in the following chapters, the narrative of modernism promulgated by those whom Wyndham Lewis called the 'men of 1914' and that was subsequently institutionalized by the New Critics, then questioned and challenged by feminist criticism, has continued to be complicated by scholarship on print culture.

But Kenner's broader point about modernist writers' engagement with technology remains productive. Laura Marcus, for example, discussing Henry James's employment of Theodora Bosanquet to operate his newly acquired Remington typewriter, has written of 'the new relationship between the hand and the machine in the context of "writing" in modernity' ('Publisher' 268). The typewriter, first commercially successful in the 1860s and making its presence felt in fiction as early as Bram Stoker's *Dracula* (1897), is described in the work of Friedrich Kittler as initiating a 'fundamental mutation in the mode of existence of our language' (Wellbery xiv). Mark Wollaeger has argued that D. H. Lawrence's ambivalent relationship towards new media and technology, in particular to the typewriter, is responsible for the 'recognizably modernist style' of *Women in Love* ('D. H. Lawrence' 75). Wollaeger also points out that at the turn of the twentieth century the word 'typewriter' could 'refer either to the machine or to the woman most likely to be working its keys' (78). Furthermore, the availability of inexpensive and small printing machinery had profound implications for writers who could not attract the interest of commercial publishers. When Harry and Caresse Crosby, who would go on to create the Black Sun Press, wanted to see their poems in print, it did not occur to them 'to submit them to a publishing house – the simplest way to get a poem into a book was to print the book!' (Crosby 156). In 1942, Anaïs Nin, despairing of getting her sexually transgressive work into print in the United States, bought a press with her lover, the Peruvian revolutionary Gonzalo Moré, for $75 (Nin 178; Dennison 120). This intimacy between writers and print technology is becoming a more salient aspect of modernist studies. Critics have drawn attention to the way in which typography itself becomes a dadaist subject in the poster poems of Raoul Haussman (Schaffner), and how Hope Mirrlees 'actively employed typography and spacing' in *Paris: A Poem* 'as part of its system of representation', in turn influencing Virginia Woolf's own understanding of the modernist page as she set the type by hand for her Hogarth Press publication of Mirrlees's poem in 1920 (Briggs 83). Suspended between the handcrafted beauties of William Morris's Kelmscott Press and the exhilaration afforded by new technologies such as the rotary press, linotype and photogravure (which will be discussed in more detail in the third section of our next chapter) the modernists plunged into a rich and strange new print cultural world which many of them also self-consciously documented and critiqued. Again, the example of Pound demonstrates with great clarity how the dynamism of new forms of print and publication attracted the attention of writers in the modernist period.

In his 'Studies in Contemporary Mentality', Pound not only anatomizes the content of what he later termed the 'elder magazines' ('Small' 690) but also pays close attention to the appearance and format of those magazines and to the indications of commercial success that imply a particular periodical 'is manifestly what a vast number of people want' ('The Strand'). For example, he draws attention to *The Strand*'s '58 pages of ads. in double column', as a sign of the financial health of the magazine. He comments too on the quality of its paper stock: 'It is thicker and uses a slightly better paper than the other 8d and 6d (olim. 6d and 4½ d) magazines on the stand where I found it' ('The Strand'). As Mark Morrisson writes in *The Public Face of Modernism* (2001), 'material markers of genre, such as price, page size, types of advertising, and frequency of publication, all contribute to a reader's horizon of expectations for a magazine' (39). We have learned from George Bornstein that the kind of materialist analysis that Pound engages in is essential to the demystification of the physical object by which modernist texts have been transmitted (*Material* 4).

Pound's anthropological study of what might be found on an English newsstand in the last two years of the First World War serves as an opening salvo in what he definitely saw as a cultural conflict. Gail McDonald reminds us that it is easy to 'lose sight of the youthful mode of *épater le bourgeois* that characterized much of early modernism' (73). Concluding his series in the *New Age*, Pound wrote 'Any aristocracy or ruling class that does not work and sweat to educate the people under it is bound to go down in blood, and I am inclined to think it deserves to' ('– ? Versus Camouflage'). In the January 1926 number of the *New Criterion*, the first after its takeover by Faber and Gwyer, Eliot proposed that a decade's worth of a literary review should 'represent the development of the keenest sensibility and the clearest thought of ten years' ('Idea' 2). In his 'Last Words', when the *Criterion* ceased publication in 1939, he wrote that it 'will not be the large organs of opinion, or the old periodicals, it must be the small and obscure papers and reviews, those who are hardly read by anyone but their own contributors, that will keep critical thought alive, and encourage authors of original talent'.

Pound had made a similar argument in his important article of 1930, 'Small Magazines'. 'The significance of the small magazine has', he wrote, 'nothing to do with format' (689). Exemplary is Harriet Monroe's *Poetry*, founded in 1911 in Chicago, which Pound characterizes as nurturing an intellectual life that the 'elder magazines' he had excoriated in 'Studies in Contemporary Mentality' had miserably failed to do. Pound surveys a number of those magazines we have come to term 'little' – *The Egoist, The Little Review, The Dial, The Criterion, transition, S4N, This Quarter, Hound and Horn, Morada* and other 'apparently tawdry and freakish' publications (704) – all of which he includes not because of their format or circulation figures but because of 'the work they have brought to the press' (701). 'Certain authors' – Joyce, Stein, Eliot, Lewis, Lawrence and Pound himself, for example – have appeared in these 'fugitive periodicals' (701) and thereby the 'history of contemporary letters has, to a very manifest extent, been written in such magazines' (702). In Chapter 2 we will explore some of the recent scholarship on women magazine editors that counters the distorting influence of what Jayne Marek describes as Pound's 'modernist patriarchalism' (*Women* 191).

Pound's 'Small Magazines' in part inspired Frederick J. Hoffman, Charles Allen and Carolyn F. Ulrich to write *The Little*

*Magazine: A History and Bibliography* (1946), one of the most significant early constructions of a typology and history of modernist print and publishing. Ulrich, head of the periodicals division of the New York Public Library, was a pioneer of what we now call library science and brought out the first volume of her *Periodicals Directory: A Classified Guide to a Selected List of Current Periodicals Foreign and Domestic* in 1932. Scholes and Wulfman cite correspondence between Hoffman and Ulrich that makes clear they did not always agree on what should be included as a 'little magazine': Ulrich provided the bibliography, but Hoffman annotated it and had the last word on what would be listed. They were guided to some extent by circulation figures, but also explained that they relied on 'qualitative' criteria:

> A little magazine is a magazine designed to print artistic work which for reasons of commercial expediency is not acceptable to the money-minded periodicals or presses. . . . Coming into use during the First World War, 'little' did not refer to the size of the magazines, nor to their literary contents, nor to the fact that they usually did not pay for contributions. What the word designated above everything else was a limited group of intelligent readers. (Scholes and Wulfman 2–3)

Almost immediately, Hoffman, Allen and Ulrich's descriptive categories were challenged. Allen had claimed in a 1943 article for *Sewanee Review* that 'about 80 per cent of our most important post-1912 critics, novelists, poets, and storytellers' had been published in the 'little magazines', a point that *The Little Magazine* repeated in its introduction (1 n2). In 1948, Paul Bixler, the librarian at Antioch College, took issue with this claim in 'Little Magazine, What Now?'. Although he acknowledged that Hoffman, Allen and Ulrich's volume was 'an "authority" to be reckoned with even when it is contradictory, confused, or dead wrong' (145), he made the point that the little magazine 'has been historically both more and less' than they allowed (147).

These earlier taxonomies of the modernist periodical have been revisited in recent scholarship, Scholes and Wulfman even arguing that 'the notion of "little magazine" prevents us from seeing what was really going on in the world of modern periodicals' (56), and seeking to correct 'a romanticized definition of little magazines as places where the aura of art was preserved by a modernist avant-garde of dedicated editors' (56). MacLeod sees *The Little Magazine: A History and Bibliography* as 'a classic example of the institutional sanctioning of high modernism's anxious and territorial mapping of its field' ('Fine Art' 184). Nevertheless, Hoffman, Allen and Ulrich's pioneering work, like that of Pound, makes clear that many of the salient issues addressed by late twentieth- and early twenty-first-century scholarship were identified and debated as early as the time of the First World War, and continued to be so for several more decades as the study of modern literature became established in universities.

It is well known that the New Criticism expounded in American universities in the 1940s drew upon tenets articulated in the 1920s by T. S. Eliot, Ezra Pound, I. A. Richards and others. Scholars such as Gail McDonald and Sharon Hamilton ('*PMLA*') have shown that the effort to establish literary criticism as a discipline with the prestige of the sciences was closely related to the strategies deployed by Eliot and Pound, in particular, in defining modernist literature as a discrete field separate from a mass culture and consumerism often gendered feminine. Pound and Eliot tried to 'validate literature by associating it with professionalism, thereby freeing it from the taints of commercialism and an amateurism that they consistently gendered feminine' (Collier, 'Virginia Woolf' 362).

Like the modernists themselves in their restless transgressions of genre, form and medium, the recent scholarship on modernism's print cultures has been eclectic and wide-ranging in its borrowings from the work of earlier textual and bibliographic scholars, from the study of Victorian print culture, from the relatively new fields of book history (which itself has gathered together several different disciplinary emphases), and the study of visual cultures. The formal experimentation that at first was identified as a defining characteristic of modernism cannot be properly separated from the material forms in which that experimentation flourished. Furthermore, attention to modernism's imbrication with the marketplace has not only refashioned our notions of what Andreas Huyssen called a 'great divide' between modernism and 'the culture of everyday life' (vii) but has also repositioned avant-garde artists of the early twentieth century as savvy exploiters of the tools of commerce. Introducing a collection of papers from a 2004 symposium on *Literary Cultures and the Material Book*, Eliot, Nash and Willison affirm that:

> Book and literary historians are now beginning to acknowledge that, in Glen Dudbridge's words, 'books [are] constructed into literatures by critics, editors, bibliographers, publishers and librarians'. Substantial evidence for this perception is the concern of the new *Oxford English Literary History* to give 'particular attention . . . to the institutions in which literary acts take place (educated communities, publishing networks and so on)', and of the *New Cambridge History of English Literature* to examine 'the materialities of textual production, preservation and circulation'. (2)

Drawing attention to Edward L. Bishop's entry on 'book history' in the 2nd edition of the *Johns Hopkins Guide to Literary Theory and Criticism* (2005), Seth Lerer points out that book history

> is now a central part of literary criticism and theory and the pedagogy of humanities departments. We find meaning in the physical appearance of the page, in typographic layout, but also in hand-written marginalia. The sociology of taste and temperament can be recovered from the economics of the book trade. Cognitive science looks to histories of reading. And old, traditional pursuits – library science, paleography, book collecting – have been charged anew with the convictions . . . 'that the status and interpretation of a word depend on material considerations, that the meaning is always produced in a historical setting, and that the meaning of a text depends on the differing readings assigned to it by historical, rather than ideal, readers'. (229–30)

This shift towards a more materialist and sociocultural approach to the literary text has had manifest effects in the academic study of literature in general. Within modernist studies the focus of critical attention has moved remarkably in the past three decades from an almost exclusive concern with the content of modernist production to a view of the text as what Jerome McGann calls 'a laced network of linguistic and bibliographic codes' (*Textual* 13). The work of McGann, Bornstein and others on the 'bibliographic code' and its role in producing meaning has influenced the majority of recent discussions of modernism's print cultures, and we devote a whole section of our first chapter to this topic. Just as textual editing has come to accept 'a socialized concept of authorship and textual authority' (McGann, *Textual* 8) and to produce many 'versions' of a text without privileging one over another, so periodical studies and book history have encouraged a greater awareness of the interplay among networks of writers, visual artists, editors, publishers, agents, marketers, mass and popular media, as well as the crisscrossing of what turn out often to be rather ephemeral boundaries between elite and mass culture in the construction of modernism. Bornstein argues in *Material Modernism*, for example, that poems by such key figures as Yeats, Pound, H. D., Moore and Eliot have been too long read in 'frozen' forms (for example in classroom anthologies) that obscure the 'richer account of them as processes rather than mere products of inscription afforded by recent version theory' (2). The new approach instigated by print culture scholarship might be exemplified by contrasting J. H. Willis's detailed and indispensable history of the Hogarth Press with Helen Southworth's edited collection on the Press and 'the Networks of Modernism'. Willis gives a thorough account of the development and commercial success of the Hogarth Press but 'mostly leaves out the complex and fascinating histories of the diverse network of authors, artists and workers involved with the Woolfs and the work that they produced' (Southworth, 'Introduction' 15). Willis maintains that 'the Woolfs cannot be said to have shaped their publications deliberately to any predetermined aesthetic or ideological end' but were guided 'as most publishers of the time' were by whatever came their way (x). Southworth and her contributors' network approach, by contrast, emphasizes 'the collaborative nature of modernism' ('Introduction' 17) to demonstrate how what was for a long time regarded as a coterie press was in fact essential to the deliberate construction of a number of different modernist discourses. The image of the Hogarth Press emerging from the work of scholars such as Claire Battershill, Alice Staveley, Nicola Wilson and Elizabeth Willson Gordon has made clear its commitment to 'young, first-time authors' (Southworth, 'Introduction' 15) as well as to bringing working-class writers to a middle-class readership, and to treating conventional publishing categories such as poetry and religion in innovative ways.

In her landmark anthology *The Gender of Modernism* (1990), Bonnie Kime Scott contended that modernism had been 'unconsciously gendered masculine' (2) until the middle of the twentieth century. In a widely reproduced illustration, 'A Tangled Mesh of Modernists' (10), Scott demonstrated that not all strands of connection among modernists 'lead to Eliot, Pound, and Joyce' (11). For all his promotion of the careers of women, as Ronald Bush points out in his contribution to Scott's volume, Pound 'frequently characterized both modernist style and culture itself as masculine achievements' (354). In *Gender in Modernism*, the 2007 sequel to Scott's earlier volume, not only do we see a larger number of women represented, but also an expansion of modernism's traditional chronology to take account of the 'missing era' of transition, 1880–1910, when suffrage literature in its diverse print forms influenced the formations of modernity to which modernism was responding. Barbara Green's work on feminist periodicals (discussed in Chapter 3) is a particularly striking example of how viewing a writer through a print cultural lens can produce a quite different reading of her work than is obtained through traditional literary critical approaches.

Earlier histories of private presses (Cave; Joost; Ransom; Wolff) and of publishing houses or the book trade (Barnes; Duffy; Unwin), as well as memoirs and biographies of publishers and editors (Crosby; Cunard; H. Ford) remain useful sources of information, but the stories they tell have been complicated by an expanded view of the modernist engagement with printed forms of communication. In a number of monographs and articles published since the mid-1980s, the economic aspects of modernist culture and the role of advertising and marketing have been brought very much into the foreground, as can be seen in Rainey's *Institutions of Modernism*. He argues that:

> The avant-garde was neither more nor less than a structural feature in the institutional configuration of modernism. It played no special role by virtue solely of its form, and it possessed no ideological privilege; instead, it was constituted by a specific array of marketing and publicity structures that were integrated in varying degrees with the larger economic apparatus of its time. (99)

Using a case studies approach, he points out that 'a modernist work was typically published in three forms: first, in a little review or journal; second, in a limited edition of recently collected poems (or as an individual volume if the work was large enough); and third, in a more frankly commercial or public edition issued by a mainstream publisher and addressed to a wider audience' (99). Although his conclusions have been challenged (e.g. by P. McDonald, 'Modernist'), Rainey's book exemplifies the sociohistorical turn modernist scholarship has taken, as does the work of scholars who have explored the marketing of modernism (e.g. Collier; Dettmar and Watt; Dubino; Staveley; Wicke; Willison et al.; Wexler). Publishers' and magazines' archives are increasingly being mined by scholars, and their documents are beginning to be available in digital form. The networks that produced and sustained modernism are being reconstructed from those archives, and this work is having a profound effect on our conceptions of the literary, requiring us to acknowledge that a modernist book, magazine, poem or novel is simultaneously a defamiliarizing art object and a commodity. Many new books and articles on these themes are appearing every year, demonstrating that attention to print culture has provoked a thorough rethinking of the history of modernism.

# 1

# Sensuous print

In her memoir *The Passionate Years* (1953), Caresse Crosby – whose Black Sun Press produced modernist limited editions renowned for the sensual appeal of their paper and design – described how in 1913 she patented her invention of a backless brassière. Having borrowed $100 to rent a room, she presented a few hundred bras 'to the public in very superior packaging (the de luxe edition blood must have already been stirring in my veins)' (74). Crosby's understanding that a book could be a luxury commodity similar to expensive lingerie can be contrasted with the view of Leonard Woolf, who argued that books are 'not a commodity which, like patent medicines, cigarettes, or mustard, the consumer buys or can be induced to buy by the skill of the advertiser' ('On Advertising' 49). The fraught relations between art and commerce became a subject of intense debate in the 1920s. By this time, the market for deluxe and limited edition books was robust, yet it was not sealed off from the popular print marketplace. The broader public's visual sense had been stimulated and educated by graphic designers and artists whose work was commissioned not only by elite presses but also by large corporations and government bodies. The turn in modernist studies towards print culture can be related to a broader tendency towards considerations of material culture and the object, exemplified in recent scholarship on twentieth-century fashion, food, shopping and advertising. In this chapter, we will focus on the materiality and visual dimensions of printed objects, and the changing ways in which these are being evaluated by critics to produce what Barbara Green has explained as 'an understanding of the affect, sentiment, and desires that bond subjects to objects and allow for the production of new subjectivities through innovative acts of consumption' ('Feminist Things' 77).

Green is pointing out how the insights of print culture scholarship coupled with those of work on material culture lead us to change the way we think about periodicals (specifically, in her study, nineteenth-century suffrage periodicals) and begin to attend not only to their intellectual content but to their physical existence as well. What Green terms 'the feminist thing', that is 'the materiality of the periodical and its existence as an object', is analogous to what we might call the 'modernist thing' – the books, magazines, posters and ephemera whose sensuous attributes have become so significant an object of interpretation in modernist studies. Jennifer Sorensen's recent work on modernist form's interaction with materiality offers a bridge between formalism and the historical approach exemplified by key modernist print culture scholarship such as Green's. Sorensen examines in detail, for example, how Henry James plays with 'complex mixed-media periodical pagescapes' in his short story 'The Real Thing' (2), and demonstrates his acute awareness of the way his text would compete for the attention of readers with the surrounding advertisements and illustrations.

In a 2006 special issue of *PMLA* on 'The History of the Book and the Idea of Literature', Peter D. McDonald remarks on 'unexpected intersections between the apparently opposed enterprises of theory and the history of the book' ('Ideas' 217). Literary theories that are focused on textuality and seem to disregard the materiality of the signifier have, Leah Price comments in her introduction to this special issue, been upstaged by book history's close attention to the page (11). McDonald points out that when Jacques Derrida famously wrote in *Of Grammatology* (1976) 'il n'y a pas de hors-texte' ('There is nothing outside of the text' or, more accurately, 'There is no outside-text'), the 'hors-texte' could be a play on the technical book-making term roughly translated as 'plate' (in the sense of a colour plate as opposed to what is set in type). The slogan thus becomes evidence of 'Derrida's sustained commitment to putting in question received assumptions about what is outside and what is thought to be inside writing' (McDonald 223, quoting Derrida 158), allying the philosopher with print culture scholarship's interpretation of every aspect of production as meaning-making.

In *How to Do Things With Books in Victorian Britain* (2013), Price refers to McDonald's treatment of Derrida's language as an example of how 'literary critics today mine other disciplines – bibliography, history of science, even archaeology – for a vocabulary in which to describe the nontextual aspects of a particular category of material object: books' (22). She notes that literary critics have by training been 'numbed' to the materiality of texts (32), but recent surveys of modernist scholarship indicate how this is rapidly changing. Michael H. Whitworth, in an annotation on 'Publishing Modernism' in his 2007 anthology of key critical texts, points out that scholars now 'approach the entanglement of art in ordinary human experience by considering the materiality of texts, the practical means by which they travelled from author to readers' (244). Bill Brown, in his contribution to *A Handbook of Modernism Studies* (2013), explains that modernism 'has increasingly been recognized as an inquiry into the fate of the object world, an account of how objects produce subjects, and an effort to encounter or affect a kind of thingness' (282). Brown, the principal exponent of what has come to be known as 'thing theory',[1] points to 'the design of books and journals as objects . . . or the insistence on the material presence of language itself' as examples of how literary modernism worked 'to dramatize its own thingness' (292). In Brown's introduction to a cluster of *PMLA* articles on 'Textual Materialism' in 2010, he refers to the work of Price and McDonald to illustrate that book history has 'affirmed the concerns raised by the most iconic of theorists: concerns about paratexts, frames, folds, borders, margins, authorship and authority, typing and printing, gathering and dispersion' (24). Print culture scholarship might, perhaps, be seen as a kind of thing theory.

If Anglo-American modernism arises from a vexed relation to the object, as Douglas Mao has argued in *Solid Objects* (1998), print culture scholarship's treatment of all aspects of production as significant must inform our understanding of that relation. Mao's exploration of the tension between modernists' 'admiration for an object world beyond the manipulations of consciousness' and their concurrent 'urgent validation of production' (11) is on the whole a philosophical inquiry, but one that inevitably takes account of the late nineteenth-century revival of handcrafts as a reaction to mechanical modes of (re)production. In *Multimedia Modernism: Literature and the Anglo-American Avant-Garde*

(2009), Julian Murphet points out that as painting moved away from representation and towards abstraction, literature – regarded as the most immaterial of arts – desired to become a 'thing' in a media ecology in which painting, photography and literature all shared paper as the 'multimedia platform par excellence of modernism' (77). Murphet reads the Vorticist *Blast* as 'one of the avant-garde's great attempts to materialize the word and dematerialize it simultaneously, in an undecidable relationship to painting that is really a profound ambivalence toward the "orchestra" of new media pushing literature and painting both toward an uncomfortable relationship with the industrial world' (124). *Blast*'s affinity with 'newsprint, posters, advertisement and graphic design' attests literature's desire to be a thing, perfectly exemplified in Murphet's opinion by the mass-marketed generic 'best-seller' (37). *Blast* continues to inspire scholars and designers: this can be seen in the 'Manifesto of Modernist Digital Humanities', a webpage which evokes the typography and iconoclastic energy of *Blast* to call for a more 'modernistic' reading of modernism and to question the positivist and realist methodologies that persist in modernist scholarship conducted in the digital environment (Christie et al.).

In *Ghostlier Demarcations: Poetry and the Material Word* (1997), Michael Davidson discusses how first Vorticism, and subsequently other Continental movements such as Futurism, Dada and Cubism enabled Ezra Pound to develop his understanding of the page as 'a generative element of meaning' rather than a space to be decorated (11). These movements taught poets how to use collage techniques and typographic innovation 'to confront the distractions of modern urban life through the multiple voices of an emerging print culture' (13). Carrie Noland remarks in *Voices of Negritude in Modernist Print* (2015) that the 'many challenges to deconstructive reading practices that have emerged in the past few decades' have resulted in numerous ways to 'understand the threat of disembodiment posed by the printed "I"' (6–7). Her study of the poets Léon Damas, Aimé Césaire and Léopold Sédar Senghor places special emphasis on their exploitation of what she calls the 'typosphere', 'that uniquely modern (post-Gutenberg) world in which paper and typeface are the matter of words' (1).

Jerome McGann claims in *Black Riders: The Visible Language of Modernism* (1993) that 'the history of modernist writing could be written as the history of the modernist book' (76). In his groundbreaking earlier work, *The Textual Condition* (1991), McGann emphasized the importance to studies of early twentieth-century book production of recognizing that William Morris's Kelmscott Press insisted on the materiality of the word: 'Suddenly letters and words were not simply counters to be manipulated for the presentation of those more important things, ideas. The letters and words were dragged back to a new presence, as if incised on the page in an apocalypse of their materiality' (85).[2] The visuality of texts has become an important aspect of print culture studies, especially in discussions of modernist poetry. Within an extended discussion of Pound's *Cantos*, McGann draws attention to the unusual typography of his most famous Imagist poem, 'In a Station of the Metro' (155). This poem receives close attention from Peter McDonald in an article evaluating the claims about reading made by Lawrence Rainey in his influential book *Institutions of Modernism* (which will be discussed in more detail in our next chapter). McDonald uses the publishing history of 'In a Station of the Metro' to demonstrate how the work of French book historians, such as Roger Chartier, and revisionist textual scholars such as McGann and D. F. McKenzie in the 1980s and 1990s 'insisted on seeing the text, not as an abstract linguistic form, but as a mediated material artifact' and therefore shifted our understanding of the 'scene of reading' ('Modernist Publishing' 231). McDonald discusses the versions of 'In a Station of the Metro' printed in *Poetry* and *The New Freewoman* in 1913 at Pound's instructions, and also the 1917 version in *Lustra*, which was its most familiar version for many years. He explains how the 1913 version 'used visual cues both to underwrite its innovative musicality and to give new importance to the medium of print itself' (234).

Modernist writers were themselves often acutely aware of the material conditions of production, with many directly involved in the publication of their works. Laura Marcus suggests, for example, that Woolf's strong sense of design in her fiction is partly due to 'her feeling for the shape and materiality of the book given to her by the processes of printing and binding' ('Hogarth' 133). In a 1919 essay titled 'Reading' Woolf's consciousness of the material conditions of literary production emerges in a metaphor that returns the printed paper to its source, prompted by her looking beyond the edge of the page to envision the book as 'not printed, bound, or sewn up, but somehow a product of trees and fields and the hot summer sky' (Hussey 253). What Mark Hussey terms Woolf's 'acute awareness of the manufactured conventions of print' (253) is an important aspect of McGann's notion of the 'history of the modernist book'. In *Black Riders* McGann points out that W. B. Yeats's 'foul rag-and-bone shop of the heart' (in 'The Circus Animals' Desertion') alludes to the medium of the writer's art: paper made from rags. The English printing industry had been transformed by the introduction of paper made from wood-pulp (7) and by the end of the nineteenth century rag paper was used only for ornamental and deluxe books (5). Yeats's publications from the Dun Emer and Cuala Presses, then, 'played a crucial role in the late nineteenth- and early twentieth-century's massive act of bibliographical resistance to the way poetry was being materially produced' (6).[3]

In *The New Bibliopolis* (2008), Willa Z. Silverman draws on Walter Benjamin's classic statement of the withering of the 'aura' of the art object in the age of mechanical reproducibility to account for how some of the bibliophiles she discusses placed the *livre de luxe* 'squarely in the domain of pure art, or even of the sacred' in an effort to detach it from other material objects being reproduced in greater quantities in the late nineteenth century, 'whether bicycles, foodstuffs, lottery tickets, or cheap paperbacks' (11). Silverman's study explores a cultural shift whereby amateur collectors became involved in the creative process, overseeing 'the selection of texts and artists to illustrate them, the choice of paper, page layout, typography, advertising, and more' (5). For many scholars of modernist print culture, the sensuous aspects of books and magazines have become inseparable from considerations of meaning.

Mark Morrisson describes how James Joyce arranged with Sylvia Beach at Shakespeare & Company in Paris to publish a deluxe edition of *Ulysses* 'with 100 signed and numbered copies on Dutch handmade paper to sell at 350 francs, 150 numbered copies on larger-sized verge d'arches paper, unsigned, to sell at 250 francs, and 750 numbered copies on handmade paper to sell at 150 francs' ('Publishing' 140). Edward Bishop has recounted how Joyce insisted that the blue of the cover had to be that of the Greek flag, so that there was an intimate relationship between the 'text' and the 'book': 'the cover was part of Joyce's project' ('Re-Covering' 24). With the 1922 Paris edition of *Ulysses* as his case study,

Rainey argues that the deluxe or limited edition 'transformed literary property into a unique and fungible object, something that more nearly resembled a painting or an objet d'art', providing an opportunity for investment to speculators in the collector's market (75). The way that many of modernism's most famous texts were produced led, in Rainey's view, to a 'new and uneasy amalgam of the investor, the collector, and the patron' (56), rather than to the creation of new readers of radically experimental work.

McGann remarks that 'fine printing work, the small press, and the decorated book fashioned the bibliographic face of the modernist world' (*Black* 7). In a number of recent articles, critics have demonstrated the way 'bibliographic codes' (which will be discussed in detail in the next section) complement and affect our reading of modernist texts. For example, Eric White explores the deluxe editions published by Contact/Three Mountains of works by William Carlos Williams, Ernest Hemingway, Gertrude Stein and Djuna Barnes as a specifically American response to the tenets of high modernism. White argues that Robert McAlmon used the 'material languages of fine press printing' to interrogate the vicissitudes of the mass market ('Continental' 290). After the appearance in 1922 of *Ulysses*, Pound proposed to William Bird, who owned Three Mountains Press, that he publish a series of short prose works in which various writers would explore modernity for a specialized audience. White explains how the typographical features and cover designs of this series are part of its ideology. Bird's 'opulent and sardonic pastoral typography' for William Carlos Williams's *Great American Novel* 'destabilizes American cultural hegemonies', and Bird's 'wraparound cover' for Hemingway's *In Our Time* intersects with the narrative of the short stories in it by presenting 'a collage of newspaper clippings, headlines and illustrations'. For White, both Hemingway and Bird create a narrative that toys with readers' expectations of print culture, 'confirming and subverting them simultaneously' (294). Michael Epp also has discussed 'the powerful impact of material book production on textual reception' in his article on McAlmon's edition of Stein's *Making of Americans*. Epp describes examining a copy at the University of Alberta's Bruce Peel Collection: 'The paper cover is a heavy, deep orange and is lettered in black ink. The cover's heavily serifed type, along with the sheer weight of the volume and its imposing color, creates a monumental effect' (286). Epp compares this book to the 1922 *Ulysses* and points out how much more challenging to the reader is Stein's because of its tight leading, dark print and thin paper (289).

Opportunities to consider these sensuous aspects of modernist texts in their early twentieth-century editions have until quite recently been limited to visits to rare book collections, but the explosion of digital humanities projects is providing greater access, albeit one that must be approached with caution. The status of the object when remediated by digital means has become a particularly pressing question within modernist studies given the enormous variety of forms that print culture takes after the late nineteenth century. On sites such as the *Modernist Journals Project* or *Blue Mountain Project* it is possible to view thousands of pages of avant-garde and other modernist periodicals, but not to discern their relative actual sizes, nor to feel such features as embossed pages. In other words, digitization dramatically alters the bibliographic code of a text, while preserving the linguistic code, and therefore raises questions about the impact of material form on meaning and interpretation. The notion of the 'bibliographic code' has underpinned research on modernism's print cultures since the early 1990s, but this topic has taken on renewed urgency in the era of digital literary scholarship. The first section of this chapter will be devoted to this topic. The second explores interactions between modernist visual and literary artists, including book illustration and cover art. This section focuses on the modernist book and on fine printing, while the third section looks at the design of more ephemeral publications such as periodicals, paperbacks and posters. We explore typefaces and typographical art as well as advertising and editorial illustration, considering the ways that commercial and technological innovations affected modernist design.

## Bibliographic codes and the study of the page

In exploring the significance of the material dimensions and visual design of modernist books and journals, the notion of the 'bibliographic code', introduced by the influential textual scholar Jerome

McGann and elaborated by other critics, is essential. McGann has discussed the bibliographic code, and its application to literary texts from various periods, in several of his books and articles. A good place to start is *The Textual Condition* (1991), a series of essays in which he explores textual variance and change, or 'the life histories' of texts (9). His aim in this book is to move beyond the exploration of textual variables by means of reading and hermeneutics, and instead to demonstrate their operation 'at the most material (and apparently least "signifying" or significant) levels of the text: in the case of scripted texts, the physical form of books and manuscripts (paper, ink, typefaces, layouts) or their prices, advertising mechanisms, and distribution venues' (11). This is the bibliographic code of a text, while the words which compose it are the 'linguistic code'. McGann argues that 'both linguistic and bibliographical texts are symbolic and signifying mechanisms. Each generates meaning, and while the bibliographic text commonly functions in a subordinate relation to the linguistic text, "meaning" in literary works results from the exchanges these two great semiotic mechanisms work with each other' (67). This, he suggests, should draw our attention to the interactive, collaborative nature of textuality and the production of meaning – this becomes obvious when we consider that, for example, the publisher is likely to have much more control over the bibliographic code of a printed book than the author does. A further stage in his argument reveals the temporal dimension in the process: 'texts are produced and reproduced under specific social and institutional conditions', and therefore, 'a "text" is not a "material thing" but a material event or set of events, a point in time (or a moment in space) where certain communicative interchanges are being practiced' (21).

McGann's work, then, is important in general terms to scholars of bibliography, print culture and the sociology of texts. Furthermore, his discussions of Pound, Yeats, Stein and others provide important case studies for scholars of modernist print. The last three chapters of *The Textual Condition* are devoted to Pound, and explore the importance of visual appearance in interpreting the *Cantos*, and the different ways in which the various ornamented and unornamented editions are likely to be read. McGann's *Black Riders* concentrates on the relationship between modernist literary styles and contemporary developments in typography and book design. His insights have been taken up in several key works on modernist print, most notably in George Bornstein's *Material Modernism: The Politics of the Page* (2001). Bornstein's definition of the bibliographic code, which is very frequently quoted, runs: 'the literary text consists not only of words (its linguistic code) but also of the semantic features of its material instantiations (its bibliographic code). Such bibliographic codes might include cover design, page layout, or spacing', together with 'the other contents of the book or periodical in which the work appears as well as prefaces, notes, or dedications that affect the reception and interpretation of the work' (6), and also, if a broader socialized context is invoked, matters such as 'publisher, print run, price, or audience' (7).

Bornstein also draws on version theory, as developed by specialists in editorial theory and textual scholarship. Scholars of Romanticism, notably Donald H. Reiman and Jack Stillinger, have been particularly influential in this area (for more recent accounts, which comment on their work, see P. Cohen; Bryant). Reiman argues that, instead of relying on a single critically established version of a literary text, scholars need reliable reproductions of each important variant version. He suggests that a version worthy of its own edition would exhibit 'ideologies, aesthetic perspectives, or rhetorical strategies' that are clearly distinct from those of other versions (*Romantic Texts* 169). Bornstein combines version theory with the notion of the bibliographic code in order to direct attention back to 'modernism in its original sites of production and in the continually shifting physicality of its texts and transmissions' (1). He argues that studying texts only in our contemporary reprintings, or in the extremely decontextualized form of the excerpt in an anthology, erases many aspects of meaning, and advocates, instead, a process of 'reading successive physical incarnations of a work to reveal its political and social contingencies' (165). His case studies include poems by Yeats, Pound, H. D., Marianne Moore and T. S. Eliot which exist in multiple forms. He explores, for instance, the trajectory of Moore's frequently anthologized poem 'The Fish', which 'largely as a result of the intervention of T. S. Eliot in the construction of Moore's *Selected Poems* of 1935 mutated from a poem heavily embedded in the First World War to an ahistorical lyric exemplifying aesthetic pattern' (3). Bornstein's discussion of Yeats appears both in *Material Modernism* and also in his chapter in *The Iconic Page in Manuscript, Print, and Digital*

*Culture* (1998), which he co-edited with Teresa Tinkle. Bornstein compares the different instantiations of Yeats's poem 'September 1913', which first appeared in the *Irish Times* in September 1913, then in two volumes of Yeats's writing published by the nationalist and feminist Cuala Press, and then in a Macmillan edition of the second volume. The effect of these transitions was to depoliticize the poem, detaching it from the events of 1913 in Ireland and reducing the force of its intervention into debates about the Dublin Strike and Lockout and about the founding of a municipal art gallery.

Additional categories have been proposed to supplement or subdivide McGann's two 'codes'. Bornstein himself introduces the idea of 'contextual codes', which he needs in order to trace the full implications of changes to the material forms of modernist texts, and also in order to trace the effects of their networks of distribution. In his essay 'What is the Text of a Poem by Yeats?', included in the 1993 book that he co-edited, *Palimpsest: Editorial Theory in the Humanities*, Bornstein writes: 'Placement of a poem within a collection occupies a middle ground between its linguistic and bibliographic codes. On the one hand, such a contextual code is bibliographic in that it pertains to the physical constitution of the volume; on the other, the contextual code is linguistic in that it is made up of words' (179). As an example, he says of Yeats's 'To Ireland in the Coming Times' that:

> The early bibliographic codes provided by the covers of *Dublin University Review* and *Poems* disappear from modern collected editions, of course, yet the quasi-bibliographic contextual codes of the surrounding poems and arrangements survive. But even those contextual codes disappear when the poem is placed in anthologies like *The Norton Anthology of Modern Poetry*. There the poem appears with a cover assimilating it to international modernism rather than the Irish renaissance, an assimilation strengthened by the appearance of the entire Yeats section between poems by the English A. E. Housman and the American Edgar Lee Masters. (183, 186)

The term 'contextual codes' has not, however, been very widely used by other critics, and is certainly not as well established as the more precise category of 'bibliographic codes'.

More recently, Peter Brooker and Andrew Thacker have suggested that a version of bibliographic codes specifically relating to magazines – 'periodical codes' (6) – can be useful. In the introduction to the first volume of their *Oxford Critical and Cultural History of Modernist Magazines*, they present periodical codes as a subset of bibliographic codes, designed to analyse features specific or significant to serial publications such as periodicity (daily, weekly, monthly and so on), place of publication, subscription and news-stand price, size, type of illustrations (monochrome, two-colour, four-colour), binding, editorial practices and payment rates for contributors. Brooker and Thacker further elaborate their system of analysis by distinguishing 'between periodical codes internal to the design of a magazine (paper, typeface, layout, etc.) and those that constitute its external relations (distribution in a bookshop, support from patrons)', noting that it is often the dynamic between these internal and external codes that yields the most insight into a magazine. They use the example of advertising, since adverts indicate 'an external relationship to an imagined readership and a relationship to the world of commerce and commodities', yet at the same time, operate 'in their placement on the page or position in the magazine as a whole, as part of the magazine's internal code' (6). At the same time as Brooker and Thacker were preparing this volume, Robert Scholes and Clifford Wulfman were writing their pedagogically oriented *Modernism in the Magazines: An Introduction* (2010). They propose a similar approach, offering a list of 'information we really need for the study of modern periodicals active during the rise of modernism' (54), including the kinds of items enumerated by Brooker and Thacker, together with points relevant to contemporary critical study, such as the availability and status of archive copies. Their chapter 'How to Study a Modern Magazine' presents a set of questions and topics to guide a close study of a single title, and these include questions about aspects of the bibliographic code.

An alternative method is proposed by Faye Hammill and Michelle Smith in *Magazines, Travel, and Middlebrow Culture* (2015). In their chapter 'Pages', they present four levels of analysis, starting with a detailed dissection of an individual page, and moving up to an account of a single issue, then a full volume (one year), and lastly an overview of the key changes which happened in the areas of staffing, visual appearance, financial stability and political outlook over the course of a magazine's lifetime. This method is specifically designed to explore the bibliographic code of commercially oriented magazines of the modernist era, which tend to have long runs and many pages of content and are rarely available in digitized, searchable form.

In other scholarship, the bibliographic code is broken down into two sub-categories: 'forensic materiality' and 'formal materiality'. These terms come from Matthew Kirschenbaum, who uses them in his account of the materiality of digital media, *Mechanisms: New Media and the Forensic Imagination* (2008). Kirschenbaum reminds us that digital objects are not immaterial, that they depend on hardware, storage equipment and inscriptions on physical surfaces. Forensic materiality, he writes, 'rests upon the principle of individualization (basic to modern forensic science and criminalistics), the idea that no two things in the physical world are ever exactly alike' (10). Formal materiality, by contrast, relates to the multiple states of a digital object. An image file, for instance, has different layers which will each be visible only when certain software is used to open the file, or certain operations are performed on it. As Kirschenbaum observes, the materiality of computing 'situates electronic textuality amid other technologies and practices of writing (indexing and cataloging, longhand, adhesives, the felt-tip pen)' (10–11). His ideas have therefore proved useful to theorists of manuscript, print and digital textuality, and particularly to those who seek to explore the relationships between paper and digital artefacts. J. Matthew Huculak proposes that we 'reappropriate the term "Forensic Code"' in order 'to describe the hidden histories of materiality that form the substrate of material modernism'. He focuses in particular on the processes of making and exporting paper, and his larger argument is that: 'The forensic code is deeper than the bibliographic code, and it seeks to define relationships among disparate uses of material – not just the "contextual codes" of producing a magazine – but also the labor practices that make such relationships possible' (166–67). Kirschenbaum's ideas are also drawn on by visual scholar and digital humanist Johanna Drucker, who argues that while critical and theoretical discussion of materiality has a very long history, 'Kirschenbaum's useful intervention came at a crucial moment, and was well positioned to shift the terms of debates about digital technology back towards attention to materiality in an approach informed by interpretative disciplines such as bibliography, critical studies, and theoretical dimensions of English literature'. Drucker takes Kirschenbaum as her starting point in her essay 'Performative Materiality and Theoretical Approaches to Interface':

> In Kirschenbaum's definitions, *forensic* materiality refers to evidence, while *formal* materiality refers to the codes and structures of human expression. The forensic elements of a document might include ink, paper, stains, fingerprints, other physical traces, while the formal elements would be the organization of the layout, design, or the style of literary composition, relations between image and text and so on. Both are available to description and analysis; neither is self-evident, each would have to be interpreted and placed in a continuum of other evidence or read in relation to other texts, images, documents and the cultural codes of their composition.

Most of the aspects of forensic materiality and formal materiality listed in this extract, would be included within the category of the 'bibliographic code', as used by McGann and Bornstein. But it is worth noting that these critics do not tend to discuss features which are specific to an individual copy of a document, as opposed to an individual edition. So they would talk about ink and paper, but not stains or annotations.

Joseph Dane in *Out of Sorts: On Typography and Print Culture* (2011) sees a problem with 'the entire notion that there is such a thing as a book, rather than a book-copy'. He argues that a 'book-copy is a material thing, a singularity, with its own history, or rather its own discrete packets of evidence that constitute such a history. . . . A book, by contrast, is an abstraction: it is the illusory "being" consequent to what is a mere dream of printing – the production of identical copies of the same thing' (14). This is what Dane had already named 'the myth of print culture', a phrase he used as the title of his 2003 book on textuality and bibliographical method. While Dane's research focuses on medieval literature, his insights are equally relevant to the early twentieth century. A nice example is provided by T. S. Eliot's hand-correction of errors in copies of his own works. On 14 September 1923, he wrote to Virginia Woolf to say that he had gone into Jones and Evans bookshop in Cheapside, which was also frequented by

Aubrey Beardsley, George Bernard Shaw and others (see Lupack 75), looking for the new Hogarth Press edition of *The Waste Land*. He reported that he had 'corrected the copies they have (they say they have sold three). There are three mistakes I left: "under" for "over" London Bridge; "Coloured" for "carven" dolphin; and Macmillan for Cambridge University Press for Miss Weston's book. I hope you will forgive me' (Eliot, *Letters* 1: 213). The copies already sold, of course, went uncorrected. In the later phases of a book's life history, it can also acquire markings or damage at the hands of readers. Annotations in book-copies can be very helpful to scholars investigating questions about audience and reader response. H. J. Jackson's *Marginalia: Readers Writing in Books* (2001) offers a wide-ranging account of annotation and its relationship to the history of book ownership from the eighteenth to the twentieth century, while her *Romantic Readers: Evidence from Marginalia* (2005) narrows the chronological scope. Jackson includes both famous and obscure readers, whereas Amanda Golden, in *Annotating Modernism* (forthcoming), concentrates on writers' annotations in their personal copies of modernist texts. These, of course, were more likely to have been preserved than copies owned by ordinary readers. For scholars such as Golden and Jackson, each annotated copy represents, in effect, a different primary text with its own forensic code.

The set of 'versions' of a text, then, can be understood to include not only its variant linguistic forms, but also its different manuscript, print or digital editions, and in addition, the individual copies of each edition. Bornstein comments that 'the literary work might be said to exist not in any one version, but in all the versions put together. In reading a particular page, we would want to know of the other versions of that page, and the first step in reading would then be to discover what other pages exist with claims on our attention' (6). He draws out the implications of this statement for editorial theory, advocating an approach which recognizes not only the constructedness of the page and the existence of multiple alternatives, but also its bibliographic code. Relating the notion of the bibliographic code back to Walter Benjamin's discussion of the 'aura' in 'The Work of Art in the Age of Mechanical Reproduction', Bornstein comments that the aura does not necessarily disappear, as Benjamin suggested, when the work undergoes mass reproduction. Rather, print and other forms of mechanical reproduction can generate a new aura, since the aura is, at least in part, a function of the material qualities of the text, its situatedness in time and space. If this aspect of a literary work is ignored, and it is 'thought of as identical merely to its words' (6–7), then the possibilities for interpretation will be restricted. Removing the aura 'removes the iconicity of the page, and thus important aspects of a text's meaning' (7).

As with so many of the themes covered in this book, the page was a subject which interested early twentieth-century writers and readers. Q. D. Leavis pointed to the effects on reading practices of twentieth-century news journalism, with its very short articles, eye-catching headlines and fixed locations for regular items: 'the mere appearance of the printed page has altered in the direction determined by Northcliffe, so that its contents are to be skimmed: the temptation for the modern reader is *not* to read properly – i.e. with the fullest attention' (226). In using the page as the basic unit of analysis, Bornstein is drawing on a broader, ongoing conversation about the history of the page, with its changing material qualities and symbolic resonances. As Peter Stoicheff and Andrew Taylor note in the introduction to their edited collection, *The Future of The Page* (2004), 'Page layout and design, seemingly modern concepts, have in fact always had a significant relationship with the semantics of a text' (9). They point to the three-thousand-year history of the page, claiming that: 'From papyrus roll to manuscript codex to printed book to hypertext, the page has shaped the way people see the world' (3). Stoicheff and Taylor identify three elements of the page that require analysis: its materials (such as parchment, vellum, tree-based paper or the computer screen); its architecture (the visual arrangement of the information presented); and its ideologies (the cultural factors which determine that arrangement). They emphasize that we tend to take these things for granted: 'The page's rectangular shape and vertical format, for instance, are so familiar to us that we cease to see them as artificial' (5), yet they must have historical explanations – possibly to do with the usual dimensions of a sheepskin, or those of a human hand holding the text.

*The Future of the Page*, which emerged from a conference held in 2000, ranges widely across medieval, Renaissance and modern culture. It includes general and theoretical material which is relevant to the study of modernist print cultures, and it also contains a chapter by Michael Groden on 'James Joyce's *Ulysses* on the Page and on the Screen'. Groden explores what hypermedia presentations of Joyce's novels, such as the electronic versions of *Ulysses* and *Finnegans Wake* on the site *Finnegans Web*, can offer to readers:

> The digital presentation retains what McGann calls the 'linguistic code' and some features of the 'bibliographic code' – fonts, paragraph layouts, line units, even page divisions. But it can also give readers options regarding whether or not to retain these – one reader might want to work with the pages of the particular print edition, another might find it more important to get all of Martha Clifford's letter on the screen at one time. It can allow readers to create much of the bibliographic code in ways that are not possible in books by making the fonts larger or smaller or by changing the font entirely. (170–71)

This essay, while fascinating, gives an effect of going back in time, with its references to CD-ROMs and Handspring computers; the effect is intensified when visiting the website (last updated in 2002) to which his discussion of digital pages refers. Indeed, discussions of digitizing modernist print always date very quickly, as the technology and terminology move on. However, despite this limitation, the continuities that can be discerned across discussions of manuscript, print and digital modernisms are an enduringly relevant aspect of print culture scholarship.

## Art and the book

Despite the numerous interactions among modernist visual and literary artists, modernist studies, as Giovanni Cianci points out in 'The New Critical Demotion of the Visual in Modernism' (2007), has often tended to neglect the visual. Cianci ascribes this to a number of causes: the brevity of a period of radical artistic experimentation cut short by the First World War and the return to more traditional aesthetic modes in the postwar period (452–54); the domestication of modernism through, for example, the critical theories of the Cambridge School in the 1920s (458–60) and, later, the New Critical emphasis on close verbal analysis and its persistent marginalization of the visual. In *The Visible Word* (1994) Johanna Drucker also notes that New Criticism and high modernist visual art criticism distorted the understanding of early modernism through an emphasis on visual art's autonomy and on the value of literature as 'a play of verbal terms . . . unsullied by such contingencies as authorship, intention, or historical circumstance' (4). The ascendance of visual culture studies since the 1980s has resulted in increased attention to modernist visual media. Yet within print culture studies, attention to the paratextual elements of modernist publications – those elements other than the main text, such as footnotes, introduction, title page and the like – has not often been directed to the work of visual artists. Diane Gillespie, for example, notes that Vanessa Bell's illustrations and jackets for her sister Virginia Woolf's books have been 'rarely discussed' (*Sisters*' 116) although they do appear in several scholarly works simply as illustrations, devoid of any commentary (332–33 n21). There has also been a tendency within scholarship on modernism to separate the productions of the European avant-garde from a more general conception of modernism, isolating discussion of the radical visual experimentation of the pre-First World War period as precursive to rather than a continuing presence in modernist forms. Yet even avant-garde productions themselves have only lately begun to receive institutional and more widespread scholarly attention.

Robert H. Davis, Jr. and Edward Kasinec point out that it was not until the 1980s that the staff of the New York Public Library (NYPL) began to mention explicitly the acquisition of work by modernist book and periodical artists, having previously tended to understand the library's mission as emphasizing textual over visual content (64). The 2007 exhibition *Graphic Modernism from the Baltic to the Balkans, 1910–1935* drew on the more than 50,000 books in NYPL's Slavonic division and exemplifies how this shortcoming has been addressed by 'the acquisition of important artifactual-quality imprints, and the scanning and digitization of large quantities of visual sources – photographs, posters, extra-illustrated books – as well as an aggressive program of advertising these achievements in scholarly journals and monographs and through exhibition' (Davis and Kasinec 64).

A 2014 exhibition at New York's Museum of Modern Art titled 'Artist/Novelist' displayed many artists' books from the Museum's collection that demonstrate not only how the codex form was manipulated and exploited in the twentieth century but also how it became the site of significant collaboration among publishers, writers and artists who worked in a variety of media. For example, the Flemish printmaker Frans Masereel's *Grostesk Film* (Berlin, 1921) is a 'wordless novel of dense, frenetic etchings' inspired by expressionist film. *Mr. Knife, Miss Fork*, published by Harry and Caresse Crosby's Black Sun Press in 1931, consists of an excerpt from René Crevel's novel *Babylone* (1927) illustrated with nineteen photograms by Max Ernst. André Breton's *Nadja* (1928) is perhaps the best-known example of Surrealist book-making, and was the first 'to incorporate enigmatic photographs and absurd captions' ('Artist/Novelist'). Not displayed in 'Artist/Novelist', but another example of the form, is the collaboration between Fernand Léger and Blaise Cendrars on *La fin du monde*, a novel based on an unfilmed screenplay by Cendrars. Léger's 'dynamic, fractured compositions create a simulation of the moving images of film as the pages of the book are turned' (Wye 72).

The work of visual artists in fact permeates modernist book publishing but has so far received sustained attention only from art historians and not from print culture scholars. Many painters and graphic artists provided illustrations or cover designs for publishers of modernist works. John Aldridge, a painter and wallpaper designer who was part of the circle around Robert Graves, illustrated Laura Riding's *The Life of the Dead* (1933). Djuna Barnes, who began her career as a reporter and illustrator on the crime beat of a number of New York City's daily newspapers (Biers 23), provided drawings for her own *Book of Repulsive Women* (1915). For her Hours Press, Nancy Cunard commissioned photomontages, drawings and typography from such artists as Yves Tanguy, Louis Aragon, Man Ray and Marcel Duchamp, and also published a book of the paintings, drawings and gouaches of Eugene McCown, who was commissioned by the Woolfs' Hogarth Press to provide the cover design for Cunard's poem *Parallax* (1925). Although there has been scant critical attention to such work within modernist scholarship to date, this is beginning to change. Contributors to Kathryn Brown's 2013 collection *The Art*

*Book Tradition in Twentieth-Century Europe* examine 'a range of exchanges' between image and text 'that experiment with the reader's physical and imaginative relationship to printed matter' (4). There has been lively critical interest in visual aspects of Harlem Renaissance print culture (which will be further discussed in Chapter 3). For example, Caroline Goeser's *Picturing the New Negro* (2007) refers to Aaron Douglas's cover design for the first best-seller by an African-American writer, Claude McKay's *Home to Harlem* (1928), to exemplify how black identity was pictured as 'newly independent and self-reliant' (6) (Figure 1.1):

> As a work of art that also functioned to advertise the book, his image embodied modern design as well as merchandising savvy. Following the tenets of modern packaging, he employed one-dimensional, silhouetted shapes in a dramatic pattern across the page, which would not interrupt the flat surface of the wrapper. He further drew on contemporary forms of art and advertising in selecting an Art Deco lettering style and employing a stylized skyscraper at left as emblems of modernity. (10–11)

Goeser points out that black artists were rarely invited to publish in mainstream magazines, and even when reviewing books by Harlem Renaissance writers, the *New York Times* chose illustrations by white artists rather than the books' available cover images (104). She notes the dearth of black-owned publishing houses, and therefore the rare opportunities black artists had for book illustration. For the cover of Walter White's *Flight* (1926), Knopf did not turn to an illustrator working for *Opportunity* or *Crisis* but used a woodcut that had been made in 1916 by E. McKnight Kauffer (123). Nevertheless, Goeser explains that book jackets afforded wide public exposure for the very few Harlem Renaissance artists who were commissioned by publishing houses, as they were carried about by readers and displayed on bookshop shelves and in advertisements (114).

Although the notion of the book as an art object has been present since scribal culture gave way to print, in the first decades of the twentieth century there was an explosion of creative work in books by artists who were better known for their work in other visual media. Often these works were commissioned by art dealers who saw a market for them in the wake of the success of late

FIGURE 1.1 *Claude McKay,* Home to Harlem *(1928), cover design by Aaron Douglas. © Heirs of Aaron Douglas/VAGA, NY/DACS, London 2014. Harry Ransom Center, The University of Texas at Austin.*

Victorian fine printing and decorated books. Ambroise Vollard, one of the most important dealers in modern French art in Paris in the early decades of the twentieth century, commissioned Pierre Bonnard to create lithographs to accompany Paul Verlaine's poem *Parallèlement* (1900) and the *Daphnis et Chloe* by Longus (1902). Vollard also commissioned illustrations by Auguste Rodin, Maurice Denis, Emile Bernard, Raoul Dufy, Marc Chagall, Georges Rouault and Picasso. In an article discussing the persistence of collaborations between visual artists and writers throughout the twentieth century, Renée Riese Hubert and Judd D. Hubert note that works by Gertrude Stein had been published by the art dealer Daniel Henry Kahnweiler before she became well-known as a writer. Kahnweiler commissioned *A Book Concluding As a Wife Has a Cow* with lithographs by Juan Gris (1926), and *The Village* with lithographs by Elie Lascaux (1928).

Illustrations had gradually been excluded from fiction for adults by the end of the nineteenth century but flourished in books intended for children. Renée Riese Hubert and Judd D. Hubert point out that nineteenth-century mimetic illustrations encouraged readers to adopt the point of view of the artist, whereas modern (and postmodern) 'graphic commentaries tend to problematize the text and thus to complicate rather than impose an interpretation' (702). Critics have recently begun to rectify the long-term exclusion of children's literature from considerations of modernism. Introducing a 2007 special issue of the *Children's Literature Association Quarterly*, Karin E. Westman notes a growing interest in the intersection of these areas of study (285). In 'Olive Beaupré Miller's *My Book House*: From William Morris to Modernism Under One Roof', Rennie Mapp identifies the influence of Morris on Beaupré Miller's 1920 children's anthology because its design follows what McGann describes as 'Morris's resistance to any interpretive separation of typeface, illustration and literary text' (Mapp 549). Mapp places Beaupré Miller's anthology 'within the cultural networks of modernist Chicago' (545), and draws particular attention to the poem 'City Smoke', in which 'the fumes from urban chimneys drift in three modes: lexical, typographical, and pictorial' (543). There is, in fact, a rich vein of children's book work within modernism, another aspect of the print cultural links between the late nineteenth and early twentieth centuries. In surveying the field from 1900 to 1985, Nicholas Paley remarks on the number of influential modernist artists who made limited edition children's books, starting with the 'extraordinary' *Dreaming Youths* (*Die Traumenden Knaben*), written and illustrated by the Austrian Expressionist Oskar Kokoschka as a commission from the Viennese Wiener Werkstätte in 1907, that is 'widely regarded as a landmark text in twentieth century book design and as one of the most important objects in twentieth century art' (Paley 266). Avant-garde experiments in typography (discussed in the next section of this chapter) also ventured into this realm, the best-known example being El Lissitzky's *About Two Squares* (*Pro dva Kvadrata*, 1922), dedicated 'To all, all children'. Paley sees this work as not only codifying many of the visual and literary developments of twentieth-century modernism but also as laying 'the foundation for later experiments in children's picture book abstraction' (266). The De Stijl artist Theo van Doesburg produced a Dutch version of *About Two Squares* in 1922, and collaborated in 1925 with the dadaists Kurt Schwitters and Kate Steinitz on *The Scarecrow* (*Die Scheuche*), a work that demonstrated how these artists had extended the experimental typography created by Lissitzky (Paley 266).

Among Gertrude Stein's works, too, are illustrated books for children. Hubert and Hubert note that she collaborated with Clement Hurd, a pupil of Fernand Léger's, on *The World is Round* (1939), and that her posthumously published *The First Reader* (1946) was illustrated by Sir Francis Rose (Hubert and Hubert 678). In 1940, Stein wrote another children's book, *To Do: A Book of Alphabets and Birthdays*, as a follow-up to *The World is Round*, but was unable to find it a publisher. Stein had herself appeared in a parodic work of 1913 that took the form of a children's reader and was created in response to the Armory Show in Chicago. *The Cubies' ABC* by Mary Mills Lyall and Earl Harvey Lyall illustrated the letter G thus:

G is for Gertrude Stein's limpid lucidity,
(Eloquent scribe of the Futurist soul.)
Cubies devour each word with avidity:
'Alone words lack sense' they affirm with placidity,
But how wise we'll be when we've swallowed the whole!'
– G is for Gertrude Stein's limpid lucidity.

Such irreverent works have also attracted attention recently, for example in Leonard Diepeveen's *The Difficulties of Modernism* (2003). *The Cubies' ABC* forms the cover illustration for Diepeveen's 2014 *Mock Modernisms: An Anthology of Parodies, Travesties, Frauds, 1910–1935*.

If book illustration in the nineteenth century was largely mimetic, depicting events and characters described in the narrative, by the 1920s the relation of the graphic to the textual had become a much-discussed question. Roger Fry described book illustration as a 'battle ground, a no-man's land raked by alternate fires from the artist and the writer, claimed by both, sometimes nearly conquered by one, but only to be half recaptured by the other. . . . The question whether true illustration is possible at all has never been satisfactorily answered' (157). Fry ends his essay with an account of woodcuts made by André Derain to illustrate Guillaume Apollinaire's *L'Enchanteur Pourissant*, published by Kahnweiler (1909). Praising his 'wonderful instinct for conceiving forms directly in terms of the gouge-stroke on the wood block', Fry says that Derain has produced 'an original poem instead of a translation' (170) that might lead a reader to anticipate more from Apollinaire than the poet was able to provide (172). What particularly interested Fry was how the modernist visual artist (using an ancient technology) is able to exploit the tension between a mimetic relation to the text and the formal autonomy of the graphic work.

In her comprehensive survey of *British Wood-Engraved Book Illustration, 1904–1940* (1998), Joanna Selborne points out that although Morris and others had rescued wood-engraving from the oblivion threatened by facsimile engraving and photomechanical processes, the late nineteenth-century fine-printing movement had paradoxically removed the medium to the 'exclusive domain of the private presses and esoteric magazines' (43). That wood-engraving and woodcuts underwent a revival in the early twentieth century was due in large part to the influence of the Central School of Arts and Crafts, in particular its School of Production, among whose notable students was the sculptor, print maker and typeface designer Eric Gill. Gill took up wood-engraving after becoming dissatisfied with designing letter forms for photomechanical reproduction in books (Selborne 60). It was the young students of the Slade School of Fine Art, however, who brought modernist aesthetics to bear on wood-engraving after being shaken by Vorticism and by the exhibitions of Post-Impressionist painting organized in 1910 and 1913 by Roger Fry in London (Selborne 85–86). Less affected, as Selborne explains, than were painting and sculpture by the 'dilemma between the use of abstraction as a means of effecting a radical break with tradition, and the need to depict contemporary life, yet in a non-representational way', wood-engraving inspired 'much of the more innovative book work and advertising in the inter-war years' (85; see also Von Lintel). Among the most successful illustrators in this medium was Gwen Raverat, who produced one of the first books illustrated with white-line wood engravings (Selborne 76). In 'Rural Modernity and the Wood-Engraving Revival in Interwar England', Kristen Bluemel, discussing the woodcut illustrations Raverat made for A. G. Street's *Farmer's Glory* (1932), together with some by Joan Hassall for Francis Brett Young's *Portrait of a Village* (1937), contests the notion that only urban modernist works can appropriately represent modernity. Bluemel sees wood-engraved books as a special feature of the flood of print concerned with relations between the rural and modernity that emerged in England after the First World War. She also discusses Raverat in her article 'A Happy Heritage', examining the curious choice of elite university presses to publish 'a culturally devalued form of poetry – children's poetry – while simultaneously attempting to signal its "elevated" status within children's book publishing through use of the old, labor-intensive art of wood engraving'. Bluemel counters the notion of wood-engraving as a nostalgic persistence of Victorian handcraft by pointing out that engraved boxwood blocks – a late eighteenth-century innovation of Thomas Bewick's – could be locked up in a chase with type to be printed. The 'aura of authenticity' bestowed by wood-engraved illustration was disseminated by 'modern, industrial processes of mechanical reproduction, mass distribution, and international marketing' ('Happy').

The modern idea of the book as an art object derived in large part from the legacy of William Morris, whose resistance to industrial modes of production led to his founding the Kelmscott Press in 1891. In *Black Riders*, McGann takes Morris as a point of departure for the study of modernism, seeing his work as a 'precursive event' for twentieth-century poetry (75). The materiality of the book, its bibliographic codes, as conceived by Morris and his craftsmen, continued to influence book design – and specifically page design – throughout the first half of the twentieth century. In 'Some Thoughts on the Ornamented Manuscripts of the Middle Ages', an unpublished essay of 1892, Morris contrasts the 'utilitarian production of makeshifts, which is the especial curse of modern times' with bookmaking in the Middle Ages 'when a book was a palpable work of art' (qtd. in E. Miller, 'William Morris' 482). Despite what Drucker describes as 'its *retardataire* stylistics and conservative promotion of anachronistic methods of production' (*Visible* 93), Morris's press 'served to sensitize the eyes of the late nineteenth-century public to the visual appearance of the page as a significant feature of literary production' (93). The influence of Morris on the arts of the book has been identified in modernist print culture scholarship concerning a broad range of literary genres and geographic locations. In a discussion of early twentieth-century developments in the production of volumes of modernist poetry in Sweden, for example, Jon Viklund draws on both Drucker and McGann to argue that, although not expressed ideologically in the manner of Morris, the increasing importance of the book artist and the use of 'expressive typography' is a parallel phenomenon to what was occurring in England at the end of the nineteenth century (302). Morris was a specific impetus for the renaissance in wood-engraving that was so marked a characteristic of modernist book production. Roger Fry's 1913 prospectus for the Omega Workshops mentions Morris directly several times in stating its antipathy to a modern industrialism that has 'substituted the machine for the craftsman and the plagiarist for the artist', thus linking Morris to the Post-Impressionism that Fry sees as having 'brought the artist back to the problems of design so that he is once more in a position to grasp sympathetically the conditions of applied art' (C. Reed, *Roger Fry* 198).

Fry founded the Omega Workshops to sell decorative arts made by painters and thus provide them an income that would allow them time to paint. It sold a wide range of products – lamps, screens, jewellery, furniture, menu cards – as well as designs for textiles. (After several business disputes, the Omega closed in 1919.) In 1915, Fry announced that the Omega Workshops would begin publishing books in addition to their other activities. A notice in the *Burlington Magazine*'s 'Monthly Chronicle' for November 1915 quotes a prospectus that specifically mentions their intention to 'employ original wood-blocks cut by the artist for the illustration and decoration of the text'. Although it produced only four books, the Omega, therefore, participated in what was a gathering wave of wood-engraved illustration that would bring the medium widespread attention by the 1920s through its presence in books, magazines and advertisements. The Omega's book publications are discussed in Alexandra Gerstein's *Beyond Bloomsbury: Designs of the Omega Workshops 1913–19* (2009) which includes colour images of each book. In that volume, published in conjunction with an exhibition at London's Courtauld Gallery, art historian Grace Brockington describes the books as making 'a statement of Fry's pacifist priorities through the high quality of their design and production' ('Omega' 62). Selborne, on the other hand, comments on Fry's lack of interest in fine printing and his unadventurous approach to typography (95). Brockington has explained that the Omega's book programme was anomalous in the history of wartime publishing, when there was general retrenchment due to paper shortages. She states that Fry was working in the tradition of 'the recent innovations of the French *livres d'artiste* as much as the British tradition of the Book Beautiful' that derived from Morris, favouring woodcut illustrations 'inspired by modern European art, rather than the medievalism of the Kelmscott Press' (*Above* 101). The last of the four Omega books was *Original Woodcuts by Various Artists* (1919). The cover was stamped with a wood block that had also stamped fabric for Omega dresses (Gerstein 157), a nice illustration of the Omega's attitude towards books as existing on a continuum of artistic productions made by hand.

When Leonard and Virginia Woolf started the Hogarth Press in 1917, the Omega Workshops often supplied them with the brightly patterned paper that became a distinctive feature of their hand-printed books. Donna E. Rhein provides a complete bibliographical description of each of these in *The Handprinted Books of Leonard and Virginia Woolf at the Hogarth Press, 1917–1932* (1985). Elizabeth Willson Gordon has explained that such 'recognizably historical elements' as woodcuts or hand-printing added a specific kind of cultural as well as commercial value to the works of unknown authors and new books alike published by the Hogarth Press ('How' 123). The Hogarth Press commissioned a great many artists during the first thirty years of its existence, but there has as yet not been very much discussion of their work specifically for book publishers, apart from that devoted to Vanessa Bell and

Duncan Grant. A brief, but useful, appraisal by Louise Buck of the work of John Banting for the Hogarth Press is a rare exception to the dearth of work on this aspect of modernism's print cultures. In *The Bloomsbury Artists: Prints and Book Design* (1999), a lavishly illustrated and comprehensive catalogue of the 'multiples' – woodcuts, linocuts, etchings, lithographs, dust jackets and book illustrations – produced by Bell, Grant, Fry and Carrington, Tony Bradshaw again noted the scarcity of attention paid to these artists' graphic work (23). Since then, David Porter has discussed in detail the involvement of the Woolfs in the visual aspects of book production ('We All'; *Virginia Woolf*). More recently, Jennifer Sorensen has brought together media theory, visual theory and thing theory to analyse three early publications of the Hogarth Press in the conclusion to her study of the interaction between modernist experimentation and its material forms.

At present, Bloomsbury – and especially the Hogarth Press – remains the focus of most scholarship on collaborations between artists and writers in modernist publishing. The collaboration between Vanessa Bell and Virginia Woolf offers a case study for the kind of modernist print culture scholarship that might be developed in the future (Figure 1.2). As Benjamin Harvey remarks in his important article 'Lightness Visible: An Appreciation of Bloomsbury's Books and Blocks', considered as a group, Bell's covers for Woolf's books constitute a 'major contribution to twentieth-century book design' (89). The earliest comprehensive treatment of this collaboration is Diane Gillespie's *The Sisters Arts: The Writing and Painting of Virginia Woolf and Vanessa Bell* (1988). Gillespie notes that Bell 'created her dust-jacket designs, like her illustrations, with a very limited palette, often no more than black with white or buff', and attributes her skill in working within these constraints to her experience as a decorative artist. Furthermore, she notes that for a book artist, because books are typically printed in black ink, 'black is usually a given. It can be, as Matisse points out, an advantage' (255). Bell used it to great effect in the black flower on the dust jacket of Woolf's *The Years* (1937).

Cloth binding had become common by the 1920s because it was insisted on by the lending libraries that were so powerful a market force in Britain (unlike in France, where the tradition of individuals purchasing the books they wanted to read meant

FIGURE 1.2 *Vanessa Bell. Woodcut illustration for 'A Society' by Virginia Woolf.* Monday or Tuesday. *London: Hogarth Press, 1922. Courtesy of Manuscripts, Archives and Special Collections, Washington State University Libraries.*

that paper covers were the norm). Cloth binding had led to dust jackets, and these soon were exploited for the purposes of advertising and branding. Bell's jacket design for the first of Woolf's novels published by the Hogarth Press, *Jacob's Room* (1922) was met with dismay by booksellers because it 'did not represent a desirable female or even Jacob or his room', but smacked of post-impressionism (L. Woolf, *Autobiography* 241). Virginia Woolf informed her sister that her design for the cover of *The Common Reader* (1925) had been excoriated by *The Star* which said that Woolf tried to live up to the decorations 'by being as revolutionary and nonsensical – a very good advertisement' (qtd. in Tony Bradshaw, 'Virginia' 290). Catherine Hollis has remarked how the distinctive lettering Bell created for her sister's name and for the titles of her books came to function as an 'authorial signature' denoting not only the Hogarth Press but the Bloomsbury Group as a whole (19–20). Gordon emphasizes this point by describing the 'triangular cross-referencing association' that linked Bell, Woolf and the Press through the sensuous aspects of book design functioning as what we would now call a brand, or what Helen Southworth has described as the 'house style' of the Hogarth Press ('Bloomsbury' 153).

The most striking example of the sisters' 'habits of competitive collaboration' (Gillespie 139) is the 1927 edition of *Kew Gardens*. Woolf's short story had first been hand-printed in 1919 with two woodcuts by Bell, the quality of the reproduction of which led to a quarrel. Woolf recorded that her sister 'firmly refused to illustrate any more stories of mine under those conditions, & went so far as to doubt the value of the Hogarth Press altogether' (*Diary* 279). As self-taught printers, the Woolfs were ill-equipped to deal with the challenges of inking engraved wood-blocks, although they persisted and eventually sought the assistance of professional printers for subsequent books containing woodcuts. Gillespie discusses the way Bell's woodcuts relate to the text of Woolf's story despite their having agreed that the illustration did not have to be 'about the story' (Woolf, *Letters* 258), and suggests that Bell and Woolf saw themselves as 'communicating in different but complementary media' (137).

The third edition of *Kew Gardens* exemplifies the kind of modernist collaborative artwork that demands a critical approach aware of how linguistic, bibliographic and other codes interact.

Gillespie infers from the layout of the twenty-one pages designed by Bell that 'Virginia or Leonard, or both, must have given Vanessa some indication of what part of the text would be on each page since the portions are relatively self-contained' (123). Like Delaunay's painting in *La prose du Transsibérien*, Bell's decorations 'penetrate into areas of the page usually reserved for text' (Harvey 106). Harvey notes that the title page indicates the book is 'decorated by' rather than 'illustrated by' Vanessa Bell, emphasizing that her work is not intended as mimetic. Woolf's text is itself altered 'in fundamental ways so as to accommodate the borders and respond to them' (107). Exemplifying what Bornstein terms 'the iconicity of the page' (7), this version of *Kew Gardens* 'puts the page – rather than, say, the paragraph – at the heart of the book's organization' (Harvey 107), a circumstance that leads to Bell's being able to exploit the surprise involved in turning the page in a manner often employed by children's book artists. For example, Harvey finds 'some surprising kinships in the playful relationship between typographic elements and illustrative elements' of Bell's decorations for *Kew Gardens* and E. H. Shepard's illustrations for A. A. Milne's *Winnie-the-Pooh* (1926), both of which treat the page 'as a kind of physical and gravitational field' (110). In an inspired reading of the page on which two working-class women's conversation devolves into nonsense (ending 'Sugar, sugar, sugar'), Harvey points out how Bell's flower divides Woolf's sentences into two, then three, then four columns, prompting a reader's consciousness of 'the (usually ignored) vertical relationships between words' and thus resulting in another version of nonsense (112).

Many significant designers provided art for the Hogarth Press and other publishers during careers that also involved them in a great variety of other fields. For example, the prolific pattern maker Enid Marx made woodcuts for *A Childhood* by Francesca Allinson, published by the Hogarth Press in 1937. Marx went on to design more covers for the Hogarth Press, and continued to work for Chatto & Windus after it bought the Press in 1946. Thus it was that the woman who designed the moquette used by London Transport until the late 1960s on its bus and Underground seat coverings also designed the dust jackets for Proust's *Remembrance of Things Past* and for the *Collected Works* of Aldous Huxley (Artmonsky 25). In 1928, the renowned graphic artist E. McKnight Kauffer created a new, somewhat abstract logo for the Hogarth Press. From then on, his design was used in all Hogarth Press advertisements, a fact that both Willis (377) and Gordon ('On' 181) see as marking a recognition on the part of Leonard Woolf that the Press was successfully developing a more commercial character. Gordon points out that this new logo was accompanied by the hiring of a dedicated traveller and an increased scope of distribution. McKnight Kauffer had already created cover designs for and illustrated works by several writers, including Lytton Strachey and T. S. Eliot. His striking photographic collage for the jacket of Leonard Woolf's psychological study of dictators, *Quack, Quack!* published by the Hogarth Press in 1935, exemplifies how for McKnight Kauffer the book jacket was 'a mini-poster' (Heller). Through its collaboration with McKnight Kauffer, the Hogarth Press became associated with the diverse network of publishers, designers, artists and advertisers for whom he had provided a graphic style emblematic of the transformed nature of print in the early twentieth century (Figure 1.3).

## Design, image and typeface

According to the historian of printing Michael Twyman, it is necessary to remind ourselves frequently that 'printing has never been limited to books'. He comments in *The British Library Guide to Printing: History and Techniques* (1998): 'Many other kinds of products, including newspapers, magazines, maps, sheet music, playing cards, religious prints, bookplates, notices, posters, security printing, forms, invitations, packaging, and even more ephemeral items than these, have had a long history in print' (17). Indeed, Twyman's earlier volume, *Printing: 1770–1970* (1970), entirely omits books in order to concentrate on ephemera. In general terms, as 'book history' has expanded into 'print culture studies', ephemera have attracted increasing attention. In modernist studies specifically, recent research has foregrounded posters, stationery, magazine illustrations and dust jackets, as well as exploring the significant influence of graphic designers on the culture of modernism. It is important, then, to consider the innovative (and also

FIGURE 1.3 E. McKnight Kauffer, Words and Poetry *by George Rylands. London: Hogarth Press, 1928. Image courtesy of the Bruce Peel Special Collections Library, University of Alberta, and the Modernist Archives Publishing Project (MAPP).* © *Simon Rendall.*

nostalgic) trends in modernist book design, which were explored in the previous section, in the wider context of other forms of early twentieth-century print. The involvement of key figures such as E. McKnight Kauffer in book art, on the one hand, and in the design of posters, advertisements and shop signs, on the other, reveals the interconnectedness of these different areas of print production, and points to their shared relationship to an expanding commercial culture.

Questions about art's connection to commerce, and about the status of the book as a commodity, were sharpened at the turn of the century by the proliferation of advertisements occasioned by new modes of printing as well as by new markets. Scholars have taken up the theme of modernism's involvement with the commercial in several different ways, and these are discussed in different parts of our book. In this section, we look at recent work on the shared visual idioms of advertising and editorial art, and on the interaction of text and image in illustrated publications. Research on the impact of commercially driven innovations in printing and typography on modernist book and periodical production will also be discussed here. In Chapter 2, the focus will shift to the ways that print products were sold, and the different financial models and business practices used by small presses, magazines and booksellers.

During the 1980s and 1990s, the history and theory of design and material culture began to emerge as a distinct multidisciplinary research field. Degree programmes, collaborative projects and publications in design history have brought together design practitioners with art historians, curators, fashion historians and even engineers. Some of these projects encompass the histories of book and magazine design, or of typography and printing. One example is the Manchester University Press book series 'Studies in Design', which includes a volume on *Design and the Modern Magazine* (2007). In their introduction, editors Jeremy Aynsley and Kate Forde observe that the magazine results 'from a division of labour between editors, advertisers, journalists, illustrators, typographers, designers, art directors and, in more recent years, stylists' (2), and therefore calls for interdisciplinary methods of analysis. 'Since magazines are composite rather than singular objects', Aynsley and Forde argue, 'they could be seen to parallel interiors, another form of complex designed entity, and in many respects they raise equivalent questions of interpretation' (2). *Design and the Modern Magazine* includes useful essays on advertising, colour and typefaces in magazines of the 1920s and 1930s. Other kinds of source for the study of modernist graphic design include the illustrated histories produced by art publishers. Two overview accounts, both lavishly illustrated, are Steven Heller and Seymour Chwast's *Graphic Style: From Victorian to Post-Modern* (1988), co-authored by two American design practitioners, and Ned Drew and Paul Sternberger's *By Its Cover: Modern American Book Design* (2005). A more specialized example is Phil Baines's *Penguin By Design: A Cover Story 1935–2005* (2005), which responds to the increasing interest in Penguin books as design icons. Exhibition catalogues are also valuable. In addition to the book art exhibitions mentioned in the previous section, several shows concentrating on modernist magazine design have attested to the growing interest in this subject. An early example is the 1985–1986 exhibition at Yale on the left-wing magazine *The Masses*, which was the basis for Rebecca Zurier's *Art for* The Masses: *A Radical Magazine and Its Graphics, 1911–1917* (1988). In 1996, *Letters from the Avant-Garde: Modern Graphic Design* by Ellen Lupton and Elaine Lustig Cohen was published in conjunction with an exhibition on 'The Avant-Garde Letterhead' at the Smithsonian Institution. More recently, Kirsten MacLeod's *American Little Magazines of the 1890s: A Revolution in Print* (2013) was produced to accompany an exhibition at New York's Grolier Club.

The history of design is closely connected with the history of new technologies. In the context of print culture, a wide range of technological developments have influenced the appearance and the material forms of the printed artefact. Among those which were invented, or made commercially viable, in the period from 1880 to 1910 were half-tone illustration, automated typesetting and offset printing; all had far-reaching consequences for modernist publishing.[4] Letterpress printing, the technique dating back to Gutenberg in the fifteenth century, is a relief process in which pieces of lead or wood, each bearing a raised character, are set in a flat bed, inked and pressed against the paper. Letterpress was still in use in the early twentieth century, but had been transformed by a series of innovations. A hand compositor could set at most two thousand characters into the bed in an hour, but the new hot-metal typesetting machines, which cast fresh characters for each job, tripled this work rate. The first Linotype machine, which produced the letters as a continuous metal line, was installed at the *New York Tribune* in 1886. About a decade later, Monotype composing machines came into commercial use. Featuring a keyboard and producing each letter individually, they allowed more scope for innovative typeface design. Offset lithography, which involves the transfer of an image from a metal plate onto a rubber roller and then onto the paper, was invented in 1903. Documents produced in this way do not show the 'bite' left by letterpress type on the surface of the paper. It was not until the 1950s that offset lithography became more economical than letterpress for short-run printing.

By 1880, images could be printed alongside letterpress text by inserting a photomechanical engraving of a line drawing beside the type. The following decade saw the introduction of the halftone process, which converted the continuous tones of a photograph into a pattern of differently sized dots. By the 1890s, it had become economically feasible to print monochrome photographs and text together, and over the succeeding decades, the quality of photomechanical reproduction improved rapidly. This innovation has been examined by media historians primarily in terms of its enormous impact on the popular print marketplace, via illustrated newspapers and consumer magazines (as we will discuss below). Literary and art historians, meanwhile, have pointed to its transformative effects on modernist practice. Julian Murphet comments in *Multimedia Modernism* that in avant-garde journals, 'literature and painting, but also photography itself, passed through the indiscriminate screen of halftone technology, which . . . managed to reproduce photographs and paintings as print, and level the terrain for words and pictures both' (77). In his case study of Alfred Stieglitz's quarterly photographic magazine *Camera Work* (1903–1917), Murphet observes that words 'had been transformed by the fact of their photographic reproduction on the printed page, in a space technically coextensive with the photographs they attended, justified and named' (63–64). The notion of words as art did not, of course, originate in the modern era, but mechanical type opened up a new area of experiment, and when it was combined with photomechanical technologies, the range of possibilities was greatly extended. The early twentieth century was an era of striking, varied and purposeful experimentation with typography.

One of the most important studies on this topic is Johanna Drucker's *The Visible Word: Experimental Typography and Modern Art, 1909–1923* (1994). Drucker emphasizes that modernist typographical experiment emerged from, rather than preceded, the innovations of commercial designers, arguing that 'the forms of graphic design that would become hallmark elements of avant-garde typography were already fully in place in advertising and commercial work by the end of the nineteenth century' (94). Her focus is primarily on the figures from continental Europe who were the leaders in typographical experiment. Prominent among them was the Futurist Filippo Tommaso Marinetti, who called for a revolution in typography that would replace the harmonious, orderly, traditional page with a mixture of different typefaces and colours expressive of flux and motion. Drucker also discusses Guillaume Apollinaire, whose *Calligrammes* (1918) presented a series of shaped poems, including one in which the words were arranged in the form of the Eiffel Tower and another, 'Il Pleut', in which almost illegible cascades of letters are designed to evoke rain (Figure 1.4).

Apollinaire was influenced by Stéphane Mallarmé, an early experimenter with typography, whose celebrated *Un Coup de Dés Jamais N'Abolira Le Hasard*, with its striking layout, appeared in the magazine *Cosmopolis* in 1897. According to Drucker, Mallarmé's inspiration for the appearance of the poem 'derived in part from his negative reaction to the habits of reading formed in response to the daily press, to the tedious patterns of verbal presentation' (56), though she also notes that he was apparently 'intrigued by the possibilities of advertising typography' (256 n4). This ambivalence was broadly characteristic of modernists, who often acknowledged the creativity evident in commercial and popular print forms while deprecating their repetitive structures and the addictive habits they encouraged in readers.

Mallarmé was also an influence on the eastern and central European artists who are associated with the flourishing of typographic experimentation during the interwar decades. Drucker gives particular attention to Ilia Zdanevich and Tristan Tzara. Zdanevich's 1923 poster for the infamous Dada event arranged by Tzara in Paris, *Soirée du coeur à barbe*, is one of the best-known examples of avant-garde typography from this era (Figure 1.5).

## Il pleut

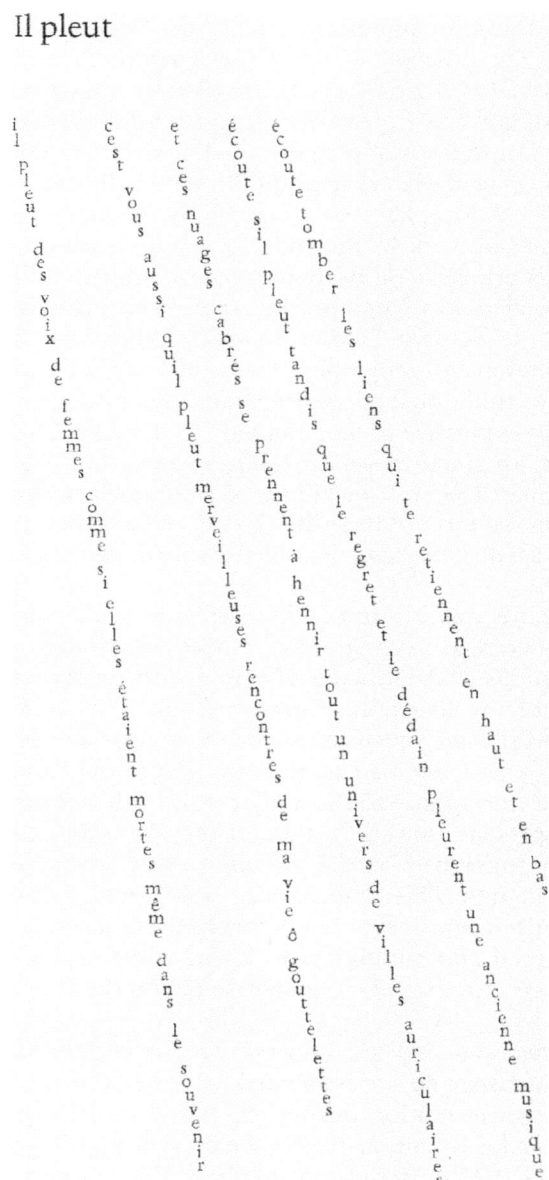

**FIGURE 1.4** *Guillaume Apollinaire, 'Il pleut' from* Selected Poems *by Guillaume Apollinaire, translated and introduced by Oliver Bernard, Anvil Press Poetry, 2004.*

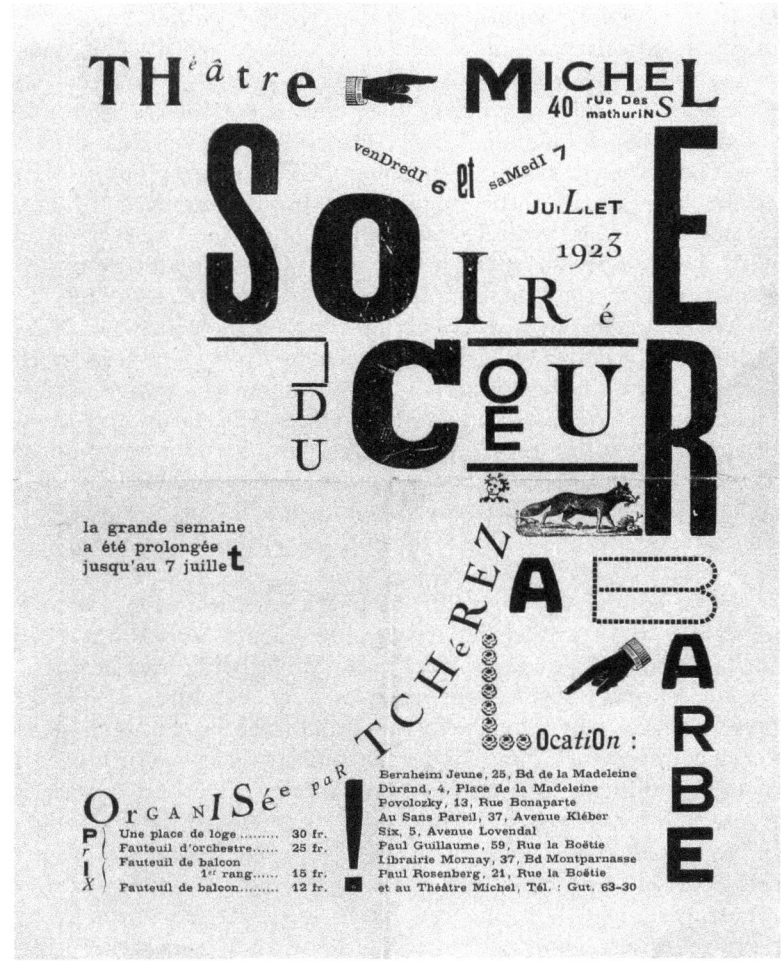

FIGURE 1.5  *Ilia Mikhailovich Zdanevich, 'Soirée du Coeur à Barbe'. Courtesy of the Merrill C. Berman Collection.*

Drucker explains that the poster uses 'paragonnage: the assortment of various sizes of type within a single word'. This fragmentation of the visual word, she notes, presents the letters as 'independent, thus intensifying the contrast between written and spoken forms of language' (189). Drucker contrasts Zdanevich's work, an esoteric rather than politicized practice, aiming solely at the 'liberation of the imagination into unknown, unfamiliar activity' (192), with Tzara's, 'which is engaged at every level with the production of language within the sites and rhetorical structures of commodity culture' (193). Tzara's much-quoted 'To Make a Dadaist Poem' wittily comments on the process of making cut-ups or collages ('Take a newspaper / Take some scissors', it begins). Tzara's re-use of texts taken from newspapers, advertisements, train schedules and similar sources was, Drucker argues, designed to explore the boundaries between art and commodity. The extracts 'bear the material traces of their original sites in their typographic form', so that 'the visual form of language ... reveals the context, history, origin of the phrases within the public sphere of printed matter' (193).

While commercial print forms provided inspiration and raw materials for avant-garde artists, the artists' experiments, in turn, influenced designers working in advertising and business. Recent scholarly discussions, such as Drucker's and Murphet's, present this as a dynamic, two-way process, seeking to revise earlier accounts which had privileged modernists as the originators of typographical innovation. An example is Herbert Spencer's *Pioneers of Modern Typography* (1969; revised 1983), which became a reference point in the field. Spencer constructs a narrative of what he calls 'the "heroic" period of modern typography', arguing that 'the revolution was carried through by painters, writers, poets, architects, and others who came to printing from outside the industry' (13). He downplays the contribution of trained professionals such as the calligrapher and type designer Jan Tschichold, who is introduced only in the closing pages as a popularizer and teacher of the new typographical techniques. Elsewhere, Tschichold, author of the landmark *Die Neue Typographie* (1928), is credited with a visionary influence on graphic design.[5] His extremely influential manifestos and printing manuals of the 1920s and 1930s codified the principles of modern typography in a way that could be followed by commercial printers. His later work, while less rigidly prescriptive, still tended towards standardization. John Clifford, in *Graphic Icons* (2014), points to the importance of Tschichold's work for Penguin Books in the late 1940s. It was he who established the colour-coding system for Penguin's paperback covers (fiction in orange, biography in blue and so on), and in addition 'he considered how the book felt in the hand, and established rules for printing, paper weight, and binding' (65).

Tschichold, whose designs always prioritized direct communication, strongly advocated the use of sans serif typefaces because of their simplicity and readability. Jeremy Aynsley, in a chapter in *Design and the Modern Magazine*, comments: 'In the 1920s the sans-serif typeface in general was interpreted as a modern design solution, associated with Constructivism and functionalism' (41). He notes that the most successful typefaces, such as Paul Renner's Futura and Eric Gill's Gill Sans, were 'designed to fit the machine aesthetic of Modernism . . . with their evident references to geometrical sources', and were intended to provide industry standards (41). Aynsley's article focuses on a less well known specialist typeface, Fashion, which is 'best characterised as *moderne* rather than Modernist', through a visual association with art deco and its luxury objects. Aynsley comments: 'The typeface is light, elegant and spatially generous. . . . Its spatial airiness, emphasising the whiteness of the page both as unused space and the space taken up, enhances a sense of luxury and extravagance' (43–44). He explores the introduction of this typeface in fashion magazines, connecting it to their simultaneous shift towards asymmetrical blocks of text, wider borders and more photography. All of these, he notes, follow the prescriptions for modernist and art magazines which Tschichold articulated in *Die Neue Typographie* (46). Numerous exhibitions held in Britain and in France in the 1920s and 1930s, as well as journals such as *Fleuron* and *Signature*, helped to promulgate typographical design. In her detailed account of the postwar British printing renaissance, Joanna Selborne sees the appointment of Stanley Morison as typographical adviser to the Monotype Corporation in 1923 as 'a turning-point in printing history' (130). Morison produced a number of typefaces that became the most commonly used in book production, and in 1932 his introduction of Times New Roman as the typeface for *The Times* 'radically affected the aesthetics of newspaper design' (130).

The term 'editorial art' can be used to refer to typography, illustration, ornamentation and other visual matter in books and magazines. Numerous critical analyses of the relationship between text and image in periodical layouts are available, and while some of these focus on popular print and some on avant-garde titles, their methods are often similar. In modernist studies, attention to the news media has not yet been extensive, but critics acknowledge the transformative effect of technologies for the reproduction of photographs. The newspapers and weekly magazines owned by the large conglomerates – notably the Northcliffe Press in the United Kingdom and Henry Luce's Time Inc. in the United States – were heavily, and increasingly, dependent on illustration. Michael North in *Reading 1922* includes a chapter on 'Tourists in the Age of the World Picture' in which he says of Northcliffe: 'He was, more than anyone else, responsible for making pictures the medium of national communication' (126). Discussion of consumer magazines is becoming increasingly prominent among scholars of modernist-era print, and most studies build on Richard Ohmann's influential account, *Selling Culture: Magazines, Markets, and Class at the Turn of the Century* (1996). Ohmann points out that the American magazines of the 1880s and 1890s, such as the *Ladies Home Journal, Munsey's* and *Cosmopolitan*, 'made halftone photoengravings a staple' (224), and emphasizes that the advertising which increasingly financed these publications was not simply an aspect of their service function, but was crucial to their lavish visual display. He argues that these magazines differed from their predecessors in ways that are visible through 'the internal relations of photographs to print' (224). Whereas in earlier decades, drawings had been used to illustrate something in the text, in the new magazines of the late nineteenth century, 'often the photographs were the point of an article, with text demoted to commentary' (224). Ohmann also points to the status of these magazines as desirable objects: 'The visual presentation of the magazine announced its own status as an elegantly made commodity that would grace a modern parlor' (224). Using a Marxist framework, he focuses on the complicated relationship between the magazine itself as product and the products that it promoted. The saleability of the magazine, and likewise of the household and personal items advertised in its pages, depended partly on visual appeal and partly on the prestige and class associations which its design, its glossiness and its colourfulness evoked.

Moving to studies of modernist magazines, an excellent example of a book which takes full account of the design and appearance of a particular title is Faith Binckes's *Modernism, Magazines, and the British Avant-garde: Reading* Rhythm, *1910–1914* (2010). Binckes notes that *Rhythm*, as well as publishing art criticism, was 'absolutely saturated with images' (131). Her chapter 'Being Graphic' relates the textual content of *Rhythm* to its many illustrations and its few, carefully selected adverts, considering the impact of these elements 'upon its status as an "art-object" and item of commercial decoration', and examining the way that the magazine managed to 'construct its graphic content as both reproducible and authentic' (14). Like Ohmann, Binckes considers the prestige of the magazine when exhibited in the home, and notes that *Rhythm* presented itself as a durable item of decoration rather than a disposable item of ephemera (154–55). At the same time, she explores the way that it used illustration to signal allegiance to a sphere of high art: '*Rhythm*'s format suggested not only recent continental *livres d'artiste*, but also the fine press titles of the nineteenth century' (131). Many magazines had by this time moved over to photography or to colour illustration, and while colour had once signalled prestige (as Ohmann describes), its increasingly widespread use 'unsettled the correlation between colour and exclusivity' (Binckes 146). *Rhythm* adhered to black and white printed artwork, celebrating a recent renaissance in black and white illustration, as seen in the work of William Morris and Aubrey Beardsley. Contributors to *Rhythm* emphasized the way that line could compete with colour as a way of expressing tone and movement. These things helped to rationalize *Rhythm*'s adherence to black and white, though the determining factor was that the magazine could not actually afford colour (Figure 1.6). Throughout, Binckes's study links the visual and design choices made at the magazine to its ideological commitments and its attempts to mediate systems of cultural value through its artwork.

Other scholars approach periodical illustration by rereading texts by major authors in their original publication contexts, demonstrating how different visual frames encourage different interpretations. For example, Adam Sonstegard's 2003 article, '"Singularly like a bad illustration": The Appearance of Henry James's "The Real Thing" in the Pot-Boiler Press', discusses an 1892 story that first appeared in the British semi-monthly

FIGURE 1.6 *Margaret Thomson, 'Rajputana Village'.* Rhythm 5.1 (1912): 5. Courtesy of the Modernist Journals Project (searchable database); Brown and Tulsa Universities, http://www.modjourn.org

illustrated magazine *Black and White*, and for American audiences, in the New York *Sun* or, through syndication, in a regional paper. The artists employed by *Black and White* and the *Sun* both drew on a sentimental and rather clichéd visual idiom. Sonstegard argues that James's text 'develops a subtle irony between the story and its periodical context', and that its narrator, himself an illustrator, provides a focus for anxieties about the way that writing and writers could be 'crowded off the page' by illustrations and by the prominently placed names of artists (180). Sonstegard concludes that James deliberately fashioned elements of his texts to be untranslatable into visual terms – 'to resist visual media' (195).

Sonstegard's argument about the way image and text compete for attention on the page takes up one of the key themes of modern periodical studies. Other scholars have pursued this via the competition between text and advertisement, often noting the shared etymology of the words 'magazine' and 'magasin', the French word for shop (see, for instance, Ohmann 224–25), and as Aynsley and Forde comment, 'the literature on the department store, another site of nineteenth-century consumption dependent on accumulation, diversity and distraction, is useful for establishing some of the key questions to be asked of magazines' (2). In the work of Catherine Clay ('What we might expect') and Catherine Keyser ('The Butter Printer'), magazine advertising for convenience food products is connected to anxieties about literary taste, and particularly about the consumption of 'convenience' forms of reading material, such as humour items or miscellaneous paragraphs. In the publications Clay and Keyser explore – such as *Time and Tide*, *The New Yorker* and the *Saturday Evening Post* – visual elements are unlikely to be understood as art, and generally function merely as a form of distraction, leading to a discontinuous reading experience.

While adverts in the print media were usually seen as diverting readers' attention from more serious cultural consumption (and were therefore avoided by many modernist magazines), advertising posters, by contrast, were often taken seriously as aesthetic objects, and some became collectors' items. In France, posters had gained recognition as an art form as early as the 1880s, while in the United States, art posters became very popular in the 1890s, and were used for both decorative and commercial purposes. In the twentieth century, posters were used as a method of promoting experimental art. Michael T. Saler's *The Avant-Garde in Interwar England: Medieval Modernism and the London Underground* (1999) offers an important account of the transport poster as a modernist form. Central to Saler's study is the figure of Frank Pick, a high-ranking transport executive who was also a founding member of the Design and Industries Association. According to Saler, Pick's design strategies, which included sculpture and architectural features as well as posters, 'turned the Underground into the culminating project of the arts and crafts movement', and did much to undo the hierarchies which placed fine art above the applied arts, as well as to further 'the avant-garde's aim of integrating modern art with modern life' (28). He explains:

> One of the earliest steps Pick took to educate the public about the new art was to commission posters for the Underground in the latest postimpressionist styles, such as fauvism, cubism, and expressionism. He hoped the Underground posters would extend the transformative potential of modern art beyond the small circles who patronized progressive galleries, as well as serve as an effective means of advertising and public relations for the corporation. The Underground had no major competitors at this time, enabling Pick to take risks that many other commercial enterprises could not afford. (99)

His approach was so successful, though, that it was emulated not only by monopolies and government bodies such as the General Post Office and the Empire Marketing Board, but also by firms such as Shell-Mex and Cunard Liners. In this way, the commercial poster became an important venue for modernist art.

Among the British artists featured on London Underground posters were Paul Nash, Graham Sutherland and Edward Wadsworth, though it was the images by the American E. McKnight Kauffer which attracted the most attention, and circulated most widely. As Saler observes, the Underground sold reproductions of McKnight Kauffer's posters, which were often purchased by students at the Royal College of Art, and copies were also sent out to provincial art schools (102). McKnight Kauffer had been profoundly influenced by the 1913 Armory Show in Chicago. His Cubist design 'Flight' (1916), which represents soaring birds in a geometric form with intersecting planes, became widely known when it was picked up by the *Daily Herald* in 1919 and used as an advertising poster. This helped to establish McKnight Kauffer's reputation as a designer, and in London, he made advertisements for Pelican Press, designed a painted sign for the Poetry Bookshop, and went on illustrate books for Nonesuch, Curwen and more mainstream presses such as Cassell, as well as carrying out the work for the Hogarth Press which was discussed in the previous section. This association with Bloomsbury modernism, as well as with the international currents of experimental painting, increased McKnight Kauffer's cultural capital and, in turn, that of the poster as genre. Mark Wollaeger, in *Modernism, Media, and Propaganda* (2006), uses the example of McKnight Kauffer to comment on 'the convergence of poster art's commercial and cultural authority' (170). Wollaeger's focus, at this point in his book, is on Joyce and propaganda, and he is one of several critics to note the interrelationships between literature and commercial visual art during the early twentieth century. He observes, for instance, that Joyce 'builds the material force of poster images into his textual practice', and points out that 'the sensuous impact of mass-produced signs is pervasive' in his work (173).

Design innovations emerging from the advertising industry influenced not only the more obviously commercial print forms of posters and glossy magazines, but also publishers' ephemera and book dust jackets, which became an important marketing mechanism during the interwar years. A good place to begin, in exploring this topic, is with Alan Powers's illustrated historical overview of book jackets, *Front Cover* (2001), which discusses the influence of modernist design, the format of early paperbacks, and the use of colour. A more in-depth study is Catherine Turner's *Marketing Modernism between the Two World Wars* (2003), which focuses on the ways that five American publishing houses promoted modernist literature in the 1920s and 1930s. Turner's broader purpose is to explore how consumer culture influenced the reception of literary modernism. She investigates the involvement of authors in promoting their books, arguing that publishers' advertisements were not 'simply gross misrepresentations of modernism created by commercial hucksters; they were created by editors, professional advertising writers, and literary authors who hoped that they could educate consumers about new styles and create a market for modernism' (4).

Turner begins with a case study of B. W. Huebsch, who was one of the first US publishers to issue modernist fiction, but who disliked the idea of culture as commodity, and did not want to sell what he saw as a great art to undiscriminating mass audiences. His adverts, therefore, were in the nineteenth-century mode of announcement rather than the twentieth-century mode of persuasion:

> Huebsch's advertisements usually included only the book's title, the author's name, a critical blurb, and Huebsch's trademark, the seven-branch candelabra with the words 'This mark on good books'. The over-decorated candelabra, with the BWH

> monograph intertwined around the base, confirmed Huebsch's affinities with Victorian culture by associating his firm with the design aesthetic of the past. In his advertisements, Huebsch used undecorated blocks of type, centered book titles and authors' names, and occasionally a plain black border. The simplicity of his design has a certain modernistic spareness, but it is hardly as visually appealing as other publishers' advertisements that featured pictures, borders, and larger print. (54)

By avoiding contemporary commercial practices, Huebsch generated cultural capital (the prestige associated with high culture), and secured his own reputation as an arbiter of taste. But several of the authors he launched in the United States, including James Joyce, Sherwood Anderson and D. H. Lawrence, soon left his firm and achieved a rather higher profile and improved sales with other publishers. (Here, Turner builds on Joyce Piell Wexler's 1997 book *Who Paid for Modernism? Art, Money, and the Fiction of Conrad, Joyce, and Lawrence*.) Turner studies the different dust jackets provided for Lawrence's novels by Huebsch and by Thomas Seltzer, to whom Lawrence switched in 1921. The jacket for Huebsch's 1916 edition of *The Rainbow* was in plain paper with black print and 'a very simple, almost stern font' (65), with no information about the book printed on the flaps or back cover. 'Such severe jackets', comments Turner, 'offered consumers no reason to buy other than what they might have read in reviews of the book or what they might be told by a salesclerk' (66–67). She contrasts this with Seltzer's 1923 cover for *The Captain's Doll*. It features three doll-like figures in primary colours, drawn in a two-dimensional, geometrical style. The cover copy exploited Lawrence's notoriety and also promoted him as a writer of genius. 'Unlike Huebsch', Turner remarks, 'Seltzer felt that the dust jacket had to do more than keep the book clean' (67). In promoting new literary styles, then, publishers drew on new visual styles.

David Earle in *Re-Covering Modernism* takes Turner's argument a stage further, discussing 'modernism as a product in the *popular* marketplace' (8), through exploration of the appearance of authors such as Joyce, Faulkner and Fitzgerald in pulp magazines and in lurid, inexpensive paperback editions. He argues that the 'visual coding of the popular paperback, seemingly oppositional to modernism, is unavoidable because of its extremity and sensationalism – even if the paperback form itself has been efficiently avoided in literary criticism exactly because of this visual coding' (159). Earle's work will be taken up again in Chapter 2, but it is worth noting here that he and Turner are only two among several critics who have lately focused on the dust jacket as a significant element of modernist print culture. Ted Bishop's 1994 article 'Re: Covering *Ulysses*' (mentioned at the start of this chapter) is a ground-breaking study which aims 'to chart the movement of *Ulysses* the book – the physical object with its various jackets, blurbs, ads and price tags – from modernist work to social document, to status object, to cultural artifact to, finally, what seems to be a kind of futures commodity in the freewheeling post-copyright market' (22). More recently, Lise Jaillant's *Modernism, Middlebrow and the Literary Canon: The Modern Library Series, 1917–1955* (2014) explores the design features of the New York reprint series 'Modern Library', which republished an impressive range of high modernist texts. Jaillant, whose book we will discuss further in Chapter 3, argues that the owners 'strove to create an image of elegant modernity for their brand' through cover and colophon design, and that the Modern Library 'combined an aura of New York glamour and intellectual sophistication with a very affordable price' (2; see also Jaillant, 'Sapper'). Magazine covers can also be studied in a similar way: for instance, in a 2013 article Gabrielle Dean gives an account of the way *The Smart Set*'s covers contributed to its 'performance of cleverness', starting with the question: 'If attitude was what *The Smart Set* sold, how could readers know it before they became readers?' As Dean points out, since this magazine 'relied more on street sales than on subscriptions, the cover had to make a visual impact that could claim the attention of both potential customers and loyal readers, concisely conveying the complex attitude that would invite further exploration' (2). The specific purposes of these various studies are very different from one another, but they share the aim of counteracting – by means of analysis of print artefacts – dominant narratives of modernism as fundamentally anti-commercial. These narratives, of course, have been discussed in depth in such studies as Andreas Huyssen's *After the Great Divide* (1986), yet they remain influential in spite of the increasing number of books and articles which demonstrate modernism's close involvement with commerce.

# 2

# Print in circulation

In *The Space and Place of Modernism: The Russian Revolution, Little Magazines, and New York* (2002), Adam McKible points out how literary scholarship has traditionally tended to compartmentalize the first two decades of the twentieth century into 'discrete monuments' such as 'the Roaring Twenties' or 'Dadaism', thereby losing 'the sense of intimate dialogue and heated disputation that marked the era' (9). The interconnected and overlapping dialogues that gave rise to what became institutionalized in academic discourse as Modernism can be rediscovered by studying little magazines of the era. McKible notes that modernist little magazines have for too long been regarded as valuable 'according to the number and quality of contributions to them by recognizable, canonical figures' (xv), with not much attention paid to the magazines themselves. Illustrating the approach of contemporary modernist print scholarship, McKible examines complete runs of four magazines (*The Messenger*, *The Little Review*, *The Liberator*, and *The Dial*) and reverses the traditional perspective by viewing individual contributions as expressive of the editorial ethos of particular periodicals. Although McKible's specific focus is on how these four periodicals 'imagined Russia as a space of transformation and possibility, hope and fear' (xiii), his study exemplifies how recent scholarship has restored to the modernist scene what he describes as 'the scattered, connected particularities of lived experience, competing but independent cultural formations, and a variety of aesthetic demands' (7). The sites from and through which modernist productions circulated have become not just the monuments of earlier histories – the 'specific, concrete location' McKible describes as 'place' – but also a 'landscape or geography of the imagination', a 'space' (8).

Scholarship such as McKible's indicates the infiltration of new cultural geographies that, as Sara Blair explains, have called 'for a more nuanced account of what it means for culture and subjects to be located' (813). Taking as her object of study 'Bloomsbury' as both global cultural phenomenon and specific London neighbourhood, Blair shows that culture and subjects 'come into being not merely in a geographical or material landscape, but in a site of social activity that produces itself and its defining relations through local, personal, and public exchanges' (813). This approach restores what have often been treated as discrete phenomena to the complex networks in which they were in fact embedded. The Woolfs' Hogarth Press, for example, is placed by Blair in an 'emergent modern publishing industry' (819) that included 'firms like Faber . . . A. and C. Black, David Fulton, the Nonesuch Press, and the theatrical publisher Samuel French' (820), all located in Bloomsbury.

The figure of the network, or web, becomes increasingly insistent in modernist scholarship from the 1990s on, though it was also present in previous decades. As early as 1969, Hugh Ford could refer in his Foreword to Nancy Cunard's account of her Hours Press to the 'network of tiny expatriate presses' that disappeared with the outbreak of the Second World War (Cunard vii). In her chapter 'At the Sign of the Printing Press: The Role of Small Presses and Little Magazines' in *Women of the Left Bank* (1986), Shari Benstock discussed 'the delicate web of interrelationships' connecting Bryher, Robert McAlmon, Margaret Anderson, Jane Heap and Harriet Weaver to Joyce (357). Although somewhat limited by her reliance on Hoffman, Allen and Ulrich's *The Little Magazine*, Benstock provides an important survey of the network of expatriate American editors and writers flourishing in Paris up to 1940. Introducing the collection *A Living of Words: American Women in Print Culture* (1995), Susan Albertine treats her subject 'not only as a hierarchy . . . but also as a network in which writing is but one of many interlinked activities' (xi). From its origins in social theory of the 1930s through its mathematical applications via graphing, beginning in the 1950s, network analysis has influenced many disciplines. In print culture scholarship, specifically, it has found purchase in the opportunities afforded by digital archives of complete runs of little magazines to plot the connections among people, places and periodicals. Similar projects are underway to map the networks obtaining among the writers and editors involved with small presses, such as Hogarth.

The notion of the 'social text' that has emerged from the conjunction of bibliography and textual studies with the historicizing tendency in literary theory and cultural studies has led to a focus on the collaborative nature of the publishing process. Darcy Cullen writes in the introduction to *Editors, Scholars, and the Social Text* (2012) that publishing involves 'the combined efforts of typesetters, proofreaders, indexers, printers, and marketers, each of which introduces a network of relationships' (3). The text, therefore, is 'no longer believed to be exclusively within the purview of the author'; rather, it is produced through collaborative – or 'social' – processes (4). For many historical periods preceding the twentieth century, book historians and textual scholars have 'created various frameworks within which to analyse the role of editors and publishers in the making of texts, manuscripts and books' (4). Although print scholarship in modernist studies has in the last two decades paid a great deal of attention to periodicals and their networks, such work is only just beginning to turn to similar issues in book publishing. It is possible that this area has been somewhat hampered by the inaccessibility of archival material, either because the business records of publishing houses are less open to researchers, or because they simply were not retained. Cullen describes how 'archaeologists of the book' must delve into 'correspondence, estate records, manuscript notebooks, newspaper clippings, reviews, and the like' to 'reconstitute for us the book publishing industry, printing methods, literary and reading practices in different times and different places' (4). An example of the challenges that researchers on modernist book publishing might face is provided by J. H. Willis who describes in *Leonard and Virginia Woolf as Publishers* (1992) how his intention to write a detailed history of the Hogarth Press was at first frustrated by 'an apparent absence of records' (xi). Eventually, through the assistance of people who had been involved with the press, he was led to 'thirty-two file boxes of Hogarth Press records containing over six hundred separate files on press authors and their books. Covered with a thick layer of grime, the boxes had not been opened in over twenty years and had been overlooked by previous writers on the Woolfs' (xi–xii). These records are now in the Hogarth Press archive at Reading University, where they have provided the basis for scholarship that offers a model of the kind of work to be undertaken on other publishing houses of the time.

The multi-university online project *Networking Women*, coordinated by Maria Camboni, takes an 'ethical stance' in its intention to 'counteract the undermining force operating in history' that has often relegated women to roles as lovers or muses. In *Networking Women: Subjects, Places, Links, Europe-America. Towards a Rewriting of Cultural History, 1890–1939*, Camboni explains that the project focuses on

> women who assisted and promoted the emergence of an (interethnic) transnational and supra-national culture, thus strengthening the interrelations within Europe, between Europe and the United States, and between their metropolitan centers (London, Paris, Berlin and Vienna, New York) and their peripheries (in particular Scotland, the South-West of the USA, the Caribees), or acting in cities like Trieste, at the crossroads of different nationalities and cultures. (8)

The women researched for the project are not viewed as 'exceptional personalities waiting to be canonized' but as 'founders of journals and publishing houses, creators of salons and theater companies, and as social and political activists: in synthesis, as critical junctions of a complex network of human, political, cultural and artistic relations worth exploring' (8–9). Such a democratic approach not only expands our understanding of what Mark Morrisson has described as the 'culture from which the texts of modernism arose' ('Publishing' 133), it can also reshape our reception of those texts themselves.

The circulation of modernist print, then, is a subject that encompasses sites of production as local as a single issue of a magazine or a hand-operated press, or as wide-ranging as the transnational networks of communication between metropolitan centres fostered by particular magazines, bookshops and publishing houses. For example, Gayle Rogers, in *Modernism and the New Spain: Britain, Cosmopolitan Europe, and Literary History* (2012), studies the Spanish magazine *Revista de Occidente*, established in 1923 by José Ortega y Gasset, commenting that it 'quickly became a premier journal of international culture. Contemporary German, British, and French texts filled its pages, alongside works by most every prominent Spanish author of the period . . . suggesting the polyglot dialogue across all of their works that the journal would host' (45). Rogers analyses *Revista de Occidente* alongside the prominent British literary magazine *The Criterion* (1922–1939), edited by T. S. Eliot. Comparative projects such as this remain relatively rare, and the majority of periodicals scholars continue to focus their research on individual titles. Comparative reading can certainly be a difficult undertaking, particularly when it crosses boundaries of nation, language, or cultural level. However, large-scale projects such as the three-volume *Oxford Critical and Cultural History of Modernist Magazines*, by bringing research on British, European and North American periodicals together into a single conversation, lay the foundations for such work, and enable larger patterns to be traced. Andrew Thacker, introducing the North American volume in the series, compares it to the first volume, which treated British and Irish titles. He notes: 'Though the chronology is roughly the same, moving from the late nineteenth century through to the period after the Second World War, the narrative of American modernist magazines is marked by different tendencies, patterns of publication, and diversity of forms' (1). For instance, one of the important differences is the much wider geographical dispersal of North American literary magazines in comparison to British ones, three-quarters of which were published in London.

In the first section of this chapter we will give an account of scholarship on networks centred on small magazines and presses. In the second section, we explore specific locations such as bookstores, libraries and cafés, and the readers who frequented them. The exchanges among readers, editors, writers and publishers in published letters and responses, as well as those now being mined in archives, provide a vivid picture of the cultural formations of modernism. Finally, we turn to what Lawrence Rainey has described as the modernists' 'fatal compromise' with a 'degraded' public marketplace (5), or what other scholars have seen as a savvy exploitation by writers and publishers of that marketplace and the fascination with celebrity.

## Networks

In a section of her introduction to *The Gender of Modernism* (1990) titled 'Connections', Bonnie Kime Scott comments on her illustration 'A Tangled Mesh of Modernists'. Created by arranging the names of authors treated in the anthology in a circle and then drawing a line between any who were connected, the mesh is an early example of the kind of visual representation of a network that might today be created by a software programme such as Gephi, Pajek or Protovis. Scott acknowledges that counting the number of strands emerging from a given author as an indicator of 'importance' gives the predictably conservative impression that Pound, Eliot, Joyce and Woolf dominate modernism. 'But', she continues, 'there are surprises, such as the extraordinary number of connections to Marianne Moore. There are other revelations. One pattern readily apparent is that women writers took a great deal of interest in one another' (10–11). Research since the 1990s on periodicals as well as on small presses has not only emphasized the multiple affiliations among the producers and sites of modernism's print cultures, but has also made visible the significant role that women played as editors. In scholarship on modernism's print cultures, the idea and image of a network have replaced earlier, more hierarchical notions of structure in explaining and figuring the complex social and professional relationships from which literary modernism arose. Introducing a special issue of the *Journal of Modern Periodical Studies* on 'Visualizing Periodical Networks', J. Stephen Murphy comments that 'Network analysis provides a new tool for literary historians, while visualizing network graphs provides a new way to reveal the social constructedness of literary history and literary value' (vi).

In recent scholarship, networks have been constructed from relations among people (editors, writers, agents, printers, readers), and among periodicals themselves. Critics have also read particular works in terms of their appearance within a network of bibliographic and other codes as they are produced from multiple sites of transmission that include little magazines, anthologies and single-authored books. As John Timberman Newcomb remarks in '*Poetry*'s Opening Door', his contribution to Suzanne W. Churchill and Adam McKible's important collection *Little Magazines and*

*Modernism* (2007), the new approach to modernist little magazines and their authors that treats them 'as productively embedded within the cultural economies, ideologies, and practices of the early twentieth century . . . can help to demystify the evaluative economies underlying the particular, perhaps peculiar, shape canonical modernism took, and help to promote the recovery of other modernisms more responsive to the diversity and specificity of their times, and ours' (86).

Relationships among the writers and editors of little magazines, in particular, have been characterized by collaboration, rivalry, antagonism or support – with all of these often evident within a single relationship. As Jason Harding comments in his study of the periodical networks within which the *Criterion* existed, 'the character of the *Criterion* cannot be divorced from the alliances and loyalties, rivalries, animosities, and friendships that mark all social relations as fully human' (7). Although memoirs, biographies and autobiographies of editors and writers, as well as histories of publishing houses and surveys of small presses, have provided valuable information, the scholarship of the last three decades has augmented such material with research in business and personal archives, and with digitizations of modernist periodicals. This has resulted in new interpretations which often resist the heroic narratives that those earlier works tended to produce. Newcomb describes the way that earlier histories 'treat the magazine field as a universe of empty space only made meaningful by the few comets who shot through it on their way to canonical glory. Most obscure rather than clarify the complex roles played by groups, institutions, and overlooked individuals in the ideological formation of American modernism' (85). While defining 'modernist' remains contentious and messy, print culture scholarship has greatly enriched the context within which this debate occurs.

Harriet Monroe, who founded the long-running magazine *Poetry* in Chicago in 1912, is an exemplary case for the way recent scholarship has reformulated previous paradigms that have often been, as Newcomb argues, negatively influenced by masculinist discourses such as that of Ezra Pound in his 1930 essay 'Small Magazines' (discussed in our Introduction). Newcomb does not want to fit Monroe into received ideas about modernism, but to reshape our notions of modernism to account for her (88). Contrary to the received notion that Pound was an avant-garde influence on

Monroe, Newcomb suggests that her publication of his poem 'To Whistler, American' in the first number of *Poetry* demonstrates that she saw in Pound a useful means of developing her magazine's avant-garde position. He sees her publication of works by Pound, Sandburg and other radically new poets as a careful strategy that worked in tandem with the editorials in which *Poetry* 'reformulated a cluster of evaluative concepts – *genius, masterpiece, tradition, form, audience* – along activist avant-garde lines' (100). Jayne Marek, in *Women Editing Modernism* (1995), defends Monroe's emendation of poems by Eliot and Pound as necessary to avoid offending the publicly acknowledged Chicago financial backers on whom her magazine depended for its survival (45). Unlike earlier critics such as Hugh Kenner, however, who constructed a narrative in which bold men like Pound fought against the prudishness of women such as Monroe, current modernist print culture scholarship has used a network approach to explore the fierce dynamism of arguments about new poetry that were conducted in the pages of *Poetry* and the little magazines that appeared in its wake.

Magazines of new verse that appeared after *Poetry* often used it as a 'foil in advancing their own styles of aesthetic radicalism' (Newcomb 9), and have consequently somewhat overshadowed the rebelliousness that is apparent when *Poetry* is considered in the context of the American poetry scene in 1912. Bartholomew Brinkman, in his analysis of *Poetry*'s bibliographic codes, emphasizes that the magazine's 'central placement of poetry on the page encourages a level of care and contemplation that was not readily available to poetry in other bibliographic formats' at the time (30). The forms of Imagism, exemplified in Brinkman's article by a close examination of Pound's 'In a Station of the Metro', 'required a format quite different from the multi-column newspaper format' common to large circulation periodicals such as the *Atlantic*. A number of little magazines 'chose to adopt *Poetry*'s small-scale format and/or its decision to isolate the poem on the page' (Brinkman 36) which 'was key for making *Poetry* hands-down *the* vehicle for the showcasing and dissemination of Imagism(e)' (33).

Many of those involved in arguments about the new poetry wrote their own versions of events that later critics then used as the basis for their interpretations. Marek discusses how Monroe's virtual excision of *Poetry*'s assistant editor Alice Corbin Henderson from her memoir *A Poet's Life* has 'changed the emphasis given

Monroe's editorship and *Poetry*'s impact on modern literature' (58). Among the achievements Marek attributes jointly to Monroe and Henderson are:

> introducing Imagism to America, encouraging the experiments of scores of modern poets, broadening the avenues of public access to poetry, and helping to encourage an international sensibility as well as reconsidering America's role in the critical debates about new work. *Poetry* argued for the existence of a distinctly American poetry and tried to display the range that such poetry could take by supporting minor as well as major poets, regional work and poetry societies, other little magazines, small-format publications, readings, prizes, and many other aspects of literary activity that are now taken for granted. (58)

Marek called for considerable analysis of the 'problems inherent to discussing what constituted an "American" literature in the early decades of modernism' (41), an analysis that recent works such as Suzanne Churchill's *The Little Magazine* Others (2006) and Eric B. White's *Transatlantic Avant-Gardes: Little Magazines and Localist Modernism* (2013) have now started to provide. Beginning in the period just before the First World War, arguments about vers libre (free verse) were a proxy for debate about what constituted a distinctly American avant-garde. Marek draws particular attention to Henderson's articles in the May 1913 and December 1916 *Poetry* that most strongly presented her ideas about the new poetry. In May 1916, Henderson mocked what she called 'A New School of Poetry', the 'I-am-it' school, reprinting lines that used the first-person from poems in the *Others* anthology and concluding her article 'We regret to say that the printer announces there are no more I's in the font' (Henderson 105). Henderson's critique of some poets' egocentrism elicited outrage from Maxwell Bodenheim and William Carlos Williams, but Henderson wrote to Monroe that she believed a 'magazine has got to have a fighting edge to it' (Marek 40). Alfred Kreymborg had founded *Others* 'in part out of frustration with Monroe's editorial interference' (Churchill 13), and Monroe editorialized in *Poetry* about *Others* as 'a haven for the wildest orgies of proud-spirited youth' (Churchill 47). Arguments about the place of regional poetry in a distinctly

American avant-garde, as well as an often conflicted relationship to European influences, were played out in editorials in *Poetry* that frequently engaged the views of other editors of little magazines and the implications for American literature of the works they published. Marek argues that Alice Corbin Henderson in particular 'helped to create a coherent critical approach to modernist writing' in a way similar to that of Pound (Marek 40).

Eric White explains how Kreymborg's strategic positioning of the poetry and prose of the writers he published in *Others* and his skillful deployment of bibliographic codes amounted to a kind of 'covert editorialising' (*Transatlantic* 37). For example, in the November 1915 issue, he reprinted before the table of contents a review of *Others* by J. B. Kerfoot that had appeared in *Life* magazine. White interprets this as signaling that *Others* 'was involved in a national debate about the new American poetics, rather than perpetuating a specialist dialogue' (38). White's important study diverges from a traditional literary critical approach that examines 'how editorial policy influences authorial agency' in seeking to explore how seeing a little magazine not just as an aesthetic object but as 'a statement of the editor's policies, poetics and cultural agenda, alters how we perceive its content' (18). In the case of *Others*, Kreymborg's 'strategic manipulation of literary space' mobilizes 'the materiality of the text, imagist poetics, free-market capitalism and the cross-cultural contact zones of early-twentieth-century America to cultivate an outwardly indigenous avant-garde from a network of transatlantic contacts' (20). The exchanges between and editorial interventions of Pound and Williams 'surface frequently in the matrices of contact that sprang up in the little magazines between 1910 and 1932' which engendered debates about 'national identity, translocation, cultural exchange and hybridity' (White 3). White traces the transatlantic movements of writers such as Pound and Williams, pointing out how their encounters with European locations informed their writing about America, playing out in magazines such as *Poetry*, *The Egoist* and *Blast* (65).

In the autumn of 1918, an 'International Episode' was instigated when Edgar Jepson derided the winners of *Poetry*'s annual prizes as 'little more than hackneyed regional writers' in an article in *The Little Review* (White, *Transatlantic* 81). His view was endorsed by Pound, and the issues were debated in two American numbers of *The Little Review*. White sets the emergence and rapid disappearance of several little magazines in the context of these transatlantic dialogues. These magazines included James Oppenheim's *The Seven Arts* (1916–1917), which became a forum for 'a new generation of nationalist writers' (83), and Robert J. Coady's *The Soil* (1916–1917), which openly embraced America's commercial culture. In 1920, Robert McAlmon joined with Williams to launch *Contact* out of a shared sense of urgency over 'the escalating influence of "foreign editors", the rise of the dada movement in *The Little Review* and the emergence of *The Dial* as the dominant literary voice in New York' (96). Their quarrel, as White explains, was not with foreign work per se, 'but rather with the level of deference shown towards "imported art" by editors of domestic little magazines' (98).

In the first number of *Contact*, Williams paid tribute in his poem 'Marianne Moore' to what White characterizes as Moore's 'networked model of literary contact' (*Transatlantic* 103). Moore had found a receptive home for her poems in *The Egoist*, despite her personal aversion to its editor, Dora Marsden. In *The Egoist* for August 1916, H. D. emphasized Moore's foreignness as an American to the magazine's English readership, yet claimed her as an ally in 'our devotion to the beautiful English language'. Churchill points out that Monroe's *Poetry* provided an American context for Moore's work but that after 1915 Moore published no more poems there until 1923, annoyed by Monroe's rearrangement and retitling of her works and by Monroe's 'unsolicited advice about how to improve her work' (146). Moore had been delighted on her first trip to New York to meet Kreymborg who introduced her to the network of poets connected with *Others*, where she published several poems. Her inclusion in the 1917 *Others* anthology brought her to the attention of Eliot who 'became an influential advocate of her work' (Churchill 154). Moore's association with *Others* gave her the confidence to make the transition to *The Dial*, a magazine that Robin Schulze describes as helping to 'change literary modernism from a form of radical dissent to a culturally central form of expression' (qtd. in Churchill 168), and which Moore edited from 1925 until 1929.

Tracking the work of writers across the numbers of a particular magazine and also across their appearance in several magazines and anthologies has allowed scholars of print culture to demonstrate the dynamic and dialogic aspects of modernist literature that became invisible following its reification in the postwar New Critical period. In 'Pressing Women: Marianne Moore and the Networks of Modernism', the fifth chapter of *Material Modernism*, Moore provides a paradigm for Bornstein's exploration of several issues relating to the networks of publication within which modernist works often first appeared. He enumerates three specific reasons that she serves this purpose: she participated fully in networks of women writers and editors but also collaborated productively with men such as Eliot and Pound; she had extensive experience as an editor herself; and her own poems 'rank amongst the most striking modernist examples of works that change their meanings as they alter both their linguistic and bibliographic codes' (83). Having traced her involvement with *Poetry*, *The Egoist* and *The Little Review*, Bornstein describes the publication by The Egoist Press of her book *Poems* (1921) at the instigation of H. D. and Bryher, without Moore's knowledge. Bryher went on to publish Moore in the magazines she founded, *Life and Letters Today* and *Close Up*, and in 1936 published *The Pangolin and Other Verse* at her Brendin Press. Moore's 'The Fish' exemplifies the role of editors as well as the influence of specific sites of publication in shaping a work's reception. Bornstein follows the poem from its initial appearance in *The Egoist* in August 1918. The appearance on that journal's front page of the names of Harriet Shaw Weaver as Editor and of Dora Marsden as Contributing Editor 'marked the poem's association with a network of female patronage', while the name of T. S. Eliot as Assistant Editor marked the work as modernist (93). The poem's next major incarnation, in *Poems*, placed it within a female network of editors and publishers, but its recontextualization, Bornstein points out, lessened the political impact of its *Egoist* publication. In his analysis of the difference between these two instances of 'The Fish', Bornstein explains how sites of circulation, bibliographic codes and the known networks of those involved in publication all affect reception. In *Poems*, 'instead of following a column on wartime Paris in an anti-war journal sold on newsstands, it follows a more introspective poem' (95); the H. D./Bryher/Weaver volume reinforces 'the foregrounding of the aesthetic: the limited edition with its pasted label and geometrically decorative cover all suggest a retreat into aesthetic intricacy rather than an advance into aesthetic engagement' (99). When the poem next appeared, in *Observations* (1924), Moore exercised editorial control that restored its political pertinence. But Eliot, whom Moore had invited to edit her *Selected Poems* (1935), 'severed the poem from its original social codings and instead inserted it into a largely aesthetic field' (99). Eliot's introduction to the volume also differently positioned the interpretative codes by which 'The Fish' would be read. Treating two of Moore's Irish poems in a similar manner, Bornstein concludes that the

> diachronic textual and political complexities of Moore's verse make clear that to read or edit merely the linguistic codes of Moore's poems diminishes them. It strips off the gender coding of the network of modernist women editors and publishers, as well as of Moore's insistence that cooperation and antagonism could operate both across and within gender, as well as across or within racial groups. (115)

Feminist revision of uncritical narratives about women's role as modernist editors marks much of the scholarship published in the field since the 1990s. In *Editing Modernity* (2007), Dean Irvine presents a 'reconfiguration of critical and literary-historical perspectives on the relationships among poetics, gender, and little-magazine production that inform women's participation in modernist literary cultures in Canada' between 1916 and 1956 (9). Other similar examples include Simone Murray's account of Elizabeth Yeats's central role at the Cuala Press, in which she directly counters the narrative promulgated by Liam Miller that pushes her 'so far to the periphery of consideration as to become invisible' (490). In her discussion of Caresse Crosby's career after the suicide of her husband, Harry, with whom she founded the Black Sun Press, Mary Lynn Broe mines Crosby's correspondence about the creation of Crosby Continental Editions to 'highlight some of the transatlantic influences on the small-press publishing industry during a rich, experimental time in the shaping of modern literature' (213). Placing Crosby in the broader context of women in print at the time, Broe details how she 'transformed the Black Sun from a limited-editions press, whose lavishly bound volumes were dedicated to the "aesthetics of romance" between husband and wife, into a commercial press that specialized in low-cost reprints and avant-garde paperbacks' four years in advance of Penguin and in direct competition with the German publisher Tauchnitz (210–11).

Although such scholarship has restored to visibility the role of women editors and publishers within modernism, the editorial work of the men who for several decades dominated the narrative of literary modernism has, of course, not been neglected. 'Editors and Programmes', Section VI of volume 1 of Brooker and Thacker's *Oxford Critical and Cultural History of Modernist Magazines*, is devoted to discussion of several influential editors who 'all faced a common dilemma in the evident decline in the readership for poetry in the immediate post-war period and its aftermath' (339): Eliot (*The Criterion*), John Middleton Murry (*The Athenaeum* and *The Adelphi*), Edgell Rickword (*The Calendar of Modern Letters*), Thomas Moult (*Voices*), Harold Monro (*The Monthly Chapbook*) and Desmond MacCarthy (*Life and Letters*). Each of these men sought to create particular readerships, aware that their periodicals existed within a complex network – or 'constellation' in Brooker and Thacker's term – of periodicals often struggling to survive.

To situate the various incarnations of the *Criterion* under Eliot's editorship in a wider historical and intellectual context, Jason Harding draws on archives, unpublished correspondence and interviews, providing a 'thickly textured account of the milieu of British inter-war literary journalism' (*Criterion* 21). Harding places the periodical within an intricate network of other publications including *The Adelphi*, *The Calendar of Modern Letters*, *Scrutiny*, and *New Verse*, demonstrating another understanding of the way the network can be conceived – as consisting of relations among publications as well as among individual collaborators and rivals.[1] Indeed, as he remarks of the controversies between Murry and Eliot, such as that about the relative merits of romanticism versus classicism, they 'are notable for the lack of any real contestatory interaction, largely a consequence of their dissemination and reception in the arena of metropolitan literary journalism' (42). Churchill, in her study of *Others*, also comments that little magazines themselves 'demonstrate how much boundary crossing occurred between various artistic circles, as well as among social and political groups and between intellectual and popular audiences' (5 n10). Accounts of the ways that editors and writers interacted within these contexts are not, however, settled.

A prevailing negative view of Eliot's role as editor of Djuna Barnes's work has been challenged by Georgette Fleischer. Fleischer takes issue with several feminist critics, with some of whom she had clashed in the letters column of *The Nation* following her review of Philip Herring's 1995 biography of Barnes. Relying on archival research, Fleischer contests the view that Eliot 'was a pernicious editor who represented *Nightwood* maliciously' (417), arguing rather that he published the novel 'despite the anticipation that it would not do well commercially and despite the danger of censorship because he identified with its spiritual crisis and because he recognized it as a work of genius' (406). Suman Gupta notes that 'a systematic examination of Eliot's interactions *as a publisher* with almost every aspiring poet of his time is yet to be undertaken' (26). Gupta examines rejection letters written by Eliot as well his marginal annotations on manuscripts submitted to Faber and Faber to infer his editorial principles. Gupta concludes that 'Eliot's creation of an institutional space in the world of publishing that acquired the reputation of nurturing and promoting "genius" conforms with the larger concerns of a literary modernism which self-consciously developed out of certain loosely formed/perceived literary groups' (34).[2]

Peter Howarth has explained how Eliot strategically used the example of the popular anthologies of 'Georgian' poetry to distinguish himself from other poets included with him in the *Catholic Anthology* assembled by Ezra Pound in 1915. The title *Georgian Poetry*, used for five anthologies published between 1912 and 1922, referred to the reign of King George V who had succeeded Edward VII in 1910. It was thus a marker of a new era, yet in its invocation of royalty, it also signalled an allegiance to traditional notions of English identity. According to Howarth, Eliot's familiarity with how Pound had constructed a collective 'Imagism' led him to understand 'more quickly than anyone else that "Georgian" was also a flag of convenience for poets of diverse interests and talents' (222). Pound had modelled the format of *Des Imagistes* on Edward Marsh's very successful first volume of *Georgian Poetry* (1912). Howarth explains that Eliot's 'reviews of his contemporaries and rivals, the Georgian poets, look like a thorough hatchet job' (221) as he pilloried their sentimentality and attributed their popularity to the poems' paying ' "a tribute to all the nicest feelings of the upper-middle class British public schoolboy" ' (222). But in an article in *The Athenaeum* in April 1919, Eliot emphasized that anthologies are primarily for the purposes of advertisement and used the example of the Georgian poets, some of whom he did admire, 'to warn other modernists against the belief that anthologies exhibited a collective artistic goal' (223). Anthologies could serve emerging poets well. As Churchill notes, Mina Loy's appearance in the 1917 *Others* anthology brought her to the attention of Eliot who then 'became an influential advocate of her work' (154). Loy appeared in that anthology alongside Eliot, Moore, Williams and Wallace Stevens, 'positioning her as part of a coterie of clear minds emerging from the chaos of the new poetry explosion' (207). Anthologies were often used, as Morrisson notes, to foster a broader collective regional or racial identity ('Publishing' 138).

Book publication, whether in an anthology or a single-authored volume, participated differently in the modernist print ecology, affording writers the chance for more sustained attention and wider circulation. Many modernist writers, unable to get contracts with major commercial publishers, began their own presses. Some of these picked up the nineteenth-century tradition of fine printing, producing expensive limited editions, while others produced more modest trade editions. Several works have surveyed the well-populated field of twentieth-century small press publishing, from Will Ransom's 1929 *Private Presses and Their Books* to Roderick Cave's *The Private Press* (1983) and Hugh Ford's *Published in Paris* (1975); in addition, memoirs of those involved in this movement abound (e.g. Crosby; Cunard). Most of these small presses had very short lives, but Leonard and Virginia Woolf managed over twenty-five years to transform their Hogarth Press from a hobby to a successfully diverse enterprise whose imprint still exists.

New scholarship on the Hogarth Press is only just beginning to make inroads on an entrenched (and erroneous) notion that it was, as Iain Stevenson wrote as recently as 2010, still a cottage industry in the 1930s, 'amateur dabbling' that would have not survived without the Woolfs' 'personal wealth and the patronage of their friends' (Stevenson 69). In fact, it was an exemplary institution of modernism: networked, influential, multifarious in its operations, yet precarious in its financial status. Once again, as in our discussion of the relationship between visual art and text in the previous chapter, there is a dearth of recent scholarship on modernist book publishing apart from the research that has been carried out on the Hogarth Press. Hogarth is unique among modernist small presses not only for its longevity, but also because it methodically broadened its list from a base founded upon modernist experimentation. The contributors to Helen Southworth's *Leonard and Virginia Woolf: The Hogarth Press and the Networks of Modernism* describe the Hogarth Press 'as an idea, a physical institution and a site of cultural capital, a node that linked together writers as disparate as [Mulk Raj] Anand, [Joan] Easdale, [Huw] Menai and [Vita] Sackville-West with emergent cultural formations like the middlebrow and globalism' ('Introduction' 21). Southworth's collection is a milestone in studies of modernist small presses that reflects in its diversity of subjects and approaches the same diversity it seeks to establish for the Hogarth Press's contributions to modernism's print cultures. As John Young remarks in his essay on William Plomer, the Hogarth Press is 'precisely the kind of economic and cultural network which now seems quintessentially modernist' (146). Young calls for a 'broader sense of the various dimensions in which [Virginia] Woolf's activities as author, editor and publisher intersected with the business and art of the Hogarth Press and thus of the specific circuits through which modernist form was produced' (146). This kind of work is now being undertaken by scholars such as Elizabeth Willson Gordon, Nicola Wilson and Alice Staveley, all of whom are involved, together with Claire Battershill and Southworth herself, in the Modernist Archives Publishing Project (MAPP). This project uses the Hogarth Press as a case study for an approach to modernist publishing that will 'move beyond isolated studies of individual houses to examine translateral networks of authors, artists, editors, press workers, and texts across different publishing venues' (MAPP). Taking into account the variety of genres and types of author published by the Hogarth Press under Leonard Woolf's management, MAPP intends to annotate, and reconfigure 'the network relations amongst these diverse texts within the wider public sphere of modernist publishing' (MAPP) as a paradigm for establishing an infrastructure by which scholars might research modernist presses from a number of perspectives.

The networks of modernism were sustained not only by institutions such as publishers and magazines, but also by the physical sites where writers, editors, agents, publishers, artists, booksellers and printers might meet one another, or where the readers of modernist texts might interact. Some of these meetings happened at the premises of publishing houses and magazines. Many more took place in bookshops, libraries, salons, cafés and galleries, and we turn to these in our next section.

## Sites of circulation

It was after a visit to one of those large and flourishing establishments where every sort of book is sold that you do not want to read; where rows and rows of the classics you wish you could read again for the first time flaunt from the shelves in gaudy leather bindings, and a whole counter labours to support the newest and dullest novels, and another is covered with monographs which instruct you minutely as to how to grow fruit-trees, catch salmon, handle golf clubs, or bicycle through the home counties. It was in one of these 'emporiums', after the usual 'We can get it for you, Madam', that I broke into open revolt and started off to The Poetry Bookshop.

– Amy Lowell (19)

In what remains to date the most comprehensive treatment of Harold Monro's Poetry Bookshop, which opened on Devonshire Street near the British Museum in 1913, Joy Grant explains that Monro wanted not just a shop but a 'Poetry House'. In common with many of the shops that sold modernism's books, magazines and other artefacts, the Poetry Bookshop held regular readings and provided a gathering place for writers and their readers. Perhaps unlike most other bookshop proprietors, however, Monro was able to offer cheap lodgings in two attics that were 'made available to needy poets, and others of sympathetic mind' (Grant 66). The Poetry Bookshop published books and journals, most famously the successful volumes of *Georgian Poetry* edited by Edward Marsh which, as Amy Lowell noted in the article quoted above, 'helped the bookshop, and the bookshop helped the book' (21). Mark Morrisson describes the public recitations of verse at the Poetry Bookshop as important to modernist poets who 'challenged the power of the conservative Poetry Society to consecrate its own poetic taste' (*Public* 56). The modernist bookshop as an important node in the networks of modernism is only now beginning to receive sustained scholarly attention, as demonstrated by Huw Osborne's anthology *The Rise of the Modernist Bookshop: Books and the Commerce of Culture in the Twentieth Century* (2015). This is the first collection to bring the insights of modernist print culture scholarship to a consideration of an institution that operates in what Osborne describes in his introduction as the 'fraught space' created by 'the twinned and competing forces of culture and commerce' (1). Some London bookshops had survived from the eighteenth into the twentieth century – Bumpus, and Hatchard's, for example. But the small modernist bookshop that appears often in the memoirs, correspondence and diaries from which derives much of what we know about it was a fertile space of exchange and production whose owners, across Europe and the United States, invariably shared with modernist writers and artists the exhilarating sense of cultural change. Osborne proposes that modernist bookshops might be seen 'as the spatial and social equivalent to an anthology or miscellany' (6) noting their many functions within networks of cultural production (2).

Discussing The Sunwise Turn, a bookshop opened by Madge Jenison and Mary Mowbray-Clarke on New York's East 31st Street in 1916, Edward Bishop explains that the owners deliberately created 'a space for *reading*, not just *buying* books' ('Sunwise' 33). Madge Jenison dedicated her memoir, *Sunwise Turn: A Human Comedy of Bookselling* (1923), to 'Mr. Clive Bell, who, though I have never seen him, founded this bookshop because he wrote a book' (Bishop, 'Sunwise' 44); she referred to Bell's best-selling *Art* (1914) in which he had explained post-impressionism in the context of Western art history. Mowbray-Clarke saw the Sunwise Turn 'as part of the Modernist movement and a movement of "Little" bookshops, like Little theatre or Little magazines' (48). As did its peers in New York, Chicago, Paris, Florence, London and elsewhere, the Sunwise Turn sold not only books, but also textiles, sculpture and other visual art, as well as publishing small editions under its own imprint, and hosting readings and literary gatherings.

A material representation of the kind of network fostered by a bookshop is a door that hung in the bookshop owned in the 1920s by Frank Shay in Greenwich Village, New York. This door was purchased in 1960 by the Humanities Research Center in Austin, Texas. Rescued by Shay from the apartment of novelist and editor Floyd Dell when his building was scheduled for demolition, the door was hung in the shop and became an autograph album signed by visitors in the 1920s. The online exhibition 'The Greenwich Village Bookshop Door: A Portal to Bohemia 1920–1925' provides information on the nearly 250 signatures that adorn this artefact, and points out that the door embodies fifty-three specific connections representing the intersecting worlds of the inhabitants of Greenwich Village bohemia and its visitors. Molly Schwartzburg explains that Shay acquired the Washington Square Bookshop in 1915 or 1916 from Albert and Charles Boni ('Frank'). The Boni brothers had opened the Washington Square Bookshop in 1913 next door to the Liberal Club on MacDougal Street, a 'politically and socially progressive organization with deep ties to the socialist magazine *The Masses*'. A door was cut between the two 'and Liberal Club events spilled regularly into the shop' ('Greenwich'). When Alfred Kreymborg's financially struggling *Others* magazine was revived in 1918, he listed the Washington Square Bookshop as its headquarters.

Gorham Munson, a literary critic who founded the short-lived *Secession* (1922–1924) and later became involved with *Broom* (1921–1924), describes the bookshop in an often-cited passage from his memoir *The Awakening Twenties: A Memoir-History of a Literary Period* (1985):

> The Washington Square Book Shop, presided over by Egmont Arrens and Josephine Bell, was during the Twenties the Greenwich Villagers' favourite shop for browsing. . . . A number of us impecunious young writers were regular patrons of its magazine stand. Magazines priced at fifteen cents to thirty-five cents we could afford, and many an exciting quarter hour was spent looking over the new issues displayed on the rack. . . . It was a very selective rack. One could not find the big circulation magazines like *American Magazine* and *Saturday Evening Post*. In Middletown, U.S.A., one out of five families received the *American*; one out of six received the *Saturday Evening Post*. But not many in Middletown ever saw the magazines on display at the Washington Square Book Shop. . . . Here were the publications of the new movements in American art and thought and literature. (87–88)

Andrew Thacker comments that 'Munson's story presents one myth of modernism that has been questioned recently, that of the advanced tastes of the metropolis (or a small subsection of it,

Greenwich Village) standing over and against "provincial" culture in Middle America.' Thacker points out that recent research on the geographies of modernist print culture demonstrates that 'contrary to Munson's view, the ideas of the "new movements" did circulate outside of Greenwich Village, to Middletown, and beyond' (12).

The young poet Hart Crane, for example, was inspired to move to Greenwich Village in 1916 when he discovered *Bruno's Weekly* in a bookshop in Cleveland (Wetzsteon 362). Guido Bruno, the publisher of *Bruno's Chap Books* and *Bruno's Weekly*, was an unofficial tour guide to the Village who became known as the 'Barnum of Bohemia' (S. Rogers 445). In 1922 The Douglas Bookshop in Detroit published his *Adventures in American Bookshops, Antique Stores and Auction Rooms*, where Bruno provided an idiosyncratic commentary on the Washington Square Bookshop, Sunwise Turn and several others. The flow of avant-garde ideas and iconoclastic art was not only in one direction, from the Village outwards. Eric White discusses how the artists' colony established by Kreymborg, Man Ray and the painter Samuel Halpert in Ridgefield, New Jersey, 'channeled an international network of modernist culture into New York' (*Transatlantic* 25), which in turn was disseminated by little magazines and small press publications sold in bookshops all over the country (Figure 2.1).

**FIGURE 2.1** *Frank Shay and his travelling bookshop, 'Parnassus on Wheels'. Harry Ransom Center, The University of Texas at Austin.*

The bookshops that carried modernist works were often opened to provide space denied by larger commercial enterprises. In England, for example, the radical feminist weekly *The Freewoman* was boycotted by W. H. Smith and Sons, 'whose virtual monopoly on rail station book stalls helped make it one of the largest distributors of journals in England' (Morrisson, *Public* 93). Drawing on Joseph McAleer's *Popular Reading and Publishing in Britain 1914–1950* (1992), Andrew Nash characterizes the years after the First World War as 'notable for an intensification of popular reading and publishing':

> The spread of public and commercial libraries and the increased sales of books in newsagents and general stores, such as Woolworths, ensured that rising production levels continued unabated by the strikes of 1926 and the slump of the 1930s. The emergence in the 1930s of tuppeny libraries which, in contrast to subscription libraries, depended for their business on books being returned quickly, increased demand for popular fiction by promoting shorter books and a greater quantity of titles. Fiction came to be marketed more and more in the form of branded goods, and in series such as the romance novels of Mills & Boon and Hodder & Stoughton's 2s. Yellow Jackets. (323, 325)

Nash explains the 'controlling power of the subscription libraries and corresponding patterns of censorship' in his case study of Chatto & Windus's practices as exemplary of interwar literary culture and bookselling. The little bookshop whose customers mingled with the writers they were interested in and whose owners often were writers themselves (as in the case of Harold Monro) was an antidote to a perceived diminishing of public taste that occasioned much anguished comment, summarized in Q. D. Leavis's tirade against 'a public which buys its literature in accordance with tastes acquired from its circulating library reading' and for whom novel-reading had become 'a drug habit' (Leavis 19).

Many independent bookshop owners were responding to what Morrisson, in his discussion of alternative publication networks, describes as a 'crisis' in the 'understanding of the modern poet's relationship to urban mass culture' (*Public* 96). The relations between small presses and small bookshops were close and symbiotic. In

1921, Leonard and Virginia Woolf briefly considered establishing their own shop for the Hogarth Press, and in 1927 discussed buying out the shop that had been opened in 1919 by David Garnett and Francis Birrell (Willis 54). When Nancy Cunard took up publishing in 1928 she had made no arrangements for distribution of the books her Hours Press produced, but had an extensive list of possible patrons. On a circular announcing the press, Cunard made sure that potential customers knew where to procure her titles other than by writing directly to her: 'Thus I listed the Warren Gallery in London, the Holliday Bookshop in New York, Edward Titus [in] Paris, and Pino Orioli [in] Florence' (Cunard 15). Such bookshops were united in their dedication to providing distribution for private press publications and often worked cooperatively with other small bookshops. In *The Business of Writing: A Practical Guide for Authors* (1922) Robert Cortes Holliday and Alexander van Rensselaer devoted a chapter to 'The New Bookshops' in which they described the owner of a 'little bookshop' as someone who usually wished his shop to stay small: 'He wins his customer's confidence; they put themselves into his hands, and are grateful to him. . . . The little bookshops co-operate with one another: getting books from each other; sending customers to each other. And, finally, there seems to be something like a conspiracy among them against, as one of them put it, "best sellers in a bad sense"' (269). The motives of a customer seeking a best-seller in a little bookshop would, they note, be suspect. In her memoir about the Gotham Book Mart, which she opened in 1919 in midtown Manhattan, Frances Steloff recalls being advised to let her customers educate her about what books to carry, and to be sure that her first customer was 'a young person' (750–51).

The best-known modernist bookshop is undoubtedly Sylvia Beach's Shakespeare & Company, founded in Paris in 1919. Beach's account in her memoir *Shakespeare & Company* (1959) of how she came to publish James Joyce's *Ulysses* has been described as part of the 'folklore' surrounding Joyce's novel by Edward Bishop in 'The "Garbled History" of the First-edition *Ulysses*'. Bishop compares Beach's narrative to the more complicated picture that emerges from archival research, providing an example of the caution with which such autobiographies must be treated by researchers. In addition to publishing *Ulysses*, Shakespeare & Company had a threefold business: 'lending books, selling books, and publishing books' (Fitch 191). Beach was the major distributor of books published by modernist small presses 'because many of the titles were censored in Britain or America or were not imported because their chief audience was the avant-garde in Paris' (Fitch 197). Unlike in England, book lending was virtually unknown in Paris bookshops at the time, but Beach offered subscriptions, or even loaned books for free to impecunious writers. The cards filled out by Beach for each book loaned are in the Sylvia Beach Papers at Princeton University's Library, and 'reveal the reading habits of the leading writers between the wars' (Fitch 192). Fitch provides a table of '1926 Sales of American Books' at Shakespeare & Company that 'reveals the fluctuating interest in British and American literature in Paris between the wars' and notes that Joyce was Beach's all-time best-seller (197).

The bookshops and cafés of modernism were the engines of its print culture, circulating newspapers, chap-books, broadsides, books and reviews, as well as art-world gossip and controversies. Mary Gluck has described the cafés and cabarets of nineteenth-century Paris as sites where the persona of the modern decadent who embodied the new culture of modernity first emerged (110). Writing of a later period, Benstock comments on how early twentieth-century Paris was romanticized in accounts of its role in the creation of modernism (4). The café, which has 'special symbolism in modernity' (Tjora and Scambler 1), has often been located in Paris, but as new geographies of modernism are constructed, other significant sites are beginning to emerge. Early twentieth-century cafés in Vienna and Florence as well as Paris are explored in Rittner, Haine and Jackson's recent collection *The Thinking Space* (2013), which focuses on the café as cultural institution. In her contribution to a cluster of articles 'Introducing Georgian Modernism' in *Modernism/modernity* in 2014, Tea Tabatadze identifies the Café Kimerioni in Tbilisi as 'part of a wider modernist phenomenon, that of the artistic cabaret-club-café, which sprung up in practically all the big cities of Europe, including Moscow and St. Petersburg, beginning in the late nineteenth century' (307). Like the modernist bookshop, the café often provided intellectual as well as physical sustenance and was tolerant of a clientele whose desire to browse and talk often surpassed its purchasing power. 'No public invitation was necessary to walk into a café' writes Cristanne Miller in *Cultures of Modernism*

(2005), her study of the poets Marianne Moore, Mina Loy and Else Lasker-Schüler (33). Miller describes the Café des Westens in Berlin that became popular with Expressionists in the years leading up to the First World War (and where, as he noted in its subtitle, Rupert Brooke somewhat incongruously wrote 'The Old Vicarage, Grantchester' in 1912) (Figure 2.2). 'Table-hopping, heated discussion, and impromptu performances were the order of the day' (Miller 33) in this rather run-down establishment that Lasker-Schüler described as 'our stock exchange where deals are closed' (Miller 34). In *Berlin Metropolis: Jews and the New Culture, 1890–1918* (1999) Emily Bilski explains this remark by describing how information about the publishing and art worlds was circulated at the café: 'What was in and what was out? Was there a chance to have a new manuscript published? What sorts of contracts had been signed and with whom?' (76). Bilski recounts that the Café des Westens employed 'a special "newspaper waiter," "Red Richard" . . . who served papers (adorned with the stamp "Stolen from the Café des Westens") as well as the latest reprint information relating to his guests' publications' (76). Prewar German café culture was, according to Bilski, highly democratic: 'Here the poor poet, the mighty critic, the powerful publisher gathered in this public place. They were open-minded about contemporary art forms and techniques . . . Above all they were opposed to nationalism, recognizing art as an endeavour that knows no national borders, requiring a free flow of creativity among artists and nations' (82). The cafés frequented by modernists, then, were sites wherein writers became readers and readers might encounter the writers whose works they sought.

Discerning reading habits and identifying readers has been the focus of considerable study by social historians and scholars of literacy, although relatively little attention as yet has been devoted to the readers of modernist literature. In researching the Hampshire Bookshop, opened in Northampton, Massachusetts, in 1916 by two alumni of Smith College who claimed that it was the first bookshop in America established and managed by women, Barbara A. Brannon discovered that the records of few bookstores have been preserved ('Building' 5; see also Brannon, 'We'). Creating a profile of likely readers has, though, long been part of the field of book history. Cathy N. Davidson notes that the classic approach to this task has been to 'examine such surviving evidence as purchase

FIGURE 2.2 *Café des Westens, Berlin, 1905*. Photograph from Kurfürstendamm: Berlins Prachtboulevard *by Peter-Alexander Bösel. Erfurt: Sutton, 2008*.

orders, account books, lending library rosters, and subscription lists in order to identify the actual readers of a given work. Once identified, these readers are then grouped by class, gender, nationality, race, profession, region, neighborhood, or religion in order to ascertain a sociological profile of a given book's readership' (18). *Reading Acts: U. S. Readers' Interactions with Literature 1800–1950*, edited by Barbara Ryan and Amy M. Thomas (2002), usefully surveys histories of reading and scholarship in the field. Examples of such projects include Janice Radway's *A Feeling for Books: The Book-of-the-Month Club, Literary Taste and Middle-Class Desire* (1997) and, in a UK context, Jonathan Rose's study of Welsh mining institute libraries between 1923 and 1952, or Nicola Humble's account of middlebrow and highbrow reading practices, which is partly derived from the surveys carried out by Mass Observation. A prominent recent example is Frank Felsenstein and James J. Connolly's *What Middletown Read* (2015), which draws on the Muncie, Indiana, public library records from 1891 to 1902, an unprecedentedly large discovery of library circulation records that can now be searched online via the 'What Middletown Read' database. 'The idea that reading experience is not rooted simply in the text but also in the context', write Felsenstein and Connolly, 'is now a central element of print culture history' (8). In studies of modernist print culture, the reader has yet to receive sustained attention, although in the interwar period there was a great deal of debate about reading and literacy, and the kinds of influences brought to bear on taste by institutions such as reviewing and book societies.

The 'Reader Critic' section of *The Little Review* provides a record of the exchange between editors Margaret Anderson and Jane Heap and the magazine's readers, but as Jayne Marek remarks, the published excerpts were 'clearly chosen as humorous and often pointed demonstrations' of this interaction (80). Letters from readers in other periodicals may also provide some insight into the public's response to modernism, but such sources obviously were shaped in their presentation by the editors who chose them for publication and they must be carefully contextualized by anyone wishing to draw conclusions from them. (Eliot, for example, had great fun inventing correspondents to engage with the articles he had published, once filling up space in *The Egoist* with letters from 'J. A. D. Spence', 'Helen B. Trundlett', 'Charles James Grimble', 'Charles Augustus Conybeare' and 'Muriel A. Schwarz' – all of whom were Eliot [*Letters* 1: 211–12].) In ' "Mind-hungers" common and uncommon', Todd Avery and Patrick Brantlinger survey a range of modernists' critical, fictional and poetic responses to what Melba Cuddy-Keane has described as 'one of the most pressing issues of the time': how to educate the reader in an era of mass production that flooded the marketplace with inferior reading materials (*Virginia* 59). Avery and Brantlinger point out that reading 'was rapidly becoming a matter for the experts, especially through the increasingly professionalized, academic practice of literary criticism and interpretation' (247). They argue that Virginia Woolf and other members of the Bloomsbury Group were particularly attuned to the 'mutual responsibilities of reader and writer', noting that in her essay 'The Patron and the Crocus' Woolf wrote that 'To know whom to write for is to know how to write' (253). Avery and Brantlinger draw attention to work on readers by scholars such as Cuddy-Keane, Anna Snaith, Derek Attridge and Kevin Dettmar who 'by unceasing historical contextualization of canonical and less-read modernist texts' are providing a clearer recognition of the 'ethical and political stakes' reading these texts engenders (259).

Examples of archival work on modernist readers' letters include those received by Virginia Woolf from a diverse range of people that are published in three volumes of *Woolf Studies Annual*. Anna Snaith introduces eighty-five letters to Woolf about *Three Guineas* (1938) from sixty-five writers from Britain, France, the United States and Canada ('Wide Circles'). In 2005, Melba Cuddy-Keane tracked down whatever she was able to discover about a 'fan' named John Farrelly who wrote to Woolf in 1940 and 1941. Despite the contention of a reviewer of a grant application submitted by Cuddy-Keane that it seemed 'very unlikely that such a limited research base can tell us anything reliable about "modernism's historical audience"' ('From Fan' 16), Cuddy-Keane finds value both in the letters from Farrelly and in her search for who he was. The largest trove of readers' letters to Woolf was published in 2006 by Beth Rigel Daugherty, who transcribed 137 letters from 121 correspondents between 1915, the date of Woolf's first novel, and 1941, the year of her death. These readers:

> 1) describe their relationship with Woolf in a vocabulary of intimacy and knowledge; 2) illustrate conventions of writing fan mail that demand apology for the relationship being assumed; 3) assert that Woolf's readership is wider and more diverse than commonly thought; 4) reflect Woolf's encouragement of youth; 5) demonstrate an enthusiastic United States response that predates the scholarship of the 1970s; and 6) demand that we rethink our construction of Woolf's audience. (4)

Daugherty proposes that to 'capture the living feel of modernism as it was being created and being read, to remove it from abstraction and hierarchies and the language of exclusion, we must posit a "tangled mesh of readers" for the "tangled mesh of modernists" we now know about' (10).

A recent sourcebook on *The History of Reading* calls for more empirical research that collates 'a range of quantifiable data, such as that offered by print runs, library circulation records, literacy figures, sale prices, average incomes, distribution networks, and advertising' (Towheed, Crone and Halsey 2), and notes that an individual's experience 'can tell us little about the broader trends and patterns of *how* a particular text was consumed' (2). The history of reading has typically been a record of what people bought or borrowed but without actual evidence that they read it. Statements to the effect that the history of reading is in its infancy have become a 'dutiful trope' (9) according to Matthew Bradley and Juliet John in *Reading and the Victorians* (2015). Nevertheless, archival work in modernist book history has sometimes been able to enrich our understanding of readers. Alice Staveley's research on Norah Nicholls, the publicity manager at the Hogarth Press in 1938, illuminates 'previously unknown production, distribution, and consumption networks behind the reception of *Three Guineas*' (296). Staveley uncovers a number of 'lost' reviews of Woolf's pacifist essay published in the journals of explicitly feminist women's organizations that Nicholls targeted in a marketing campaign to increase Hogarth Press sales. These reviews throw 'unexpected light on a huge repository of modernist women's print culture' that had been unnoticed in specialized archives or copyright libraries, providing yet another example of how print culture scholarship can alter received critical opinion even of widely discussed modernist works. Most significantly, Staveley argues that the 'rhetorical communities' which Nicholls created 'rippled outwards in ways that allow us to see, if we ever doubted it, how book reviews form their own "interpretative communities" reflecting and shaping the desires, aspirations, and objectives of their target readerships' (319). Molly Abel Travis pointed out in *Reading Cultures: The Construction of Readers in the Twentieth Century* (1998) that reader-response and reader-reception studies promoted the understanding of readers 'in terms of specific political and historical situations' (1), and urged scholars to consider the process of reading as a form of individual agency (60). Travis's analysis of 'the cultural effort invested in rendering Joyce's *Ulysses* readable' (23) reconstructs the way the novel circulated among differently constructed types of readers upon its publication in the United States in 1934. Recently launched empirical studies such as *The Reading Experience Database*, *The Australian Common Reader* and *Reading: Harvard Views of Readers, Readership, and Reading History*, together with pioneering work on readers, such as Richard D. Altick's *The English Common Reader: A Social History of the Mass Reading Public 1800–1900* (1957), and the continuing scholarship on Victorian readers provide a rich context as well as methodological models for continuing study of modernist readers and reading.

## Finance, marketplace, celebrity

> The present venture is a modest effort to give to poetry her own place, her own voice. The popular magazines can afford her but scant courtesy – a Cinderella corner in the ashes – because they seek a large public which is not hers, a public which buys them not for their verse but for their stories, pictures, journalism . . . We shall be able to print poems longer, and of more intimate and serious character, than the popular magazines can afford to use. The test . . . is to be quality alone.
>
> – Harriet Monroe (27)

Harriet Monroe's much-quoted opening editorial in *Poetry* magazine is one of several contemporary programmatic statements which place literary 'quality' in opposition to financial profit. Monroe's play on the word 'afford' contrasts little magazines, which cannot afford (pay for) glossy, colourful printing, with large-circulation titles, which cannot afford (risk) publishing difficult or controversial material in case they alienate subscribers or advertisers. *Poetry* itself, though, is an anomaly. It is the modernist magazine that survived modernism, and that is still on sale – and still dedicated to new poetry – today.

Information about the history of *Poetry* as an enterprise is therefore easier to obtain than it is for many other literary magazines: as a going concern, it has an interest in preserving its own archive. *Poetry* is often discussed, not only in the context of modernist-era print, but also in that of today's American little magazines. For instance, Anderson and Kinzie include two pieces on *Poetry* in their sourcebook *The Little Magazine in America: A Modern Documentary History* (1978). One, 'The Care and Funding of Pegasus', is by Joseph Parisi, who in 1978 was an associate editor of *Poetry*, and later served as editor-in-chief. He writes that the 'financial and administrative affairs of the magazine' are 'a complex, evolving story often as entangled as its literary correspondence and relationships'. Describing *Poetry* as 'singular in its economic resourcefulness' (217), Parisi notes that in 1912, the annual budget of $5,000 came from pledges that the well-connected Monroe obtained from eminent citizens of Chicago by 'appealing to their civic pride' (218). Funding via patronage has been in use in many literary cultures since the Renaissance, and it remains essential to *Poetry*'s survival. As Marjorie Garber comments in *Patronizing the Arts* (2008): 'With certain exceptions – like the $100 million-plus donation that the heiress Ruth Lilly made to *Poetry Magazine* in 2002 – literary patrons are less visible today than in previous decades and centuries' (13). *Poetry*, then, remains exceptional.

At the same time, the case of *Poetry* only reinforces the well-known fact that literary publishing is, almost by definition, an unprofitable business. Although influential, long-established and high-profile, *Poetry* is nevertheless sustained by philanthropy, not commercial viability. Many of the little magazines of the modernist era expected to lose money, even seeing this as honourable, since it proved that they were not motivated by a desire for financial gain. Some relied on donations or on the free labour of devoted staff, and others on cross-subsidy from more profitable publishing ventures, on corporate money or on institutional sponsorship, such as that of universities. Larger magazines, by contrast, were increasingly funded by advertising which, as early as the 1890s, had begun to replace newsstand and subscription sales as their primary source of income. A similar division operated in relation to publishing houses. Small presses were often privately funded or partly dependent on a network of supporters or subscribers, while larger presses relied on commercial sales. Critics and book historians are exploring these different financial models as part of an ongoing investigation into the material substrate of modernism and its relationship to notions of literary value.

Sources for the study of these topics are various. In terms of archival material, the papers of some individual authors, editors and booksellers, and – less frequently – of presses or magazines have been preserved. Examples of the latter include the Cuala Press archive at Trinity College, Dublin, and the *Dial* papers at Yale. In terms of published resources, studies of the book trade can yield important economic detail – for instance, J. H. Willis's *Leonard and Virginia Woolf as Publishers* (1992) includes an appendix giving profit and loss figures for each volume published between 1917 and 1938, and he also explains the subscription plan which Leonard Woolf established 'to suit his need for a small amount of working capital and a list of regular buyers' (48). Hugh Ford's *Published in Paris: American and British Writers, Printers, and*

*Publishers in Paris, 1920–1939* (1975) covers Contact, Seizin, Carrefour, Three Mountains, Obelisk and other small presses.

Equally important are first-hand memoirs, such as those by and about Sylvia Beach, Caresse Crosby, Nancy Cunard and Harriet Shaw Weaver, which offer insight into the histories of Shakespeare & Company, the Black Sun Press, the Hours Press and *The Egoist*. Many of these mid-century narratives are, however, considered by later scholars to be biased or incomplete. When using these memoirs, whether in volume form or via modern sourcebooks such as Anderson and Kinzie's or Travis Kurowski's *Paper Dreams: Writers and Editors on the American Literary Magazine* (2013), it is important to be aware of the nostalgia which often permeates them. Indeed, Anderson and Kinzie note in their introduction:

> It may be that the modern world is no longer as receptive to intelligent meditation as it may have been through the 1940s, and that our culture will no longer support the literary judgements of a relatively small number of literate commentators. It may be that the advances in publishing technologies and the conglomerations of their economies militate against the cultural coherence of the past. Or it may be, too, that such coherence is an inevitable function of nostalgia. (4)

A narrative of decline, whereby post-Second World War publishers and magazines no longer live up to the ideals of those thriving in earlier decades, is prevalent in many retrospective accounts.

Scholes and Wulfman, in their guide to studying modern magazines (Chapter 6 of *Modernism in the Magazines*), provide checklists of the data that a scholar needs in order to begin to understand an individual magazine and how it was positioned in the marketplace. As well as items related to the editorial and production side of things, they list pricing, circulation and advertising content, three crucial factors in determining the financial basis on which a magazine operated (54–55; 146–48). Magazine prices, and price variations, are rarely recorded in bibliographic studies but can usually be found on the covers of archived issues. Prices are key indicators of the status and likely audience of a periodical. Commenting on the British print marketplace at the start of the twentieth century, Scholes and Wulfman point to the difference between sixpenny weeklies, such as *The New Statesman* or *Spectator*, sixpenny monthlies, which published popular fiction, and one-penny weeklies, offering more miscellaneous content to a mass audience: 'we can see that the category "sixpenny weekly" names a weekly magazine selling at a monthly price, which, therefore, must be a weightier magazine containing deeper thought for a smaller audience' (50). As to the proportion of advertising content, this can be roughly calculated by counting pages. The likely revenue from advertising, while not easy to work out exactly (unless accounts have been preserved), can be categorized on a scale from substantial to modest, according to whether the advertisers are, for instance, large manufacturing firms taking out full-page ads, or publishers and booksellers purchasing space for small notices.

Circulation figures are the most elusive part of the economic dataset. Figures for selected titles in particular years are given in bibliographic guides such as Frank Luther Mott's, Edward E. Chielens's, or Alvin Sullivan's, and in survey studies of popular magazines such as David Reed's, Theodore Peterson's and Mike Ashley's. Scholes and Wulfman advise on how to use such sources (45–48; 62–63, 71), but do not point out the unreliability of some indicators of audience size and growth. Here, it is helpful to turn to another methodological model for periodical studies, by Charles Johanningsmeier. It appears in volume 6 of the *Oxford History of Popular Print Culture* and centres on ways of collecting information about readers of American magazines:

> To learn the actual numerical circulation of a periodical, one must go beyond editors' and publishers' claims, given their vested interest in inflating circulation statistics: the higher the claimed circulation, the more they could charge for advertising space. Before the creation in 1914 of the Audit Bureau of Circulations (whose reports are generally reliable because misreporting to this organization could lead to stiff penalties for a periodical's publisher), the best source for reliable periodical circulation figures is N.W. *Ayer and Son's Newspaper Annual* or George P. Rowell's *American Newspaper Directory*, both of which included circulation figures for newspapers and magazines. (598–99)

Directories such as these, designed to help companies decide where to advertise, also existed in other countries – in the United Kingdom, for instance, there was *Mitchell's Newspaper Press Directory* (1846–1907) and *Willing's Press Guide* (1928–).

Recently, the editors of the *Oxford Critical and Cultural History of Modernist Magazines* have compiled tables of prices for selected British magazines in their first volume (Brooker and Thacker, 'Introduction' 24–25) and of circulation figures for selected American magazines in their second (Thacker 17). In the third volume, covering continental Europe, there are no tables, but the general introduction provides a helpful summary of the sources of finance that European magazines drew on:

> Some magazines were successfully self-financed by wealthy individuals, for example Marinetti and Picabia. . . . In Spain, the magazines *Vell i nou* and *Revista nova* were both founded by the art promoter and editor Santiago Segura. Otherwise, external private or corporate money played a role. Thus, the Norwegian *Exlex* (Lawless) edited by Ragnvald Blix was funded to the tune of 300,000 Norwegian Krone in 1918 (over £630,000 or $980,000 in 2012) by friends in the textile industry . . . A subsidy from UFA (Universal-Film AG) enabled Hans Richter to launch *G* . . . In yet another direction, Antonio Gramsci's *L'Ordine Nuovo* became, from 1921, the official Communist Party paper. (Brooker 20)

Brooker's account draws attention to the motivations, whether related to politics, profit or prestige, of those who financed magazines. Various chapters in all three volumes of the *History* explore the ways that the interests of funders influenced, or were in tension with, the contents of the magazines they sponsored.

More generally, economic information is increasingly used by scholars to inform their interpretative accounts of modernist publishing. In this respect, two foundational studies, that appeared almost simultaneously, are Wexler's *Who Paid for Modernism?* (1997) and Rainey's *Institutions of Modernism* (1998). Wexler comments that her book is 'not publishing history' but 'a study of the ways ideology and models of authorship interact with social institutions to shape literary texts' (xxi). Her research centres on the archive of J. B. Pinker, the agent for Conrad, Joyce and Lawrence, and part of her argument is derived from comparison of the print runs, sales and profits of different editions of these authors' books. She contends that modernist writers used 'complex forms that seemed inaccessible to many readers as a way to demonstrate indifference to money and devotion to art. Since it was also necessary to earn a living by writing, however, modernists cultivated patrons and readers by generating publicity in the popular press' (123).

Rainey uses income and circulation statistics (taken from published sources) to compare *The Dial*, *The Little Review* and *Vanity Fair*, the three magazines that were considered for the US publication of *The Waste Land*. *Vanity Fair* generated $500,000 per year in advertising revenue, and devoted over half its space to paid advertising, in comparison to under 20 per cent in *The Dial*. Of *The Dial*, Rainey writes:

> Its subscription list was some two and a half times larger than the *Little Review*'s: 6,374 in 1922 (compared with the average of 2,500 for the *Little Review* in 1917). Its ratio of advertising to circulation revenues was not 1:10 but 1:3 (specifically, $9,100 to $31,400) . . . But above all, the *Dial* was supported by massive patronage: its deficits for the three years from 1920 to 1922 were . . . paid for directly by Thayer and Watson at the rate of $4,000 per month from each. Nothing is more revealing than comparable figures for the *Little Review*, which in 1918 was supported by a syndicate of four donors whose contributions totaled $2,350 per year. (92–94)

Rainey says of the three magazines: 'Each represented a moment in the growth and triumph of modernism' (91). He proposes that *The Little Review*, which had published the early work of the then unknown Eliot, represented modernism's past, as 'a literature of an exiguous elite', while *The Dial*, where *The Waste Land* actually appeared, was modernism's present, 'a form of production supported by a massive and unprecedented patronage' and *Vanity Fair*, which helped turn Eliot into a celebrity over the following months, 'looked forward to modernism's future, to the ease and speed with which a market economy could purchase, assimilate, commodify, and reclaim as its own the works of a literature whose ideological premises were bitterly inimical towards its ethos and cultural operations' (91).

Rainey's work has provided a starting point for many other scholars. For example, Alan Golding's 2005 article on the relationship between *The Dial* and *The Little Review* considers 'how the shaping of taste by modernist magazines is a collective project, not a matter of the atomized influence of single publications' (43). Most critics have defined these two periodicals in opposition to one another, with *The Dial* positioned as more ordered, authoritative and commercialized, and *The Little Review* as more eclectic, politically engaged and controversial. Golding, however, argues that they 'needed each other to accomplish their cultural work' (43). Although *The Little Review* eventually became antagonistic towards *The Dial*, they nevertheless jointly shaped an emerging poetic canon, because: 'The *Dial* helped to canonize what the *Little Review* helped to discover, and thus in some sense the *Little Review* exercised its influence *through* the *Dial*' (46). They shared contributors and were influenced by some of the same people (notably Pound); they ran adverts for one another, and *The Dial* helped *The Little Review* financially.

A different business model was used by *The Smart Set*, which was somewhat anomalous in that its editorial policy was adventurous, yet it reached as many as 30,000 readers. Sharon Hamilton explains the financial situation which made this possible:

> *The Smart Set*'s most influential joint editors and part owners, in the period 1914–23, H. L. Mencken and George Jean Nathan made so much money from their own book publications and freelance writing that they published the magazine essentially without concern for profit, and invented sources other than advertising (of which they attracted very little) with which to subsidize it, including publication of the dirty fiction magazines *Parisienne* and *Saucy Stories* and the journal that would go on to become the most famous detective magazine of all time, *The Black Mask*. This freedom from financial controls (and also, therefore, from a certain degree of self-censorship) meant that *The Smart Set* could publish stories that dealt frankly with the realities of modern life. ('American Manners' 227)

These stories included work by Dorothy Parker, F. Scott Fitzgerald, Eugene O'Neill and Sherwood Anderson. Volumes of *The Smart*

*Set* from 1913 to 1922 have now been digitized by the *Modernist Journals Project*, and the magazine is attracting increasing attention for its role in the development of both celebrity culture and New York modernism, as well as for the connections it reveals between literary and pulp publishing. David Earle includes a chapter on *The Smart Set* in *Re-Covering Modernism* (2009), pointing out that Joyce began his American publishing career there, with two stories from *Dubliners* that appeared in 1915 alongside the work of pulp authors (Figure 2.3). Earle also notes Joyce's appearances in interwar reprint magazines and postwar men's magazines, anthologies and paperback editions. The example of Joyce is just one of many that Earle uses to demonstrate 'how slanted our history of the movement is in regard to the *forms* of modernism', since critical accounts are still 'reductively based upon the material forms that those early literary historians thought worthy of archiving: the little magazine, manuscripts, and first editions, rather than reprint magazines and literary digests, reprint and circulating library hardback editions, pulp magazines, and paperbacks' (3).

There is another gap in the archive, in addition to those mentioned by Earle. Prominent magazines with a national circulation often published modernist writers, and these titles are preserved in research libraries – but often in an incomplete form. In his 2011 article 'The Mess and Muddle of Modernism', Sean Latham comments on the difficulty experienced by the MJP in accessing complete runs of more mainstream titles to digitize:

> Most issues of *Scribner's Magazine* in the period from 1910–1922 contain hundreds of pages of advertising . . . gathered together in distinct sections of the magazine and numbered separately from the rest of the letterpress. This practice reflected the larger culture's uneasiness with this new rhetorical form and made it easy for libraries to remove the ads . . . The result has been the widespread destruction of this vital portion of the archive, and because of the independent numbering system for advertising pages, the hole itself is not even visible in the bound runs that have been preserved. (416–17)

The advertisements are valuable, not only from the point of view of cultural history, but also because they reveal how the magazine was

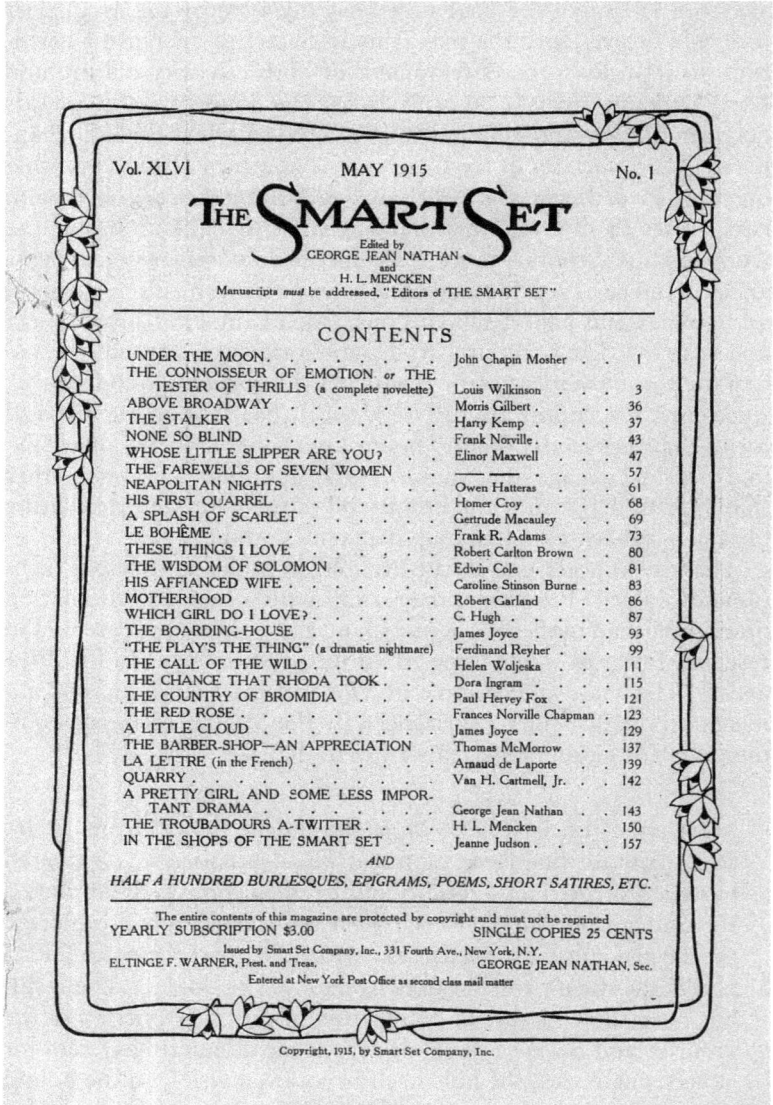

FIGURE 2.3 The Smart Set *May 1915 Contents. Courtesy of the Modernist Journals Project (searchable database); Brown and Tulsa Universities, http://www.modjourn.org.*

funded. The volume of advertising in a magazine such as *Scribner's* shows that it had adopted the business model developed by the American print entrepreneurs of the 1880s and 1890s such as Frank Munsey and S. S. McClure – that is, to sustain a loss on the low cover price and thereby build a large circulation which could be used to attract advertising. As Richard Ohmann points out in his study of the golden age of American mass magazines, readers bought a commodity 'that commodified *them* as well – presented their attention, their needs, their aspirations, their anxieties, as use values to unseen third parties' (80). Therefore, advertisements can provide insight into a magazine's target audience, offering clues about gender, class fraction, age range and geographical location.

While most scholarship on print advertising focuses on periodicals, the use of advertising in books, on endpapers, dust jackets or spare pages at the back, should also be noted. Most frequently, adverts were for other titles available from the same publisher, a practice that had been established by Victorian publishers. Consumer advertising, for products such as patent medicines and food items, also appeared. These were mostly found in inexpensive volumes of fiction and in novels published in parts, which would have advertising sections wrapped around them. As Simon Eliot notes in 'A Prehistory for Penguins': 'Most paperback and paperback equivalents in the nineteenth century carried advertisements of one sort or another' (14). This practice was carried over into the twentieth-century paperback. Phil Baines, in *Penguins by Design*, notes that early Penguins carried pages promoting other available titles, adding: 'In February 1938 the first commercial advertisements appeared, and the revenue they generated helped keep the cover price at the original sixpence for a time. The use of adverts declined rapidly from about 1944' (32). All these kinds of adverts give insight into the way publishers were trying to position each new title in the marketplace.

Alongside research on the way that publishing enterprises were funded, another strand of work in this field looks at the business from the other end, exploring the ways that modernist authors made a living. A repeated pattern is that of an author publishing in both small-circulation venues, which would earn prestige, and also in popular formats, which would earn money. In some cases, an individual text might move from a small-scale to a more profitable venue: for instance, Simone Murray comments that 'all of Cuala's publications by W. B. Yeats served as hand-printed precursors to the mass-market editions produced by commercial firms' (494). Karen Jackson Ford, in her essay 'Making Poetry Pay' in Dettmar and Watt's *Marketing Modernisms*, notes that Harlem poet Langston Hughes 'had the good business sense to understand that the poem could be . . . commodified. Poems could be published individually in magazines and newspapers, gathered together for a volume, reprinted in later volumes or anthologies, interpolated in prose, sung on the stage, recited in personal appearances, submitted to writing contests, and recycled yet again for a *Selected Poems*' (276).

In other cases, an author might produce different types of text suitable for different publication venues. In current critical discussion, there is much interest in as Thacker puts it, 'the appearance of writers of high symbolic capital in magazines with large sales' (19). He mentions Virginia Woolf's essays in *Good Housekeeping*, Theodore Dreiser's publications in *Munsey's*, and Willa Cather's in *McClure*'s, adding that other writers contributed to medium-circulation magazines – Pound, Joyce and Ford to *The Smart Set*, Eliot to *Vanity Fair* and *Vogue*. Thacker asks: 'does this boost the symbolic capital of the magazine or somehow lower that of the authors?' (20). Several critics have focused on this question, whether by studying the variety of authors published by an individual magazine or publishing house, or by tracing the trajectory of an author through print venues of varying repute. A nice example of the latter approach can be found in Scholes and Wulfman's account of Pound's rather scattergun approach. In 1905, Pound had one of his early poems rejected from *The Bibelot* for being 'insufficiently modern', while the following year, he had one accepted by the mass-market *Munsey's*. And then, in 1908, when he was in Venice, Pound sent his father back in America some stories and travel writing with instructions to try to place them in the following magazines: 'Try first on "Outlook". Then if not accepted Everybodies, McClure, Cosmopolitan, Book News in order".' In 1913, he withdrew some poems submitted to *Poetry* and sent them instead to the better-paying *The Smart Set* (41). This analysis leads up to Scholes and Wulfman's much-quoted insight: 'Modernism happened in the magazines all right, but it didn't happen only in the little ones' (41).

Among the larger magazines that are attracting increasing interest from scholars of Anglophone modernism are *Vanity Fair* and

British *Vogue*, particularly during the editorship of the highbrow Dorothy Todd (1922–1926). These titles were positioned between elite and mainstream cultures, and mediated modernism for a mass audience. Discussion of *Vanity Fair* and of other American 'smart' or 'slick' magazines such as *The New Yorker* and *Harper's Bazaar*, was stimulated by the publication of Michael Murphy's essay on the rise of the slicks in Dettmar and Watt's 1996 collection, as well as by Rainey's *Institutions of Modernism* and Nina Miller's *Making Love Modern: The Intimate Public Worlds of New York's Literary Women* (1998), which attends to 'the periodical forms of popular modernism' (88). An important later study is Catherine Keyser's *Playing Smart: New York Women Writers and Modern Magazine Culture* (2010), which contextualizes the 'smart' magazines through comparison with Harlem journals including *The Crisis* and *Opportunity*, and with women's fashion magazines, daily newspapers and little magazines. Keyser's account reveals many shared preoccupations, as well as shared staff and contributors, among these different types of periodicals, and shows that this facilitated exchange across cultural boundaries.

Nicola Luckhurst's *Bloomsbury in Vogue* (1998), a pamphlet in the Bloomsbury Heritage series, describes the showcasing of Bloomsbury in Dorothy Todd's *Vogue*. *Vogue* did not publish modernist poetry or fiction, but it gossiped about modernists, photographed them and visited their houses, in effect marketing high culture to an audience extending far beyond the intellectual elite. Articles by Jane Garrity, Aurelea Mahood and Christopher Reed have explored this theme further. Garrity describes the Bloomsbury Group as a 'mass market phenomenon', and 1920s *Vogue* as 'a fascinating cultural hybrid' (30). Christopher Reed counters Garrity's claim that the magazine evinced no homoerotic sensibility in this period, arguing that in fact '*Vogue*'s extensive coverage of literature and the arts became a guide to an emerging canon of queer modernism'. He mentions articles in *Vogue* by and about André Gide, Jean Cocteau, Marie Laurencin, Edith Sitwell and Gertrude Stein ('Design' 381–82). Mahood explores the 'complex dialectic between high culture and fashion' (38), discussing *Vogue* contributions by Sitwell and Richard Aldington, and concluding that their essays introduce an aspirational, middle-class audience 'to what was originally a "restricted" or minority culture'. The perceived elite status, she argues, was the source of modernism's appeal for this audience, something which suggests 'the need for further consideration of the location of the popular press in the construction of our received and now challenged constructions of high modernism' (46).

This, indeed, is an emerging theme in the new modernist studies. For example, Karen Leick, in her 2008 *PMLA* article, 'Popular Modernism: Little Magazines and the American Daily Press', proposes that 'examining the ways popular audiences understood modernism rather than the way modernists understood popular culture reveals that there was an increasingly intimate exchange between literary modernism and mainstream culture in this period and that, in part because of the rise of celebrity culture, modernist writers and texts were better known and, indeed, more popular than has been acknowledged' (126). Leick argues that the modest circulation figures of American little magazines such as *Broom*, the *transatlantic review* or *The Little Review* 'fail to reflect the astonishing cultural influence of these publications', since their content was remediated and gossiped about in newspapers and mass-market magazines such as *Life* and the *Saturday Evening Post*. Leick notes that, for example, in the 1920s the *New York Times Book Review* ran a weekly 'Current Magazines' column that reported on the contents of modernist magazines alongside those of glossies such as *Harper's* and *McClure's* (123). She also explores the many parodies of modernist writers that appeared in the mainstream press. These parodies, though expressing ambivalence, puzzlement or downright hostility towards figures such as Stein or Joyce, did not harm their reputations or sales. Indeed, as Leick observes, it is incorrect to suggest that the success of *The Autobiography of Alice B. Toklas* turned Stein into a household name: 'the reverse is nearer the truth; it was because Stein was a household name that *The Autobiography of Alice B. Toklas* became a best seller' (137). Leick's article crystallizes some of the arguments which have been made at greater length in several books on early twentieth-century literary celebrity, notably monographs by Aaron Jaffe, Loren Glass, Faye Hammill and Jonathan Goldman, as well as an edited collection by Goldman and Jaffe. All of these draw on the methods of print culture studies, using periodical archives and authors' and publishers' papers in order to explore the way that reputations were built and cultural capital generated via practices of networking, collaboration, editing and reviewing.

The different topics considered in this chapter are of course difficult to separate out. Many critical accounts explore the way that modernist networks centred on particular sites of circulation, or the way that they intersected with commercial and popular cultural formations. An example of a discussion which brings all these elements together is Peter Brooker's introduction to the third volume of the *Oxford Critical and Cultural History of Modernist Magazines*. He observes, 'In addition to the work of the magazines, the talking shops of cafés, booksellers, and studios gave added voice to a metropolitan or transmetropolitan counter-public sphere, and were aided by independent publishing houses and gallery outlets.' Among the examples he cites are publishers such as Edizione di Poesia in Milan, Malik Verlag in Berlin, Éditions Gallimard in Paris and *Edition 69* in Czechoslovakia, as well as exhibitions staged at the Salon d'automne in Paris and the Galeries Dalmau in Barcelona. Brooker draws particular attention to *Der Sturm*, which was at the centre of a 'thoroughgoing independent and mobile institutional network', because its founder, Herwarth Walden, also established galleries and tours, and published books (19). Brooker comments, 'These combined outlets functioned so as effectively to sidestep the apparatus of conventional publishing houses and exhibition venues. At the same time, the proximity of established publications and of new print media and the marketing techniques of an advancing commodity culture caution against drawing a stark dichotomy between avant-garde experiment or "amateurism" and the "professional" mainstream' (19). Many earlier studies of modernism did attempt to maintain the 'stark dichotomy' that Brooker describes, but in recent decades, work on modernist print culture has increasingly emphasized the crossover between modernist and mainstream cultures, and the tendency of readers, as well as writers, artists and editors, to move across the range of printed forms and cultural levels. In the next chapter, the question of cultural level will be taken up in relation to the educational or uplifting purposes of certain print ventures, while questions of advocacy and activism will be explored in relation to politically committed publishing enterprises.

# 3

# Purposeful print

This chapter focuses on literary and publishing enterprises with a distinct, socially grounded aim, whether in the area of education and uplift or politics and activism. Self-improvement is the keynote of the print initiatives discussed in the first section of the chapter: the book clubs, digests, reprint series and paperbacks that brought high culture to an expanding literate public. These cultural formations, often described as 'middlebrow' because they aimed to widen access to canonical writing, to mentor readers in their choices, or, more broadly, to encourage self-culture, provoked immediate resistance because of their alleged standardization of taste. An important concern of recent criticism has been, as Janice Radway puts it, to understand 'the particular ways in which middlebrow culture managed and controlled those it addressed so successfully' (12). In the second section, we turn to the political causes embraced by modernist-affiliated publishers, editors, authors and artists. These included women's suffrage, black self-determination, socialism and anti-colonialism. The interactions and possible tensions between modernist aesthetics and political radicalism were intensively debated during the period, and this is an important strand in current critical discussion, though the emphasis shifts according to geographical and temporal contexts. In the study of American magazines, for instance, race is a predominant concern, while in a European context, discussion of radical politics and anarchism is more salient. Another aspect of the relationship between politics and print is the question of, as Meredith McGill describes it, 'state investment in and control of the circulation of texts' (390). Politicians and legislators – often abetted by individual citizens or collectives – decide what types of print to protect via copyright regulations, and what types of print to suppress via obscenity regulations. Recent scholarship reveals not only the extent to which modernist print production was distorted by these twin forces of control, but also the range of productive strategies of resistance adopted by authors and publishers. This is the focus of the third section of this chapter, which is quite concise because there is a separate book on 'Modernism and the Law' in the New Modernisms series.

Our two main sections below are titled 'Educational print' and 'Political print', and certain types of print enterprise fall fairly naturally under one or other of these headings. The first covers middlebrow institutions of culture while the second includes magazines, pamphlets and publishing enterprises centred on protest, reform or group advancement. Yet the themes of 'education' and 'politics' are, of course, impossible to separate completely, since education is itself a political matter, and can be used as a political strategy. In the sphere of the middlebrow, efforts to organize the reading and develop the tastes of middle- and working-class audiences inevitably get caught up in debates about whether mass literacy furthers democracy or facilitates social control. In projects of class or racial uplift, education is a key method of achieving political aims, and activist publications usually aim to teach their audiences in order to motivate them. For example, as Trevor Joy Sangrey notes, the pamphlets put out by the Communist Party USA on contemporary issues such as the Scottsboro trial 'highlight the similarity of the aims of education and propaganda' (134).

Sangrey's essay appears in Rachel Schreiber's collection, *Modern Print Activism in the United States* (2013), which emerged from two panels at the 2011 Modernist Studies Association conference. This book is an excellent starting point, since it indicates some of the newest directions in the study of political print. In her introduction, Schreiber defines print activism as 'print media's role in social and political activism throughout the long twentieth century . . . the central vehicle by which activists on all points of the political spectrum . . . spread their opinions, elicited support, created networks among like-minded individuals, and attempted to establish cohesive group identities for the larger world' (2). She argues that since activism is today largely conducted online, 'print activism can now be periodized as a twentieth-century phenomenon, one that is inherently modern not only in its contributions to modern culture but also for the ways that it enabled American moderns to connect with one another' (1). Some essays in the volume focus on publications affiliated to specific causes – the Reform Press of the late nineteenth century, the suffrage press, Ku Klux Klan publications, Communist pamphlets, gay and feminist magazines and even the Student Non-Violent Co-ordinating Committee's 1968 wall calendar. But mainstream publications, too, could advance particular causes, and the collection also contains essays on the meaning of Mother's Day in *Good Housekeeping* and on the Cold War in the *Ladies' Home Journal*. These two case studies could easily be taken up in the context of either educational or political print. In general, though, critics tend to discuss consumer magazines more in relation to education and aspiration than to politics, since they appeal primarily to a desire for individual self-improvement rather than group advancement.

This question of where to 'place' mainstream publications raises one of a series of methodological and theoretical issues related to early twentieth-century 'purposeful print'. First, does the history of reformist and 'improving' publishing really belong to modernist print culture studies, or should it more properly be understood as 'popular print'? After all, many activist publications used the rhetorical and sentimental techniques of popular fiction, while middlebrow educators tended to inculcate a relatively conservative version of literary taste. For this reason, research on popular print can provide useful resources and frameworks for analysis of such material. For instance, volume 6 of the *Oxford History of Popular Print Culture* (2012) includes general chapters on 'The Magazine Revolution', giving an overview of labour and reform titles, and on 'The Changing Face of Publishing', describing the 'thriving reform and alternative press' in turn-of the-century America (Zboray and Zboray 34), and there are also separate chapters on suffrage and labour themes. On the other hand, publications designed to voice protest or to achieve social change might be understood as, by definition, articulating a minority position, and theories of modernism can therefore be equally useful in interpreting them. Modernist little magazines and small presses were often very politically engaged, while modernist artists and writers frequently contributed to radical publications. As well, even the most genteel of the middlebrow publishing enterprises presented challenging literary texts to their audiences: the Book-of-the-Month Club sent out titles such as Elizabeth Bowen's *The Hotel* and Richard Wright's *Native Son*, while the Modern Library reprinted titles by Faulkner, Joyce and Woolf. These examples show that, of course, print culture history cannot be divided into tidy streams of 'popular' and 'modernist'; indeed, some of the most invigorating recent research focuses on the way that these streams converge and diverge.

A second issue is the way that the category of the 'political' can work to obscure the aesthetic dimension of writing and art that appeared in print venues associated with activism. For example, as Michael Bibby points out in a 2013 article on the racial formation of modernist studies: 'The New Negro Renaissance is typically viewed as congruent with but distinct from modernism and, until the early 1970s, New Negro literature was most often addressed by scholars in sociological rather than literary journals' (486). In later decades, scholars have argued that art that was purposeful should not automatically be devalued in aesthetic terms. Equally, art produced by groups that might be classed as minorities or as oppressed is not always activist art. These issues, indeed, were much debated in the modernist era itself. The little magazines that were most committed to aesthetic experimentation explicitly distanced themselves from political affiliation. In an article on the avant-garde Paris-based magazine *transition*, David Bennett comments:

> In their introduction to the first issue, the *transition* editors had identified the community that their magazine addressed, not as a diacritical community of social, political, national, or economic interests, but as a 'disinterested' constellation of individuals united at the level of aesthetic sensibility. 'We should like to think of the readers', the editorial explained, 'as a homogeneous group of friends, united in a common appreciation of the beautiful, – idealists of a sort'. (491)

This notion of a community of taste, Bennett continues, had strategic value: 'Art, so redefined, could transcend or erase the political, economic, and historical boundaries against which it had defined its own "autonomy"'. In more directly practical terms, it was through an appeal to this community of taste 'that Jolas defended his editorial policies against Lewis's imputations of communist sympathies' (491). Yet, according to Mark Wollaeger, modernists' efforts to isolate aesthetic emotion from political concerns could never wholly succeed, since there was an underlying affinity between modernist and propagandist discourses. 'Modernism and propaganda', he writes, 'were sometimes agonistic, sometimes allied, and sometimes nearly indistinguishable', while on a formal level, 'both try to make meaning effective through ambiguity' (*Modernism* xiv).

In methodological terms, the study of print in action often requires intensive recovery work. The importance of research on advocacy periodicals was acknowledged as early as 1982, in Brian Harrison's essay 'Press and Pressure Group in Modern Britain'. Efforts are ongoing to unearth forgotten printed materials associated with migrants and immigrants, women's groups, racial minorities and specific causes such as, for instance, anti-vivisection (see Susan Hamilton). An exemplary project is James P. Danky and Wayne A. Wiegand's collection *Print Culture in a Diverse America* (1998), which covers topics ranging from the Italian immigrant press to African-American literary societies. Recovery work is needed, too, in respect of middlebrow print initiatives. The founding studies in this area are Joan Shelley Rubin's *The Making of Middlebrow Culture* (1992) and Janice Radway's *A Feeling for Books: The Book-of-the-Month Club, Literary Taste and Middle-Class Desire* (1997). Among the most recent examples is Patrick Collier's *Modern Print Artifacts: Textual Materiality and Literary Value in British Print Culture, 1890–1930s* (2016), which explores widely read but little-discussed print forms such as literary weeklies and poetry anthologies. These, like book clubs, performed a function of selecting and recommending reading materials (ranging from challenging to accessible texts) for middle- and working-class audiences. Research on topics such as these exemplifies some of the ways in which modernist studies has expanded its remit. On the one hand, scholars are investigating a range of print forms which, while not focused on art or literature, did circulate alongside modernist publications and were likewise addressed to minority audiences. On the other, they are exploring how modernist texts fare when they are re-presented as 'improving' reading for large audiences.

Among the theoretical models which have been applied to the kind of print forms we discuss in this chapter are theories of counterpublics, social movement theory and the idea of reading communities. Accounts of publics and counterpublics, notably those by Nancy Fraser and Michael Warner (both building on the foundational work of Jürgen Habermas) are often cited in print culture scholarship. As Sean Latham writes in 'The Mess and Muddle of Modernism': 'The explosion of print culture in this period created opportunities to address increasingly diverse, emergent publics as well as to fashion new counter-publics that often took shape on the intensely dialogic pages of magazines' (411). The notion of 'publics', as Latham uses it, points to the commercial opportunities offered by niche publishing of books and periodicals. This is taken up by, among others, Joyce Wexler, who notes: 'Throughout the modernist period, the financial interest of a publisher did not depend on bestsellers. It was more profitable for a firm to issue many books aimed at various segments of the market than to invest heavily in a few titles' (8). Latham's use of 'counter-publics', however, points more towards an oppositional model of resistance and protest. As Mark Morrisson discusses in *The Public Face of Modernism*, commercial publishing facilitated niche publishing and this was then exploited by radical groups in order to generate counterpublics. In an American context, for example, as Jean M. Lutes observes:

> Many suffragists, socialists, labour organizers, and racial and ethnic minorities established their own newspapers. Few of these alternative presses existed to make money. . . . One of the most fiercely needed counter-publics was the one fostered by the black press. Driven in part by the surge in lynchings that occurred in the late nineteenth century . . . some 1,219 black papers were launched between 1895 and 1915. (105)

These print forms may have been 'alternative', but that does not mean that they were located entirely outside the mainstream, communicating only with readers who were already committed to their causes. George Hutchinson, in *The Harlem Renaissance in Black and White* (1995) points out that: 'Black writers found their various niches within the diversifying publishing system; they were not all of one mind, nor did they all publish in the same places. However, the places in which they did publish were interconnected, making up a varied, dynamic network that challenged the cultural status quo' (8). Radical voices often reached wider audiences than might be expected, by means of publishing across a range of venues and gaining a perceived legitimacy through the medium of print.

In *Feminist Media History: Suffrage, Periodicals and the Public Sphere* (2011), a book with a strong emphasis on methodology, Maria DiCenzo, Lucy Delap and Leila Ryan advocate the application of social movement theory to media history. They argue that traditional histories of women's movements, because they rely on theories of counterpublics, tend to foreground struggle among different organizations and groups: 'While the concept of "counterpublics" stresses a relationship (an oppositional, antagonistic one between existing entities of some kind), the extensive literature on social movements stresses processes, methods, and change' (30). This is helpful to scholars focusing on the publications associated with women's campaigning, particularly in terms of understanding their gradual alterations over time, and their role in sustaining networks.

While the notions of both counterpublics and social movements normally imply a purpose of resistance or activism, the idea of a 'reading community' can work in a more normative sense: to legitimize constructions of nation, for instance. The phrase 'reading community' derives from Benedict Anderson's highly influential idea of 'imagined communities' which, along with his related argument about what he calls 'print capitalism', is frequently invoked by book historians. Leslie Howsam, in *Old Books and New Histories: An Orientation to Studies in Book and Print Culture*, provides a helpful summary of these ideas, explaining that Anderson's formulation of imagined communities

> is largely based on characterizing national identity in terms of reading. People who read the same text, whether a newspaper or a novel, especially if they read it at about the same time, are in a sense constituting themselves as a community, although they are unknown to each other as individuals. For Anderson, 'the book was the first modern-style mass-produced industrial commodity'. (58)

This notion of the 'reading community' can be usefully applied to documents that will be read at approximately the same time by many different people, such as daily papers or novels sent out by a book club. The notion of fostering community cohesion through reading is not always seen as wholly coercive. Janice Radway, in her study of the American Book-of-the-Month Club, writes admiringly that 'the elaborate and eloquent reader's reports written by the club's editors about every manuscript they evaluated for selection . . . fostered the definition of an imagined community of general readers, both within and without the club, who were . . . captivated by books in all their immense diversity and by the manifold pleasures of buying them, owning them, reading them, and using them' (6). Some critical discussions of women's monthlies likewise emphasize their potential to forge productive connections among readers who never met in person. This is particularly relevant to women in isolated rural communities, and recent work on Canadian magazines such as the *Western Home Monthly* (see McGregor) and *Canadian Home Journal* (Hammill and Smith) explores this question of readerly belonging. In our next section, we focus in more detail on these types of educative print enterprise.

# Educational print and the middlebrow

'The Book Clubs . . . are instruments not for improving taste but for standardising it at the middlebrow level' wrote Q. D. Leavis in 1932 (229). The American poet and fiction writer Delmore Schwartz took a different view, commenting that the Book-of-the-Month Club 'has been invaluable in widening the audience for serious literature' (qtd. in Rubin 97). These comments encapsulate a debate that was very prominent during the interwar years. The new mechanisms for bringing high culture to large audiences were seen by some as democratizing, and by others as a threat to the status of literature as an emblem of a higher civilization. Much of the critical work on middlebrow print cultures explores this debate and, importantly, relates it to the material form of the book. Megan Benton, in a 1997 article on book ownership and cultural identity, notes that in the 1920s books, both as specific texts and as physical objects, were increasingly understood to express the values and social status of their owners. Benton argues that, while elite or highbrow readers criticized 'ordinary' readers for treating the book as a commodity, both groups were equally inclined to use books as markers of cultural identity: 'Sometimes color, size, or binding were the chief qualities considered; at other times genre or specific authors and titles rendered the desired effect, selected as a brand-name assertion of personal style' (271).

The special significance that the book took on in the 1920s was partly an effect of the new media that flourished at this time. Radio, film, newspapers and mass-circulation magazines provided accessible entertainment and information, provoking anxieties that books would eventually disappear. But, instead, Benton notes, the distinctive qualities of books were thrown into relief: they 'offered more extended, intimate engagement with texts, their format ensuring a permanent and enduring "ownership" rather than the ephemeral contact provided by the other forms'. Benton concludes that the 'cheap plenitude . . . of the era's burgeoning mass media helped to distill rather than dilute the traditional cultural stature of books' (272). In more recent critical work, the word 'intermedial' has emerged to name the ways that different forms of printed, aural and visual media interact, and this has become an important theme in discussion of modernist-era print. Examples include Debra Rae Cohen's work on *The Listener* magazine and its relationship to BBC broadcasting, or Will Straw's on the way that print media 'developed new forms of graphic extravagance nourished by the cultural proximity of print to electronic media like cinema and radio' (22). This new research builds on the pioneering studies of middlebrow culture, which gave particular attention to relationships among book culture, periodicals and broadcasting.

The two founding, and much-cited, studies are Joan Shelley Rubin's *The Making of Middlebrow Culture* (1992) and Janice A. Radway's *A Feeling For Books: The Book-of-the-Month Club, Literary Taste, and Middle-Class Desire* (1997). Rubin's background is in history and Radway's in English studies; each book combines methods from literary analysis and cultural history, and Radway adds an important element of autoethnography, exploring her own experiences as a book club member. There are many convergences between their arguments. Neither proposes that individual texts and authors can necessarily be categorized as middlebrow (or high or lowbrow). Rather, they see the middlebrow as a set of institutions and reading practices which mediated between elite literary cultures and mass audiences, a process that was fraught with tension. They present institutions such as book clubs as sites where notions of value were negotiated, rather than taken for granted. This was because these institutions combined a stated purpose of guiding and educating readers with a commercial imperative. For example, Rubin says of Dorothy Canfield Fisher, an influential member of the Book-of-the-Month Club's first selection committee: 'As she presented it, the Book-of-the-Month Club became a nonprofit organization, a kind of mail-order public library akin to the adult education and museum outreach programmes she advocated throughout her career' (130). Yet the club 'aimed from the start at well-heeled college graduates' (98). Some of the other projects that Rubin examines, notably Charles W. Eliot's 'Five-Foot Shelf' (the Harvard Classics), were intended to provide a liberal education for working people. But this initiative, too, was highly profitable.

Rubin's discussion is wide-ranging, covering not only book clubs and publishers but also literary reviewing in accessible venues such as *Books* and the *Saturday Review of Literature*, book programmes on the radio, and outreach from universities, notably the 'Great Books' programme at Columbia. Initially an undergraduate course designed by Professor John Erskine, 'Great Books' was later popularized by him via the lecture circuit, magazine articles and his *The Delight of Great Books* (1927). Rubin explains that Erskine's use of a grand survey, ranging from the Greeks to John Stuart Mill, instead of the periodized classes that were more usual in English departments, 'enabled students to find joy and meaning in literature, provided their teachers would allow them simply to relate it to their own lives' (165). This aligned Erskine's reading practice with that of the general reader rather than the academic specialist. This democratizing aspect of his work, Rubin notes, somewhat counterbalances the 'reassertion of white Anglo-Saxon Protestant superiority' which is evident in his selection of an all-white, all-male canon and in his insistence that immigrants ought to become familiar with the Western literary tradition (177).

Rubin includes a chapter on the nineteenth-century genteel cultural formations that, she argues, represented the origins of middlebrow culture. Radway, by contrast, sees the middlebrow as 'a historically specific organization of cultural production that appeared only in the twentieth century when cultural entrepreneurs wedded a particular notion of culture to the production and distribution apparatus associated with supposedly lower forms'

(367 n4). Both critics explore the relationship between modernist and middlebrow cultures, a theme which has become prominent in later work. Rubin focuses mostly on the ambivalence of middlebrow critics and book club judges towards experimental writing. On the whole, they exhibited a preference for accessible materials, but some of them were more open to challenging contemporary literature, and encouraged readers not to fear it. In Radway's account, middlebrow culture was an effect of the dominance of modernism, both as aesthetic practice and, through its influence on academia, as critical practice. She proposes that middlebrow institutions and ways of reading offered an alternative system of literary value, prioritizing affective responses to texts above attention to their formal qualities. One of her key insights is that 'despite the traditional claim that middlebrow culture simply apes the values of high culture, it is in fact a kind of counterpractice to the high culture tastes and proclivities that have been most insistently legitimated and nurtured in academic English departments for the last fifty years or so' (9–10).

Both critics comment on how the ideological dimensions of middlebrow culture related to its material manifestations, though it is Radway who theorizes this most explicitly. They also discuss the stratification which emerged in the publishing industry, and the way that 'brow' categories became a marketing strategy, allowing for targeted promotion of appropriate types of books to distinct audiences. This line of argument has been further explored by Kim Becnel, in *The Rise of Corporate Publishing and Its Effects on Authorship in Early Twentieth-Century America* (2008). This book, heavily dependent on Rubin and Radway for its critical framing, offers case studies of a series of authors with successful publishing careers (Djuna Barnes, Pearl Buck, Lloyd Douglas and William Faulkner). These examples, Becnel claims, demonstrate that 'the cultural hierarchy that the publishing industry helped to create has done more to facilitate communication by introducing writers to their audiences, and vice versa, than to corrupt or dilute art and literature' (2). Becnel tends to replicate, rather than critique, the moral discourse that was used by early twentieth-century commentators in order to describe, on one side of the debate, the uplifting or healthful effects of 'good' reading or, on the other, the compromising of critical standards that book clubs, radio book chat and paperback publishing supposedly caused.

Radway, Rubin, Becnel and numerous other scholars of middlebrow print concentrate on the United States, but many of the cultural institutions they describe had analogues in the United Kingdom. Nicola Wilson, in an article on Hugh Walpole, Virginia Woolf and the Book Society, provides a helpful summary of the British book clubs:

> The Book Society was established in 1929 by Walpole . . . and the novelist Arnold Bennett. Modeled on the American Book-of-the-Month club (established 1927), it was the first book club to operate in Britain – it would be followed by the Book Guild (1930), the Left Book Club (1936), and the Readers Union (1937). . . . Set up as an 'aid to the busy reader', the Book Society sent a new, full-price book to its members each month, which they could either keep or exchange for one of its other recommended titles. The subscriber received a copy of the publisher's edition of the chosen book, not a specially printed and/or bound edition (as with the Readers Union). . . . The books chosen were intended to be a worthwhile read and not too complex for the average reader. (244)

Owing to their large memberships (the Book Society reached ten thousand by the mid-1930s) and extensive publicity, book club selections were highly influential, affecting library purchasing and changing the fortunes of publishing houses. From her research in the publisher's archives, Wilson provides a detailed account of the financial advantage to the Hogarth Press of having two of its novels, Vita Sackville-West's *The Edwardians* and William Plomer's *The Case is Altered*, selected by the Book Society. She also explores the complicated negotiations surrounding their selection of Woolf's *Flush*, which was initially judged to be too short to be sold to members at the usual rate, so had to be produced in a special edition with added illustrations.

The Book Society was not actually the first book club in Britain, though it was the first one established on the monthly choice model. The *Times Book Club* dated back to 1904, and as Ashlie Sponenberg points out, its practice of selling retired library books at cheap rates was controversial because it violated the Net Book Agreement (19).[1] Victor Gollancz's Left Book Club (LBC), established in 1936, likewise annoyed traditional booksellers by making its titles available exclusively through the club. Yet the aims of the LBC were not commercial: as historian James Jupp comments, it was 'primarily an educational body with a political purpose'. He quotes from an introductory leaflet stating that the club aimed to help all those struggling against Fascism and for world peace by giving them 'such knowledge as will greatly increase their efficiency' (Jupp 86). The LBC was unusual in serving the function of a social network: the *Left Book Club News* included information on the meetings of neighbourhood reading groups, many of which were organized by 'self-educated sympathizers' (Sponenberg 19). The club received a certain amount of scholarly attention during the 1970s but there has been little discussion of it since then, though an anthology based on its selections appeared in 2001 and several archival collections are available. The Right Book Club (RBC), set up by Christina Foyle of Foyle's bookshop in 1937 and established partly in reaction to the LBC and to the broader proliferation of socialist and communist writing in the 1930s, is much less well known. Terence Rodgers, in a 2003 article on the RBC which also provides one of the most up-to-date commentaries on the LBC, observes that the RBC has been written out of the history of the 1930s, and has no official archive (1). Paraphrasing a letter he received from Foyle in 1987, Rodgers says that her purpose in establishing the RBC was 'to foster a renewed interest in democracy among the ordinary public, to stimulate interest in Conservative thought and to ... give non-socialist authors a public' (2). Rodgers points out that 'the RBC unashamedly modelled itself on its rival', even mimicking the distinctive typeface used by the LBC, and this emphasized the direct competition or conflict between them (3).

While the book clubs provided the newest books to their subscribers, other print enterprises focused on making previously published works more easily available and better known. Many initiatives focused on the classics, and a few on contemporary work. Book series were particularly important. Mary Hammond, in *Reading, Publishing and the Formation of Literary Taste in England, 1880–1914* (2006), explains that from the mid-nineteenth century onwards the 'cheap classic series was an important manifestation of the lower-middle classes' drive toward self-education and self-fashioning. It was also part of a corresponding drive on the part of publishers to realise the economic potential of this vast new market' (86). Her chapter on W. H. Smith explores their production of cheap reprints for sale on railway bookstalls, and their focus on reading material that people would be happy to be seen with in a public space. 'In the early days of their monopoly', she notes, 'Smith's was pursuing a shrewd marketing policy as well as performing what they saw as a public service when they insisted on stocking only the "inoffensive" literature which was a part of middle-class consensus' (68). She goes on to discuss Routledge's rather less restrained Railway Library, offering 'brightly-coloured pocket-sized reprints, jammed with small print and adverts and sporting a dramatic illustration on the front cover' (86). A shift took place around the turn of the century, with the establishment of more aspirational series such as Oxford World's Classics in 1901. According to Hammond:

> Despite its genesis in the railway library of the 1860s . . . the classic library series, though also cheap and reliant upon non-copyright single-volume works, very quickly came to stand for something quite unrelated to travel and transience, and took on a very different set of cultural meanings. These meanings are rooted in self-help, the rise of the suburban bourgeoisie, and a subtle shift in the position of the publisher in the literary field. (86)

The sober, edifying but inexpensive volumes in 'classics' series represented 'both the zenith of mass publishing and a contradictory desire for cultural distinction' (86). Collectible book series became immensely popular. Maureen Duffy, in her history of the Methuen list, points to the commercial potential of uniform series: 'If the punters could be persuaded to begin collecting them, the chances were that they would go on indefinitely' (31). She notes that the series that Methuen set up in 1904 ranged from facsimiles of Shakespeare folios, at twelve guineas for a set of four, through to sixpenny paperback editions of Dumas's fiction (31). (A guinea, twenty-one shillings, was a monetary value particularly associated with the purchase of luxuries; a sixpenny publication was cheap.) Series such as these were promoted using a rhetoric of education and self-improvement, but also in terms of the decorative value of sets of books.

An in-depth account of the book series and its relationship to cultural hierarchies can be found in Lise Jaillant's *Modernism,*

*Middlebrow and the Literary Canon* (2014). This book analyses The Modern Library, a reprint series focusing on recent literature that was established by Albert Boni and Horace Liveright in New York. In 1917, as Jaillant explains, while many out-of-copyright classics were available in cheap formats, contemporary literary works were not usually affordable for lower-income readers. She cites the example of Samuel Butler's *The Way of All Flesh*, available for $1.50 in E. P. Dutton's 1910 edition. On the Modern Library's first list, this book was included at 60 cents, along with work by Wells, Wilde, Hardy, Maupassant and Dostoyevsky. Jaillant writes that 'the Modern Library was the first American uniform series to sell a broadly defined literary modernism to a large audience' (1). In 1925, it was bought by Bennett Cerf and Donald Klopfer, who continued to include controversial texts on the list. As Jaillant argues, 'middlebrow producers played an ambiguous role, trying to explain "difficult" literature to their middle-class audiences while also developing an identity of their own by engaging with the mass market' (5). In elaborating her notion of 'New York middlebrow', she productively links book and periodical publishing: 'The Modern Library shared three main characteristics with the smart magazines: an emphasis on cultural pedagogy, a collision of different cultural tastes, and a participation in the emerging celebrity culture' (15). She demonstrates these arguments through case studies of five authors published in the Modern Library series: Wells, Anderson, Woolf, Cather and Faulkner.

Cultural pedagogy was likewise central to the various series launched by Penguin Books, founded in 1935 by Allen Lane. Penguin focused initially on fiction, but its Pelican imprint, launched in 1937, was for non-fiction and had a more explicitly educative purpose. Penguin is primarily recognized for what David Cannadine describes as 'the extraordinary simplicity and audacity of Lane's original conception: persuading other publishers to sell to him the paperback rights of their hardback titles, which he would then re-issue . . . in a format which sold many times more copies than the original edition' (105). The firm also commissioned many significant works, as Penguin Specials, Pelican originals or volumes in its educational series. As the most prominent and innovative among Britain's middlebrow publishing enterprises, Penguin has attracted extensive critical attention. Some of the studies centre on Penguin's founder; the most recent are Steve Hare's *Penguin*

*Portrait: Allen Lane and the Penguin Editors 1935–1970* (1995) and Jeremy Lewis's *Penguin Special: The Life and Times of Allen Lane* (2005). Others focus on aspects of design; these are cited in our section 'Design, image and typeface' in Chapter 1. A 2013 collection, *Reading Penguin: A Critical Anthology*, emerging from the Penguin Archives Project, provides a multifaceted account of different aspects of Penguin's activity and influence. Cannadine's essay appears in this volume, and another contribution, by Simon Eliot, explores Penguins as material objects, possessing 'a certain sort of reassuring flimsiness' (1). As he explains: 'Flimsiness and cheapness means you can risk going beyond your normal fare and trying something new. If it doesn't work, you can give it away or throw it away' (2).

Nicola Humble, writing in a middlebrow-themed issue of the journal *Modernist Cultures*, explores Penguin in the context of interwar reading practices. She notes that their publication of authors such as Hemingway, Forster and Huxley meant that texts formerly seen as highbrow were 'effectively transmuted into the middlebrow' through commodification:

> The strength of its series identity worked to dissolve the status differences between various forms of literature. Penguin books were classy enough for people not to be ashamed to be seen with them, digestible but intellectually stimulating, and inexpensive enough to allow virtually anyone to build a library of significant contemporary writing. A powerful tool of self-improvement for many thousands of working- and lower-middle-class readers, these books heralded the beginning of a reading culture in which class and brows were both increasingly irrelevant. (57)

Humble's assessment of Penguin is congruent with Radway and Rubin's accounts of American middlebrow publishing; all three see these enterprises as broadly beneficial to a reading public eager for access to intellectual culture. Other critics apply the term 'middlebrow' to Penguin in an almost opposite sense, suggesting that the firm exhibited a resistance to the intellectual. Stefan Collini, in an article on the publishing of literary criticism between 1930 and 1960, comments: 'Indeed, during the first 15 or 20 years of Penguin's existence, its avowed address to "the intelligent general reader", or even sometimes "the people", could occasionally have a slightly middlebrow edge to it, scorning the kind of "over-intellectualized" writing which could only appeal to a tiny or specialist audience' (659). Because of this range of possible implication, care is certainly needed when using the term 'middlebrow'. But in the context of print culture studies, it is most commonly used in the sense defined at the start of this chapter: that is, to refer to print forms that aimed to bring high culture to large audiences and to encourage self-improvement and upward mobility.

These forms included periodicals as well as books. Several weeklies were devoted to helping readers to negotiate the burgeoning print marketplace, while many general-interest titles included book columns. Both Jonathan Wild and Patrick Collier have discussed the literary paper *John O'London's Weekly*, launched in 1919, with Wild focusing on its relationship with the reading public and Collier on the models of authorship it presented. According to Wild, the founding editor, Wilfred Whitten saw

> that a significant market existed for a publication pitched towards a readership ready to develop its taste for and knowledge of 'good' books. Although various other publications of this period specifically catered for a bookish audience – notably the *Times Literary Supplement* and *The Spectator* – Whitten understood that the putative readership he intended for his weekly would consider these established periodicals dry and scholarly. . . . Whitten set out with *JOLW* to create a paper dedicated to books that would neither patronise its readership by adopting a schoolmasterly tone, nor assume that the process of instruction was entirely unnecessary. ('Insects' 51)

*John O'London's* was in some respects similar to the penny paper *T.P.'s Weekly*, where Whitten had previously worked. *John O'London's* folded in 1916, but wartime conditions expanded the size of the reading public and generated a new enthusiasm for literary activities as well as for self-culture. As Collier explains, '*John O'London's* fashioned itself as a force for cultural education. Correspondingly, it imagined its reader as an autodidact interested in print culture not merely as a consumer but as an aspiring writer. *John O'London's* thus invested in a self-help ethic that pulled it towards affiliation with the grandiose claims of correspondence schools' ('*John*' 99). David Carter, who has conducted extensive research on histories of Australian print, notes that readers there had access to British and American titles such as *John O'London's* and the *Saturday Evening Post*, but that there were also local publications which contributed to the development of a specifically Australian book and periodical culture. He points to magazines such as *All About Books for Australian and New Zealand Readers*, established in 1928 ('Modernity' 146). In *Always Almost Modern: Australian Print Cultures and Modernity*, Carter comments that *All About Books* embraced a variety of aims: 'to produce more readers and sell more books; to produce better readers (and sell more *good* books); and to produce an Australian book culture based on "sound literary judgement" ' (161). This last phrase is quoted from a 1934 issue of the magazine, and points towards its claim to literary taste, as opposed to academic expertise.

Aspirational periodicals such as these can usefully be included in a discussion of 'modernism's print cultures' because they were important in the literary landscape of the era, and because they did pay attention to modernist writing. For instance, in 1920 *John O'London's* celebrated the work of both Virginia Woolf and Dorothy Richardson (Wild 62 n35), while the first issue of *All About Books* reviewed Woolf's *Orlando* (Carter, *Always* 156). Other commercial magazines responded to a broader notion of modernism, encompassing design and fashion, in the context of a preoccupation with contemporary taste. In their study of Canadian magazines and middlebrow culture, Hammill and Smith examine discourses of expertise and difficulty, arguing that the women's, family and society titles they focus on 'sold themselves on the basis of the expert knowledge of their contributors in areas such as dress, interiors, health and beauty, cookery, domestic economy, reading, and shopping' (133). They also note that 'although haute couture was the form of high culture which most appealed to these magazines, modern art also received attention, particularly from the Francophone magazines' (134). A whole other area of research centres on mass-market print forms which did not respond to modernism or literature at all and did not serve an explicitly educational purpose, though they may have had nationalist or other ideological goals. While this type of work is somewhat beyond the scope of this book, it is very useful for learning about adjacent areas of the print marketplace, which often impinged on, or overlapped with, the middlebrow print discussed in this section. A representative example of such scholarship is David Welky's *Everything was Better in America: Print Culture in the Great Depression* (2008), which covers newspapers, magazines and books, and uses the term 'mainstream' in preference to 'mass-market' or 'popular'. 'Mainstream print culture consists of written material that has a national reach', writes Welky. This was achieved through distribution (including, for newspapers, the use of syndicates and wire services) and through ideological strategies – that is, 'creating an illusory national culture to which all readers belonged' (4). Welky includes profit-driven print forms that tend to be omitted from studies with a more literary orientation: comic strips, for instance, as well as celebrity-focused magazines such as *Life*, crime and romance novels, and also the hugely popular *Reader's Digest*, which was founded in 1922 and provided condensed versions of periodical articles and, later, of books.

Many of the print initiatives described in this section still exist. Columbia retains a 'core curriculum' in liberal arts, and its 'Literature Humanities' course is explicitly based on Erskine's programme. Penguin Books is celebrating its eightieth anniversary, though it merged with Random House in 2013. The *Times* still has a book club, though it is conducted as an online meeting point for 'real world' book groups around the country. Other contemporary enterprises recreate or reinvent early twentieth-century approaches. In her article on the London reprint publisher Persephone, Urmila Seshagiri argues that the firm has succeeded by 'merging modernist cultural practices with the demands of literary culture in the twenty-first century' (245). It combines feminist recovery work with a strong emphasis on the book as artefact: the printed endpapers reproduce historical and modern textile designs. Persephone also organizes lectures, tours and afternoon tea events, as well as publishing what Seshagiri describes as 'a metamodernist little magazine, *The Persephone Biannually*' (245). Seshagiri presents Persephone as a late institution of modernism (243), though given that it prioritizes pleasurable, accessible fiction, as well as emphasizing the importance of owning beautiful books, it might also be understood as a middlebrow institution. At the same time, its feminist orientation gives it a political force: in addition to recovering the work of neglected women authors, Persephone has also republished suffrage novels by Constance Maud and Cicely Hamilton. In the next section, we turn to the subject of print culture and politics in the modernist era.

## Political print

Cary Nelson describes his foundational study *Repression and Recovery: Modern American Poetry and the Politics of Cultural Memory, 1910–1945* (1989) as 'an effort to revise our notions of the social function of poetry', by means of recovering 'marginalized or forgotten poets – particularly women, blacks, and writers on the left' (xi), as well as 'rereading the almost universally suppressed political poetry of the period' (26). Nelson's book uses extremely wide-ranging print-cultural archives research to force a re-examination of what academic Modernism has canonized. In 1989, most of the poems discussed had never been republished, so he includes many illustrations in order to allow readers to see them in their periodical or pamphlet contexts. In the twenty-first century, access to a good proportion of these materials is available via digitization projects, and the conversion of printed material into databases has allowed for new methods of searching and reading across magazines and ephemera which were not available in the 1980s. Nevertheless, Nelson's insights and methods remain highly relevant to contemporary print culture scholarship. He was among the first to call on modernist scholars to 'shift attention from the poets of the canon and return to the journals of the period' (71), in order to recover not only individual poets but also the 'anonymous poems distributed as part of the mass social movements of the past century' (75). Much recent research continues to focus on uncovering lost texts by well-known authors or earlier versions of famous poems. Nelson's argument, though, is that 'all the poetry from 1910–1945 merits reexamination, even the genteel poetry of the mass circulation magazines' (26), because it can help us understand the cultural work that poetry could do in the period. He contends that: 'English professors should be pressed to explain why, for example, the poetry sung by striking coal miners in the 1920s is so much less important than the appearance of *The Waste Land* in *The Dial* in 1922', and adds that 'the effective suppression of popular art forms – in our case, jazz, the political poetry of mass social movements, and song – and the rejection of the uses to which nonacademic audiences put literary texts are explicit expressions of class relations' (68).

One of the mass social movements that has come into focus in recent print culture scholarship is feminism, and especially the campaigns for women's suffrage. Some of this work focuses on particular countries – for instance, Barbara Green concentrates on Britain and Mary Chapman on America. Yet as Lucy Delap and Maria DiCenzo point out in an essay on the Anglo-American feminist press: 'Participation in the women's movement of the nineteenth and twentieth centuries was centrally a reading experience, and print culture proved to be an element that easily crossed national boundaries' (55). Among the examples they discuss is *The Freewoman*, launched in 1911 and edited by Dora Marsden and Mary Gawthorpe. This British journal, Delap and DiCenzo note, made a transition from periodical to pamphlet as American suffrage organizations reprinted individual articles. Conversely, issues of the American *Forerunner*, published from 1909 to 1916, 'circulated as scarce and treasured items in Britain'. This scarcity meant that the magazine was still being read after it had ceased publication, and 'back issues of the *Forerunner* were consulted as if they were an encyclopedia or bible' (62).

According to Delap and DiCenzo, modernism is not the best critical lens to use for understanding the suffrage press, since the 'preoccupation in modernist studies with the status of authors, literary production, cultural criticism, formal experimentation and aesthetic value make it a problematic point of departure for understanding developments in social and political spheres' (50). Mary Chapman, on the other hand, argues that suffragist discourse can be productively read alongside contemporary literary texts, using similar methods of analysis. Her book *Making Noise, Making News: Suffrage Print Culture and US Modernism* (2015) aims 'to chart a relationship between radical politics' print cultural reform efforts and modernist literary experimentation' (13). Focusing on the concept of 'voice', she points out that suffrage publicity stunts, as well as written texts, dramatize women's voicelessness in the public sphere through particular types of utterance, or non-utterance: quotation, ventriloquism and stylized silence. In the nineteenth century, some of these strategies were used in oratory, but when suffrage campaigners gained access to mass print media, their discursive moves became even more sophisticated. Chapman argues that 'the ventriloquist and citational core of suffragist discourse . . . resembled later literary modernist experiments in voice while also substantially revising understandings of authorship' (16). Part of her analysis focuses on the periodicals sold on the street by suffrage 'newsies' and the eye-catching 'news bags' they carried. She comments:

> I read early twentieth-century suffrage materials as both politically modern and aesthetically modernist, by demonstrating the rhetorically and typographically 'loud' figures that characterize both modern suffrage advocacy magazines like the *American Suffragette* and modernist little magazines like *BLAST*. By affiliating themselves with the new, the news, and noise, these suffragists fashioned themselves and their print cultural products not as marginal but as central, indeed as representative voices of modern America. (23)

Chapman also explores the way that the suffragists' political opinions were promulgated via the mainstream media and commodity culture. Their messages could be projected 'onto sites that were not editorially willing to entertain these perspectives' (18), as in the photographs of demonstrators carrying banners that appeared in anti-suffrage daily papers such as the *New York Times*. In 1910, campaigners even provided retailers with paper bags stencilled with suffrage slogans, so that customers would – willingly or unwillingly – carry their messages through the streets.

Barbara Green, in her essay 'Feminist Things', also explores the material culture of the suffrage movement. Focusing on the promotional strategies of campaigners, many of which were borrowed from the world of commerce, she builds an argument about women's creative contributions to the development of early twentieth-century print and material culture:

> Attention to the thinginess of suffrage culture may change the way we think about suffrage papers. Suffrage journals – along with manifestoes and leaflets – also functioned as objects in and of themselves. Sold with collectibles in suffrage bookshops, displayed on coffee tables in the home as signatures of political

conversion, used as physical evidence in public trials, carried as badges or signs of affiliation on the street, the suffrage periodical was often the first object that a potential convert came in contact with as she became radicalized. (67)

Another of Green's essays, in the 2012 'Mediamorphosis' special issue of *Modernism/modernity*, presents a valuable discussion of correspondence columns in the avant-garde *Freewoman* and the feminist weekly, the *Woman Worker* (later renamed *Women Folk*). Letters columns, as Green notes, 'certainly count as some of the more ephemeral aspects of weekly papers', which, of course, are themselves relatively ephemeral publications, and are not likely to circulate after the period in which they appeared (462). Yet they are highly valuable for print culture scholars, as they offer some information, albeit fragmentary, about readers and the ways in which they interacted with periodicals. Drawing on Lauren Berlant's notion of intimate publics, Green demonstrates that the 'correspondence page as intimate public sphere showcases a variety of responses to women's culture, not just consumption and identification (shopping and feeling) but also the production of new (often politicized) subjectivities' (466).

Suffrage publications made a major contribution not only to the political history of this era, but also to its literary history. They were spaces for activism, but also venues for creative texts. Bruce Clarke, in a chapter on *The Freewoman* and its successor, *The Egoist*, in Churchill and McKible's *Little Magazines and Modernism*, describes them as presenting a 'close concatenation of unprecedented political and literary feminisms' (124), and examines their influence on authors including H. D., William Carlos Williams and Rebecca West. Chapman's book offers several case studies of authors who engaged with suffragist discourse. Among them is Marianne Moore, whose suffrage journalism and suffrage-inspired poetry, according to Chapman, 'show us an unfamiliar side of the avant-garde writer whose context is not only the aestheticized environment presumed by New Criticism but also the political foment of the Progressive Era, an author who finds her literary voice (and positionality) by imitating the citational discourse of the campaign to secure women a voice in politics' (146).

Tensions between the aesthetic and the political are a central aspect of the history of the Harlem Renaissance, with opposing points of view about art's role in countering the historically negative depiction of African Americans focalized by W. E. B. Dubois's 'Criteria of Negro Art' in *The Crisis* (October 1926) and Alain Locke's 'Art or Propaganda?' in *Harlem* (November 1928). Simply put, in their 'great debate' DuBois claimed that art must serve a social purpose, and Locke that art must be free to serve its own ends. George Hutchinson acknowledges the diversity of opinion among black intellectuals about critical standards, but emphasizes the consensus that 'aesthetic experience could be a powerful impetus to the destruction of social convention, the awakening of new types of consciousness, and the creation of new forms of solidarity across traditional boundaries' (*Harlem* 13). In his introduction to the *Cambridge Companion to the Harlem Renaissance* (2007), Hutchinson explains how in the 1980s understandings of the movement began to shift at the same time as a revaluation of modernism also got underway (9). Although numerous intellectual discourses have contributed to this shift, several elements of print culture that we have discussed in this book play a significant part in recent scholarship on the Harlem Renaissance and the place it occupies in more broadly conceived studies of the African diaspora.

Locating the Harlem Renaissance in time and space has proved vexing, but there is a growing tendency to see it as a prominent manifestation of a much broader 'Negro Renaissance'. The editors of a special issue of *Modernism/modernity* devoted to the Harlem Renaissance believe that most would agree on 'the centrality of print culture, especially magazines, to this period of unprecedented literary and artistic expression' (McKible and Churchill, 'Introduction' 430). The special issue, 'In Conversation: The Harlem Renaissance and the New Modernist Studies', begins with a questionnaire modelled on a symposium conducted by *The Crisis* in 1926 and one in the final issue of *The Little Review* in 1929. Among the respondents to McKible and Churchill's questions about scholarship on the Harlem Renaissance, Barbara Foley argues that its usual focus on cultural and artistic 'flowering' deflects attention from the 'crucially important postwar political roots' of the movement (439). McKible and Churchill themselves raise the question of whether merging modernism and the Harlem Renaissance 'risks erasing a history of racial exclusion' (431). This question is confronted directly by Michael Bibby in his contribution to the special issue. According to Bibby, New Critical constructions of modernist poetry have informed a continuing racist construction of form that excludes the work of black writers from considerations of modernism. That is, 'the category "modernist poetry" has been constituted in modernist studies in such a way that it is possible to produce detailed, sophisticated research on this poetry without ever acknowledging the racial diversity of its history' (491).

In their overview of black print culture, *Propaganda and Aesthetics: The Literary Politics of African-American Magazines in the Twentieth Century*, first published in 1979, Abby A. and Ronald M. Johnson sought to 'fill a considerable gap in literary history' left in the wake of Hoffman, Allen and Ulrich's *Little Magazines*, where only *Fire!!* and *Challenge* received a brief mention. In more recent accounts of modernist magazines, Harlem periodicals are positioned more centrally: for instance, there are three chapters about them in the North American volume of *The Oxford Critical and Cultural History of Modernist Magazines*. One of these, by Martha Nadell, argues that, unlike the more secure organs of political organizations, short-lived magazines such as *Fire!!* (1926) and *Harlem* (1928) adopted the strategies and tone of modernist magazines. Wallace Thurman started both magazines but only managed to produce one issue of each. Nadell notes that he consciously modelled *Fire!!* on such little magazines as *Blast* and *The Little Review*. Thurman assailed what he perceived as 'the New Negro establishment which insisted on policing the novels, poetry, painting, and illustrations of the period', and demanded that creative work be understood as an agent of social change (Nadell, 'Devoted' 805).

Black identity was, and remains, a crucial nexus of the tensions between aesthetics and politics in an American context. Although the vast majority of magazines and publishing houses for black writers were in New York, the population of Harlem itself comprised many who had migrated there from other parts of the United States or from other countries. Lara Putnam describes the 'overwhelmingly literate and highly internationalist' newcomers who moved to Harlem after the First World War, noting that dozens of 'British Caribbeans played leading roles in radical politics, literary production, or both, founding or editing periodicals including the *Voice*, the *Crusader*, the *Emancipator*, *Opportunity*, the *Messenger*, and the Universal Negro Improvement Association's *Negro World*' (470). In *The Practice of Diaspora: Literature, Translation, and the Rise of Black Internationalism* (2003), Brent Hayes Edwards signals a shift away from critical emphases on 'U.S.-bound themes of cultural nationalism, civil rights protest and uplift in the literary culture of the "Harlem Renaissance"' (3), pointing out that the 'New Negro' movement expressed a '"new" black internationalism' (2). The First World War had dealt 'a serious blow to the prestige of "white" civilization' (Hutchinson, 'Introduction' 6), and black soldiers returned from Europe to the United States ready to fight for their own rights. When the *Nation* ran a series of articles titled 'These United States' (1922–1925), claiming inclusiveness but excluding blacks from consideration, *The Messenger* responded with its own series, 'These "Colored" United States' (1923–1926). Adam McKible has argued that although it 'is one of the great achievements of Harlem during its "Renaissance", *The Messenger*'s vision of black America is clearly not limited to the magazine's site of production' ('Our (?) Country' 132). A large number of black writers and visual artists travelled widely in the postwar period, and many spent time in Paris, a city, Edwards argues, that 'resonates in the cultures of black internationalism because it came to *represent* certain kinds of crossings, certain extensions of the horizon' (3). Claire Oberon Garcia details a 'black feminist modernism' that emerged from discourses circulating through Paris, Harlem and the Antilles (35). New understandings of modernism inevitably transform old understandings of the print culture of the early twentieth century. The Pan-Africanism that was a salient feature of black writers' work unites Harlem Renaissance creativity with both the politics and aesthetics of the wider diasporic culture. As Carrie Noland argues in *Voices of Negritude in Modernist Print: Aesthetic Subjectivity, Diaspora, and the Lyric Regime* (2015), Negritude authors understood that they could be most influential by following the path of writers such as Langston Hughes or Jacques Roumain, 'respected diasporic writers who published in English or French in an attempt to reach out to a Pan-African (rather than regional) audience' (11).

Langston Hughes had travelled to Spain in 1936 to report on the civil war for the *Baltimore Afro-American*. Like other African-American journalists, Hughes saw the Spanish Civil War through the lenses of race and international socialism. Michael Thurston explains that Hughes drew these black and red perspectives together not only through his war reporting but also in his poetry readings at the front, in radio broadcasts, and in the poems he began to publish in the International Brigades' *Volunteer for Liberty* as well as in American periodicals such as *New Masses* and *Esquire* (143). Addressing the Second International Writers' Congress in Paris in 1937, Hughes 'explicitly connects the treatment of blacks in the United States with international fascism' (154). Thurston points out that the publication history of Hughes's speech is unique among his writings:

> Published in the *Volunteer for Liberty*, the *Crisis,* and *The Negro Worker*, the essay reaches readers primarily concerned with left politics and literature, with the Spanish Civil War, and with issues of interest to American blacks. In both its content and circulation, Hughes's address brings together the components of Spain's significance and the constituents of his audience, an audience of which the black press, and its readers in turn, formed a crucial component. (155)

Looking outside the United States for comparisons to the situation of African Americans was not at all unusual. Rachel Farebrother, surveying issues raised by scholarship on the *Crisis*, notes that Du Bois wrote a series of articles about the Indian struggle for independence. Farebrother describes Du Bois's internationalism as complex and shot through with tensions: his 'essentialism, his insistence upon a global alliance cemented by shared "blood" and family bonds, brings his internationalism back into line with a concept of identity that seeks to uphold racial separation and difference' (121). The ideology of racial uplift, in its focus on the 'race man', was often in thrall to patriarchal values, but as a more complex picture of the *Crisis* continues to emerge, other elements present there have become more visible.

Jayne Marek has shown how 'black women added dimensions of gender and class awareness to the debates over identity, heritage, and politics' circulating during the Harlem Renaissance ('Women Editors' 106). Marek exemplifies this by explaining how Jessie Fauset's literary editorship of the *Crisis* (1919–1926) benefited female writers (see also Zackodnik). Farebrother furthermore identifies the 'wide-ranging multimedia format' (108) of the magazine as a topic of particular interest to recent criticism. In her case study of 'The *Crisis*, Easter 1912', Ann Ardis uses the methodologies of periodical studies to model 'a way of reading a literary text's bibliographic and contextual codes that treats the periodical issue as the primary object of study' (32). Following insights derived from scholarship on the British feminist periodical press, Ardis considers that modernism is a limiting framework within which to consider the 'aesthetic heterogeneity' of the *Crisis* (36). *The Crisis* was not seeking to position itself in relation to transatlantic little magazines. Looking at the periodical as a whole reveals the dynamic interrelations of its various elements, as well as its 'dramatic visual and editorial transformations even during its first few years of publication' (26). Its advertisements, for example, strike Ardis as 'a key ingredient of this magazine's dual commitment to protesting racial injustice and affirming the achievement of African Americans' (34). As Todd Vogel remarks in the introduction to *The Black Press: New Literary and Historical Essays* (2001), the public sphere of free actors postulated by Jürgen Habermas that has been critiqued by Houston Baker and by Nancy Fraser for what it excludes from consideration (7) also does not account for the fact that 'print does not do its work alone' (8): the issue of how the black press functioned distinctively within its community of readers is a question that modernist print culture scholarship is now taking up.

Maureen Honey stresses the racial diversity of the new poetry movement of the interwar period, pointing to the inclusiveness of Monroe and Henderson's *Poetry* anthologies from 1917 to 1946 (442). Recent studies such as that of Caroline Goeser on the interplay between text and image in Harlem Renaissance books, magazines and other print artefacts restore this diversity through detailed explorations of how black writers and artists contributed both to the little magazines of the Negro Renaissance and to mainstream, white-owned publications. In *Picturing the New Negro: Harlem Renaissance Print Culture and Modern Black Identity* (2007), Goeser provides a generously illustrated account of how black illustrators and writers negotiated the racist stereotypes of American print cultural ecology to fashion a modern black identity that was legible both to African American readers and the dominant white culture. Goeser's is one of several recent works to focus on the collaboration between visual artists and writers of the Harlem Renaissance. Others include Anne Elizabeth Carroll's *Word, Image, and the New Negro* (2005), which provides close readings of five illustrated publications: *The Crisis, Opportunity, Survey Graphic, The New Negro* and *Fire!!*; M. Genevieve West's *Zora Neale Hurston and American Literary Culture* (2005), which includes discussion of book covers and marketing art work; and Martha Jane Nadell's *Enter the New Negroes: Images of Race in American Culture*, which discusses what she terms 'interartistic' (8) work in black print culture of the 1920s to 1940s.

Goeser focuses much of her discussion on illustration, a form that has a long association with political critique. She draws attention to the use of illustration animated by leftist politics in the *Masses* and the *New Masses*, to both of which the black artist James L. Wells contributed regularly. Wells is one example of how Harlem Renaissance illustrators and political cartoonists (such as Albert E. Smith) should be 'considered part of the broad artistic context for the political prints of the 1930s' (Goeser 14). Using Aaron Douglas, the most prolific Harlem Renaissance illustrator, as a case study, Goeser argues that black illustrators developed a 'double-voiced narrative' (ix) whereby images actively participated with text. Douglas, who wrote to Langston Hughes in 1925 that he no longer wished to make 'white art painted black' (1), set himself to develop a 'new racial language' that would communicate effectively to a broad audience without relying on the stereotypes that pervaded print culture (20). In his commercial work, Douglas exemplifies for Goeser a pattern of subversion of such imagery as he cleverly advanced his efforts 'to refashion black identity in modern terms' through skillful exploitation of the interplay between art and commerce (25).

As these examples indicate, left-wing and black print cultures overlapped significantly in America. George Hutchinson provides a taxonomy of several periodicals that he believes were important to the institutionalization of the Harlem Renaissance, according to 'the main imperatives of their cultural politics: instruments of African American uplift and reform organizations (*The Crisis* and *Opportunity*), mainstream weeklies of the moderate left (*The Nation* and *The New Republic*), quarterlies of the bohemian and radical left (*Masses-Liberator-New Masses* and *Modern Quarterly*), and quarterlies of iconoclastic satire (*The Messenger* and *American Mercury*)' (*Harlem* 135). Other American left-wing journals of the 1920s and 1930s include *Good Morning, The Freeman, The Modern Quarterly, Blast: A Magazine of*

*Proletarian Short Stories, The Windsor Quarterly, The Rebel Poet, The Anvil, Dynamo* and *The Partisan Review*. All these are covered in the North American volume of *The Oxford Critical and Cultural History of Modernist Magazines*, in the four essays comprising the section on 'A Revolutionary Message'. This in turn is part of the 'Radical Voices' part of the book, covering about a quarter of its length. A comparison with the other two volumes is revealing. The volume on Britain and Ireland does not include any section on political print, although there are individual chapters on 'Art and Politics in the 1930s', covering *The European Quarterly, Left Review* and *Poetry and the People*, on 'Interventions in the Public Sphere', covering *Time and Tide* and *The Bermondsey Book*, and on Irish revolutionary print. Other chapters touch on questions of democracy, war and discord. But the volume does not use politics as an organizing principle, and does not give the impression of a flourishing radical print culture in Britain. As to the European volume, this is subdivided by country and city. The section on Germany includes by far the most discussion of left-wing and activist print, though essays on Milan's revolutionary magazines and Russian socialist titles are also included. These tables of contents do not, of course, reveal the precise extent of leftist periodical publishing in each country, but they are suggestive in terms of where such activity was concentrated, and they also tell us a lot about the emphases of recent research. Some areas of current work are omitted, however. For instance, there is no coverage of Spanish Civil War magazines, or of Canadian Communist, popular front and labour periodicals (web resources on both topics are listed in our 'Toolbox' section at the back of this volume). In a 2015 article titled 'Assembly Lines: Researching Radical Print Networks', Andrea Hasenbank focuses on *The Canadian Labor Defender*, which offers insight into the strategies of print activism in Depression-era Canada. As it includes an extensive reviews section commenting on other proletarian pamphlets and newspapers, it is also a valuable bibliographic resource in itself. Left-wing literature and print culture is becoming a salient theme in Canadianist research: Hasenbank builds on several important studies, notably Candida Rifkind's *Comrades and Critics: Women, Literature, and the Left in 1930s Canada* (2009) and Jody Mason's *Writing Unemployment: Worklessness, Mobility, and Citizenship in Twentieth-Century Canadian Literatures* (2013).

In a US context, the labour poetry of the fin de siècle is explored in an essay by Cary Nelson in Jani Scandura and Michael Thurston's collection *Modernism Inc: Body, Memory, Capital* (2001). Nelson's piece 'takes up not only neglected or forgotten poems but also marginalized audiences for poetry' (Nelson, 'Politics' 269). The essay is preoccupied with the material forms in which labour poetry appeared. A key example is Edwin Markham's 1899 'The Man with the Hoe', which 'became one of the anthems of the American labor movement', and was first published in the *San Francisco Examiner* (269) and later reissued as an illustrated supplement to the paper's Sunday edition:

> Already oddly positioned within William Randolph Hearst's sometimes melodramatic newspaper, the poem has its inner tensions further exacerbated by the *Examiner*'s richly contradictory fin-de-siècle presentation. . . . Unashamed of stylistic contradiction or cheerfully eclectic, the accompanying images mix elements of a Victorian scrapbook with art nouveau and Edwardian book illustration. . . . Nowhere in the illustration are there factory owners or workers to be seen. (271–72)

Ephemera such as union poem cards are also considered in the essay, but the analysis remains preliminary since, as Nelson comments: 'The history I want to narrate is as yet unwritable because we do not have ready to hand either the full range of modern poetic texts taking up the issues of work and its exploitation or the distinctive and ephemeral way the poetry was published and used at various moments by distinct audiences' (269).

In terms of British culture, several critics have discussed the contributions of the Hogarth Press to public debate about political issues, another sign of its unusual position among modernist small presses. Diane Gillespie identifies Leonard Woolf's increasing involvement with periodical networks as the reason for the Press's prominence in the public sphere, focusing her essay on a controversial review by him of several books on religion that led to a 'Questionnaire on Religious Belief' published in both the *Nation and Athenaeum* and the *Daily News* in 1926. The results of that questionnaire then formed the basis for a book by R. B. Braithwaite published by the Hogarth Press, *The State of Religious Belief* (Gillespie, 'Woolfs' 84). In addition to the publications that reflected Woolf's own interest in international affairs, the League of Nations and imperialism, the Hogarth Press frequently published books that contributed to debate about specifically English political issues (Willis 239–41). Anna Snaith describes the Hogarth Press as 'a key disseminator of anti-colonial thought in the interwar period' ('Hogarth' 103), noting also that it published the first book in English by a Muslim, and by a Kikuyu (117, 119). Snaith emphasizes that the 'political force' of the Press derived from its pamphlet series. Ursula McTaggart points out that pamphlets were typically avoided by publishers because it was hard to profit from their sale, but that Leonard Woolf was committed to the form (72). In his autobiography, Woolf comments on the difficulty of placing Hogarth pamphlets in traditional bookshops or at railway station bookstalls, but through their consistent subject matter and uniform appearance Hogarth series such as the Day to Day Pamphlets made a significant contribution to public discourse (McTaggart 73). In a pamphlet by C. L. R. James, *A Case for West Indian Self-Government*, McTaggart sees an example of how the Hogarth Press 're-inscribed the English sphere of discourse' by both exposing it to 'international conversations and influences' and also by insisting that 'English' discourse must include colonial voices (74). Indeed, the notion of 'voice' – gaining a voice, developing a voice, including diverse voices – is what connects all the types of politicized print discussed in this section. As Mary Chapman notes, voice 'is one of the oldest tropes that democratic Western culture has, both for participation in the public sphere and for literary style'. She adds: 'These two meanings of "voice" – as political and literary self-expression – converge in the early decades of the twentieth century'. This was because print activism by, for example, women, minority ethnic groups, left-wing organizations and working-class people demanding a voice in public debate coincided, as Chapman puts it, 'with an adjacent campaign among aesthetic modernists to renovate literary style through formal experiments in voice, perspective and intertextuality' (12).

# Copyright and censorship

The conjunction of formal experimentation incorporating different kinds of voices in works of literary art with the emergence of vocal print activism in the modernist period was confronted by the efforts of the state to control expression through the legal mechanisms of censorship and prosecution for obscenity or sedition. In the popular imagination, modernist literature is often most widely associated with a handful of celebrated obscenity cases, notably those concerning James Joyce's *Ulysses*, D. H. Lawrence's *Lady Chatterley's Lover*, and Radclyffe Hall's *The Well of Loneliness*. These cases for decades were the scaffolding for a narrative of writers' heroic resistance to government censors and a sexually repressive society, a narrative that has been challenged and complicated by more nuanced, archives-based scholarship. Censorship on the grounds of obscenity, libel, blasphemy or political sedition has become one of two primary legal contexts for the study of modernist print. The other is copyright, an area of law which had considerable impact on the ways in which modernist literature was produced and circulated nationally and internationally. Censorship and copyright are now often seen as tightly entwined in a legal framework with which all participants in the production of print had to negotiate as copyright was (and is) granted by the same state apparatus that determined what was allowed to be published and what would be suppressed.

In their overview of US publishing from 1860 to 1920, Zboray and Zboray explain the importance of the passage of the 1891 Chace International Copyright Act in the United States after fifty-five years of agitation: 'Cheap, pirated editions of European works virtually vanished, to the benefit of legitimate publishers of standard editions' (31). The Chace Act granted rights to foreign authors, but only if the work was produced in the United States within a defined period and two copies were deposited with the Copyright Office: these requirements were known as the 'manufacturing clause' and had far-reaching repercussions for twentieth-century writers outside the United States. Robert Spoo, in his indispensable monograph *Without Copyrights: Piracy, Publishing, and the Public Domain* (2013), points out that the next significant change to US copyright, in 1909, revised the 1891 act by permitting works not written in English to escape the manufacturing clause.

With Michel Foucault's trenchant essay 'What is an Author?' as a significant influence, critical legal studies and cultural studies began to pay close attention to copyright in the early 1980s. In *The Copywrights: Intellectual Property and the Literary Imagination*

(2003), Paul Saint-Amour identifies the persistence in copyright law of a Romantic conception of the 'individual genius-creator' as at odds with the 'dynamic and intersubjective model of meaning or value' (6) that has become the intellectual currency of our own time. Saint-Amour discusses how several nineteenth- and twentieth-century writers engaged creatively with copyright in their fiction. Taking her cue from Saint-Amour's reading of the 'Oxen of the Sun' chapter of *Ulysses* as the performance of 'an encyclopedic range of fair use borrowings from its many source texts' (18), Celia Marshik discusses the influence of copyright on Virginia Woolf's nonfiction in 'Thinking Back Through Copyright', her contribution to Saint-Amour's edited collection *Modernism and Copyright* (2011). Marshik points out that in *A Room of One's Own* Woolf quotes from works in the public domain, but 'when she turns to her own moment, Woolf avoids quoting extensively from protected works by *inventing* contemporary novelists and their writings' (72). Marshik also argues that Woolf's strategic emendations of her first two novels when they were to be published in America make clear her awareness of copyright law. Despite this awareness, however, Woolf 'probably never knew that her intellectual property remained vulnerable despite her revisions' (68) because *The Voyage Out* and *Night and Day* did not comply with the requirements of the manufacturing clause.

The arcane American copyright laws enabled 'bookleggers' to produce pirated editions of or to publish excerpts from the work of authors who were outside the United States. The most famous of these pirates was Samuel Roth, whose career has been documented by Jay A. Gertzman in *Bookleggers and Smuthounds: The Trade in Erotica, 1920–1940* (2011). In his biography of Roth, *Infamous Modernist* (2013), Gertzman relies on the archive of Roth's papers deposited at Columbia University in 2005 to argue that his subject has received a 'bum rap' from literary history (xvii): 'What Roth did was not illegal. Rather, it violated the protocols of mutual fair dealing between publishers and authors' (xiv). In a detailed account of Roth's dealings with James Joyce, Spoo presents an image of Roth that radically revises how he has been depicted in the annals of modernism.

B. W. Huebsch, the publisher of some of Lawrence's banned works in the United States, had explained to Joyce that although publishing *Ulysses* in France would allow Joyce to preserve the text as he wanted it, he would forfeit his US copyright. Allowing Huebsch to publish it would preserve his copyright in the United States, but at the expense of expurgating the text to satisfy American censors. Huebsch also pointed out to Joyce that book pirates in the United States would in any case emend the text to avoid running afoul of the law, so either way Joyce lost if he published first in France (Spoo 66–67). As Spoo points out, 'the true proximate cause of Lawrence's and Joyce's copyright woes was that they had not complied with the 1909 act's manufacturing clause' (86). Roth wrote to Joyce in May 1922 on the letterhead of his proposed *Two Worlds* magazine, a project described by Spoo as 'a force for diffusing an archly eroticized version of modernism in a country bound by moral prohibitions and conventional reading habits' (7). The prospectus that was printed all the way down the right side of this letterhead (which Roth continually revised) distinguished between a book, which is 'accepted as something accomplished, beyond revision', and a magazine, the tradition of which 'is alive with the hazard that underlies the firmness of the printed word' (Gertzman, *Infamous*, 64). The only magazine 'ready to print the best being written in English', the prospectus went on, is *The Little Review*, but it has 'often had to disappear from view'. Roth initially proposed to publish *Ulysses* in a single issue of his magazine, suggesting that he had not in fact seen the 730-page 1922 Paris edition when he made his overture to Joyce.

In 1922, Roth did not have the funds necessary to launch his magazine, and the recent conviction on obscenity charges of *The Little Review*'s editors, Margaret Anderson and Jane Heap, for their publication of the 'Nausicaa' episode of *Ulysses* also factored into his decision to delay publication (Gertzman, *Infamous* 65). In 1926 Roth began to publish excerpts from *Ulysses* in *Two Worlds Monthly*, bringing about an international protest mobilized by Joyce and Sylvia Beach.[2] Joyce's subsequent lawsuit against Roth which Spoo explains was for the unlawful exploitation of his name in advertisements, 'became a means by which Joyce altered public perception of *Ulysses* and furthered his growing reputation as an avant-garde innovator'. 'Together with the international protest', Spoo continues, 'the lawsuit marked a significant moment in the development of modernism as an engine for generating authorial celebrity' (7).

Gertzman argues that Roth was not only interested in making money from 'prurient titillation' but also wished 'to broaden the horizons of middle- and working-class readers from the heartland of America, as well as city dwellers who worked in offices and stores and in the professions' (*Infamous* xviii). As Loren Glass claims in 'Redeeming Value: Obscenity and Anglo-American Modernism', '*Ulysses*'s modernist credentials were affirmed by its entry into the middlebrow marketplace, and this paradox was sustained by the successful marketing of modernism in the publishing industry and the canonization of the new criticism in the academy that mandated the moral "disinterest" of literary value' (349). Samuel Roth provided what Spoo describes as 'a slightly delayed, oblique modernism, an evening edition of the morning news, a bringing together of "two worlds", Europe and America, in magazines that promised an increase of "gaiety", a more vivid living in the moment, an experience of candor, sophistication, and entertainment, in equal parts' (89).

Ezra Pound did not sign Joyce's letter of protest against Roth (Spoo 191). Pound was an outspoken critic of American copyright laws, seeing them as an aspect of capitalism's triumph over culture (Spoo 71). In 1918 in the *New Age*, he published proposals for an international copyright law that would reward authors for their labour but not obstruct the wide dissemination of their works. Pound, who, along with Arthur Symonds and Ford Madox Ford, had agreed in 1922 to become a contributing editor of Roth's *Two Worlds*, was acutely aware that modernist works had to cross borders if culture was to be reformed. Both copyright and obscenity laws hindered the transmission of works Pound deemed vital to the modernist project, and in the December 1914 number of *The Little Review* he quoted at length Section 221 of the US Criminal Code, pointing out that 'it is well that the citizens of a country should be aware of its laws', in this case 'the amazing, grotesque, and unthinkable, ambiguous law of our country' (Pound, 'Classics' 33).

Although censorship has long been a significant topic in discussions of modernism, the ways that writers engaged creatively with it has recently become a particular focus. In *British Modernism and Censorship* (2006), Celia Marshik develops the notion of a 'censorship dialectic' that 'shaped modernism by encouraging or forcing writers to take up censorship as a theme in both their non-fiction prose and creative writings; it pushed writers to meditate on their own productions and to explain themselves in documents that provide vital insights into specific works and into modernism in general' (5). Marshik criticizes earlier works such as Edward de Grazia's *Girls Lean Back Everywhere* (1992) for promoting 'the myth of modernism's triumph over censorship' (207 n12). With that caveat in mind, however, de Grazia does provide an entertaining account of several celebrated cases. In her study, Marshik discusses D. G. Rossetti, G. B. Shaw, Woolf, Joyce and Jean Rhys. Of these, Woolf was in a unique position because she was a publisher as well as writer. English obscenity statutes made printers themselves liable, which was often the reason writers could not find publishers who would produce their work, leading many of them to private press publication outside the country. Marshik comments that the Hogarth Press 'paradoxically enmeshed [Woolf] in the very "fear and suspicion" she sought to escape. Indeed Hogarth placed Woolf inside a panopticon wherein she and her husband Leonard were forced to police themselves lest the real police launch a prosecution for obscene libel' (11). Writers' intentions often were stymied by printers who balked at setting particular words in type: prominent examples include Joyce's refusal to delete the word 'bloody' from *Dubliners* when the printer objected, and the refusal of the printer employed by Elkin Matthews to print certain poems in Pound's 1916 collection *Lustra*. Libel law was closely related to obscenity law, as Sean Latham demonstrates in *The Art of Scandal: Modernism, Libel Law, and the Roman à Clef* (2009). Like Marshik, he points to the way that writers, including Joyce and Wyndham Lewis, responded creatively to these restrictions 'by writing deliberately defamatory works lightly cloaked in the roman à clef's "conditional fictionality"'. Latham adds: 'Like the laws of obscenity and copyright that Joyce and Lewis also incorporated and critiqued in their works, so too does defamation play a vital role in their exploration of the limits of fiction and the legality of literature' (86).

Some writers and their publishers used visual and typographical strategies to draw attention to the operations of the censor. When John Sumner of the New York Society for the Suppression of Vice threatened to confiscate e. e. cummings's *The Enormous Room*, the book appeared with every instance of the offending word 'shit' 'laboriously inked out of every copy by hand' (North 150). Andrew Nash, in his study of Chatto & Windus, reproduces a page from Richard Aldington's *The Death of a Hero* (1929) to show how Aldington had 'arranged for objectionable passages to be asterisked out in a defiant gesture of resistance to the implicit censorship of his work' (331). Aldington's novel was available from circulating libraries, such as Boots or W. H. Smith, only upon request, but his next book, *The Colonel's Daughter* (1931), was effectively removed from wide circulation when Smith, and then Boots, refused to make it available at all (Nash 328). In 'Circulating Morals (1900–1915)', Nicola Wilson explains the power of libraries to restrict the availability (and, therefore, the print runs) of books, especially after the creation in 1909 of the Circulating Libraries Association to coordinate the views of the six main libraries. In 'Boots Book-lovers' Library and the Novel' (2014), Wilson draws on the Chatto & Windus archive at Reading University to examine the specific impact of the Library on the revisioning process. Paul S. Boyer, in *Purity in Print: Book Censorship in America from the Gilded Age to the Computer Age* (2002), explains that ' "book censorship" in the late Victorian era was not primarily a matter of obscenity laws or of suppressive attacks by specific groups. It was simply the sum total of countless small decisions by editors, publishers, booksellers, librarians, critics and – occasionally – vice societies, all based on a common conception of literary propriety' (20).

By the early twentieth century, resistance to this climate of repression was steadily growing. Peter Keating adduces the example of Gilbert Cannan's *Round the Corner* (1913), to which the circulating libraries objected: 'Martin Secker immediately counter-attacked with advertisements proclaiming it "*Not* an immoral book", one that he was "proud to have issued", and urging the public to insist on the right to decide the matter for itself' (280). Seeing issues of censorship and control as part of a longer print cultural history extending back into the nineteenth century has contributed to a reformulation of some of the accepted narratives about well-known modernists. In *Slow Print* Elizabeth Miller suggests that the challenge of writers such as Joyce and Lawrence to obscenity standards

> looks different when we consider it as the tail end of a slow print revolution that began as an effort on the part of radical writers, editors, and printers to seize the means of print production. Such a perspective would challenge, for example, Joyce Wexler's

argument about Joyce and Lawrence that 'the marketing genius of modernist authors inspired them to defend erotic fiction as art and sell it as smut' (91). If we read 'obscene' modernists in the context of changing rhetoric around free print . . . the turn toward sexually outré topics seems to follow a shift of emphasis from class radicalism to sexuality in mechanisms of state suppression. (301)

Rachel Potter makes a similar point about the long history of writers' strategies of engagement with censorship in *Obscene Modernism: Literary Censorship and Experiment 1900–1940* (2013). She builds on the research of such scholars as Adam Parkes, Allison Pease, Paul Vanderham and Marshik to argue that resistance to censorship to some extent mirrored 'the censorship networks that controlled the dissemination of books' in the United States and England (4). The operation of these networks in England is discussed in detail by the contributors to *Prudes on the Prowl: Fiction and Obscenity in England, 1850 to the Present Day* (2013), a collection Potter edited with David Bradshaw and for which she provides a useful overview of changing practices regarding obscenity in her introduction.

Censorship is not solely a matter of determining obscenity. The suppression of political ideas unwelcome to the government was facilitated in the United States by the passage of the 1917 Espionage Act. This act's 'banning treasonable material from the mails led to the suppression of fifteen magazines' (Baggett 176). In England, the 1914 Defense of the Realm Act permitted the government to seize and destroy pacifist pamphlets. Baggett argues that the entry of the United States into the First World War in April 1917 established a specific political context for the US Post Office's confiscation on the grounds of 'indecency' of *The Little Review* in October that year when it published Wyndham Lewis's 'Cantleman's Spring-Mate'. Lewis used the story of a soldier's rape of an English woman as an allegory about the morality of war. Anderson and Heap's outspoken support of Emma Goldman since 1914 had already cost them a great deal of financial support, as well as the loss of office space when landlords who found their politics seditious evicted them. To the authorities of the first half of the twentieth century, modernist art was often associated with blasphemy, pornographic indecency and political radicalism, categories whose boundaries could be quite porous. As Meredith McGill remarks in 'Copyright and Intellectual Property: The State of the Discipline' (2013), more research on 'the relations between obscenity, property, and circulation would both contribute to the study of copyright and help to underscore the importance of pornography to the history of publishing more generally' (416). Censorship and copyright are imbricated in modernism, and as the interest of modernist studies in its own disciplinary history grows, so does interest in the shaping effects on modernist literature of these legal regimes. Commenting on her legal challenge to the Joyce estate's 'program of private censorship' of quotation from Joyce's sexually explicit letters to Nora Barnacle, Carol Loeb Shloss states that although the case was 'ostensibly about determining the parameters of fair use, it was catalyzed by the Joyce estate's attempts to shut down *all* language about certain subjects that it wanted kept in silence and darkness' (253). Censorship and copyright thus extend their influence beyond the modernist period into our present moment. Contemporary changes to copyright are of particular concern to scholars because the subjects of their research can move in or out of the public domain depending on the passage of new laws, a situation of special difficulty for projects in the digital humanities that seek to make modernist works freely available online.

# Conclusion

Scholarship on modernism's print cultures has emphasized the collaborative 'making' of modernism by the various actors who wrote, edited, illustrated, published, marketed, translated, reviewed and read modernist texts. Our survey of recent scholarship on modernism's print cultures takes as its primary focus what Sean Latham describes as a 'golden age of print culture' ('Mess' 408). That 'golden age' in fact stretches back into the mid-nineteenth century, to what Richard Menkes has argued in *Telegraphic Realism: Victorian Fiction and Other Information Systems* (2008) is Victorian realism's response to new technologies of communication (3). It also stretches forward into the current moment, when the affordances of digital technology have profoundly affected what it is possible for scholarship to do, at the same time as raising compelling questions of methodology that, in turn, force us to revise our ideas of what modernism was in the first place. In the inaugural volume of the New Modernisms series, Latham and Rogers announce that 'there is no such thing as modernism', because it continues to be a 'mobile, expansive, and unsettled concept' (1). Over the past two decades, the study of modernism's print cultures has contributed significantly to the demise of a Modernism enshrined, for example, in the anthologies assigned each year to thousands of undergraduates that represent the movement as an elitist formal experiment, willfully obscure and produced by people who had nothing but contempt for the rapidly expanding reading publics of the time. As our discussion of the diversity of material forms and the close relations of such forms to the commercial marketplace has shown, the 'great divide' between modernism and the masses has turned out to be a chimera.

If, as Ann Ardis has argued, 'a transformed culture of print, not film, is the first as well as the most important new media form of the twentieth century' (Ardis, 'Staging' 31), scholarship on that new form has in the last two decades seen 'methodological convergences of periodical studies, book history, media history, and material culture studies that are enriching our understanding of modernism's complex relation to the media ecology of modernity' (Ardis, 'Mediamorphosis' v). In particular, much of the ferment around modernism's print cultures has been driven by the emergence of periodical studies in the last decade, the modernist version of which owes a great deal to earlier scholarship on Victorian periodicals. (The *Victorian Periodicals Newsletter*, now renamed *Victorian Periodicals Review*, was founded in 1968.) Scholarship on periodicals from the late nineteenth century up to the year in which copyright determines when a title enters the public domain has been enhanced by a number of digital humanities initiatives, listed in our 'Toolbox'. The material turn in modernist studies has often, paradoxically, been enabled by digital representations of objects, a remediation that has elicited a great deal of discussion as virtual 'archives' obviate the need for expensive travel to special collections but also replace the tactile experience of confronting the physical object of study with its virtual image. Announcing 'Etant-donnés', a 2013 'meta-modernist symposium' at the University of Cork, the organizers questioned the undue fetishizing of the object in modernist studies, and asked if it was perhaps time 'to reimagine the archive' in a time when 'pilgrimages to archives' might no longer be necessary (Hayden et al.). James Mussell has commented that 'one of the curious effects of the digital moment is the way it has enhanced the aura of the archive' ('Repetition' 344), yet he suggests that 'A more productive approach is to rethink digital resources as offering representations of whatever it is that the archival objects *also* represent' (354). In light of the expansion of scholarship on modernism's print cultures enabled by digital humanities projects, however, we may conclude that the digital does not 'erase' print but has actually materialized it as a distinct set of cultural, historical and technological practices. As Anouk Lang has remarked, 'DH methodologies don't erase considerations of materiality but rather can foreground them by offering new and provocative optics, and thereby force us to think about them, and how to represent them, with a set of tools and a vocabulary that we haven't had to use before.'

In 1926, T. S. Eliot suggested of a literary review that 'the bound volumes of a decade should represent the keenest sensibility and the clearest thought of ten years' (2). Patrick Collier has recently assessed all the issues published to date of the *Journal of*

*Modern Periodical Studies* to develop a close analysis of scholarly trends. Collier concludes that 'we do not have a consensus on the object of knowledge in modern periodical studies, or even much in the way of explicit discussion of it' (93). He finds that modern periodical studies, while it has succeeded in expanding its purview to previously under-studied or un-studied periodicals, has nevertheless often reproduced 'well-established *topoi* such as surrealism, cubism, Dada, the Harlem Renaissance, etc.' (95) rather than creating new knowledge about how magazines shaped modernity in unexpected ways. As we pointed out in our Introduction, Lucy Delap and Maria DiCenzo have argued that 'a change of perspective – from a literary focus on *content* to a media history focus on circulation, or a historical focus on transnational exchanges of ideas' would lead critics to see features of print cultural objects that are obscured by using 'modernist' as the main category of enquiry. Collier asks what might be gained by periodical studies were modernist literature and art not relied on 'as the central touchstones of the period' (96). As an example, he reads a special issue of *JMPS* on anarchism and asks 'What might be visible about the print culture of Anarchism if modernism were dropped from the critical foreground? What aspects of anarchist culture are best understood through other literary styles or rhetorical constructs?' (96) Such questions and critique demonstrate the destabilizing effects of print culture scholarship on the category of 'modernism' itself.

This scholarship has begun to refashion our notions of the literary as researchers now are becoming accustomed to read magazines in their entirety, and to analyse the complex interrelations of all their elements – size, paper quality, circulation, cost, advertisements, typography, juxtapositions, editorial intention and so on. Books also are increasingly being studied not solely for their content but as objects in a marketplace, their reception conditioned by graphics and other 'paratextual' elements, marketing, reviews and the status of their publisher. Research now being undertaken in the business archives of publishing houses will further our understanding of the relations between modernism and the marketplace, expanding the definition of 'literary' criticism as it absorbs the insights of textual studies, book history, periodical studies, visual studies and cultural studies, all of which contribute to the field of print culture scholarship.

Inevitably, new contexts and new objects of study lead to new interpretations and new ways of reading, thus affecting pedagogical methods. Several online projects devoted to periodicals invite the scholarly community's assistance or are continually updated and added to through their use in university courses. Examples include the virtual 'Newsstand: 1925', to which David Earle's students contribute annually, and the 'Index of Modernist Little Magazines' maintained by Suzanne Churchill at Davidson College, where students contribute to the ongoing expansion of the site. The 'Cover-to-Cover Initiative' of the Modernist Journals Project asks for assistance in identifying libraries that have complete runs (including advertising sections) of any of the journals on a core list of twenty titles the MJP regards as crucial to the study of modernism. The MJP has been consciously constructed as a resource for teaching as well as for research, providing on its 'Teaching with the MJP' pages lesson plans, classroom projects, tools, sample syllabi and assignments, as well as an instructional wiki. Latham has also described the MJP as an enabling counternarrative to the 'distinctly masculinist' modernism of Eliot, Pound and the New Critics, stressing that a digital archive should not be treated like an anthology from which users selectively attend to already well-known works or writers ('Mess' 425).

In the same special issue of *Tulsa Studies in Women's Literature* in which Latham's 'Mess and Muddle' appears, Amanda Sigler provides an example of how our understanding of canonical modernists is altered when their work is replaced in its original context of publication. Focusing her study on the publication of Virginia Woolf's short story 'Mrs Dalloway in Bond Street' in *The Dial* of July 1923, Sigler explores the advertising practices and marketing language of the periodical in relation to Woolf's narrative about shopping and gift-giving. She demonstrates that Woolf's contributions to periodicals brought her into ever more imaginative and intense engagement with the demands of commerce, thus rendering Woolf herself analogous to *The Dial*, which 'struggled between artistic purity and commercial necessity' (Sigler, 337). Placing the 'material concerns' of Woolf's fiction back into the 'material context' of its publication opens the work to a reading that exemplifies how print culture scholarship is not only adding knowledge to our understanding of modernism, but also transforming what we thought we knew about canonical writers such as Woolf. As

J. Stephen Murphy remarks, a pedagogy focused solely on textual interpretation risks losing the valuable insights from literary history that the materialist emphases of print culture scholarship and digital humanities provide (xii–xiii).

Digital humanities also provides new modes of access to print objects for textual research that reflects the turn to notions of the social text. Staying with the example of Woolf, 'Comparing Marks: A Versioning Edition of Virginia Woolf's "The Mark on the Wall"' (McGinn et al.) offers a 'case study of small-scale digitization' and models an approach that could be applied to numerous similar literary examples. Using Juxta Commons and Text Encoding Initiative (TEI) annotations, this project is careful to honour Woolf's own fluid attitude towards her texts, 'resisting finality in flux' (McGinn et al.). Because the various 'witnesses' of 'The Mark on the Wall' are presented horizontally, visitors to this site can compare the differences among several versions of Woolf's sketch published between 1917 – as one of two stories in the inaugural publication of the Hogarth Press – and posthumously in 1944, without any sense that one is privileged over another. Methodologically, 'Comparing Marks' builds upon the approach of Helen Southworth's edited collection *Leonard and Virginia Woolf, the Hogarth Press, and the Networks of Modernism* in its attention to 'the hybrid quality of the Press', and its 'often disconcerting mix of professional and amateur practices' (Southworth, 'Introduction' 2). As with all the most successful modernist DH projects, 'Comparing Marks' refocuses attention on the material text by embedding digital images of the pages of each version of 'The Mark on the Wall' in a critically informed context.

Any survey of scholarship such as this book makes inevitably has to create divisions that may strike some readers as artificial or strained. The integrated scholarship on a particular topic or period has in some cases been distributed across more than one of our categories to serve the demands of our book's organizational structure. Thus, for example, discussion of illustration in books and magazines of the Harlem Renaissance might appear either in a section on graphics or in one on politics, or in both. Print culture is an interdisciplinary field. We were sometimes made sharply aware of this when a trip to the library to collect books for a particular section might involve visiting several different shelf marks, or even floors, according to how the various books had been catalogued: under book history, textual and bibliographic studies, literary criticism, media studies or even sociology. Our book provides a guide to the scholarship of the last two decades on modernism's print cultures, but we do not enter into arguments of our own with that material. Our argument is simply that research on print culture has had a transformative effect on modernist studies.

One of the most significant among those effects has been to dissolve boundaries: those between avant-garde and mainstream, between high and low culture, between art and commerce and even to some extent between the visual and the textual. In consequence, as the New Modernisms series itself exemplifies, 'modernism' is being reintegrated into the richly variegated early twentieth-century culture of which it was a part. Seeing this culture as a whole allows us to relate together such apparently disparate artefacts as an Imagist anthology, an advertisement in *Vanity Fair*, a poster on the London Underground, and the *Prose du Transsiberien*, and to explore them all in a single critical framework. One effect of this is a kind of rehistoricizing of the familiar and a making visible of what had been obscured by older paradigms of criticism and teaching. What is made visible is a world in which print was the dominant media form, spilling beyond the covers of the codex and moving out onto walls and into the street.

# NOTES

## Chapter 1

1 See the special issue of *Critical Inquiry* on 'Things', edited by Brown, 28.1 (2001), especially his introduction, 'Thing Theory', 1–22.

2 The Kelmscott Press was founded in 1891 by William Morris to produce beautiful editions of his own works and those of his favourite authors. Morris designed typefaces, produced his own paper, and bound the books by hand. Kelmscott titles were influenced by medieval illuminated manuscripts and early printing. Morris was concerned to restore the close relationship between art and society figured in handcrafted production that had been threatened or eliminated by the technological innovations of the nineteenth century.

3 Dun Emer, founded by Yeats and his sister Elizabeth in 1904, evolved into the Cuala Press in 1908 (see Murray, 'Cuala'). Cuala produced elegant editions of the work of innovative contemporary writers, whereas Morris's Kelmscott Press focused on reprinting lavishly illustrated classics.

4 On the technical and economic history of these processes, a good place to begin is with guides to printing such as Twyman's or Pankow's, or general volumes on the history of the book. See, for instance, Eliot and Rose's *A Companion to the History of the Book* (especially Banham's chapter on the industrialization of the book); or volume 4 of the *Edinburgh History of the Book in Scotland*, which has a substantial section on 'Production, Form and Image' (Finkelstein and McCleery).

5 See, for instance, Raizman (192) on Tschichold's 'mission' to reform and analyze the language of page design. Ruari McLean's 1975 book on Tschichold remains the most detailed account of his career; its valuable appendix presents English translations of Tschichold's essays on subjects including the placement of type, the mass-production of the classics and his reforms at Penguin.

# Chapter 2

1 Matthew Chambers, in *Modernism, Periodicals, and Cultural Poetics* (2015) builds on Harding's work, extending the analysis into the mid-century period in order to explore the 'networks of exchange within and between different literary periodicals that condition the types of poetry published and the kinds of poetic discourse that come to cohere and predominate' (2). His particular focus is on poetry's role in 'solidifying an ethnolinguistic English identity' (1). This book appeared too late for us to incorporate a full discussion of it. A related study, also focusing on the mid-century period, is James Gifford's *Personal Modernisms: Anarchist Networks and the Later Avant-gardes* (2014). This book, while not primarily a work of print culture scholarship, does consider the importance of periodicals within political and literary networks.

2 In 1996, Ronald Schuchard showed that Eliot's own prose was 'as vulnerable to the anarchic state of international publishing as any of his contemporaries' (171) as he struggled throughout his life to 'shape and reshape his canon for the marketplace' (172). At the time, Schuchard commented that only a scholarly edition could remedy the 'unscholarly textual situation' of Eliot's American prose publications; the first three of a projected eight volumes of a critical edition of *The Complete Prose of T. S. Eliot* have so far been published by Johns Hopkins and Faber.

# Chapter 3

1 The culmination of several efforts throughout the nineteenth century to control the retail price of books, the Net Book Agreement came into effect on 1 January 1900. Booksellers agreed to sell books at set prices and if they sold them at less, the publisher would refuse to supply them. See Barnes; Stevenson.

2 The Modernist Versions Project makes available some images of Roth's magazine at http://web.uvic.ca/~mvp1922/portfolio/samuel-roth/

# TOOLBOX

# Resources for studying and teaching modernism's print cultures

## Reference sources, bibliographic guides and survey studies

Abrahamson, David and Marcia R. Prior-Miller, eds. *The Routledge Handbook of Magazine Research: The Future of the Magazine Form.* New York: Routledge, 2015.

Arnold, John and Martyn Lyons. *A History of the Book in Australia. Volume 2: 1890–1945.* Brisbane: U of Queensland P, 2001.

Ashley, Mike. *The Age of the Storytellers: British Popular Fiction Magazines, 1880–1950.* London: British Library, 2006.

Black, Fiona, and Patricia Lockhart Fleming, eds. *History of the Book in Canada. Vol. 2: 1840–1918.* Toronto, ON: U of Toronto P, 2005.

Bold, Christine, ed. *US Popular Print Culture 1860–1920.* Vol. 6 of *The Oxford History of Popular Print Culture.* Oxford: Oxford UP, 2012. [Includes a 'Selective Chronology 1860–1920' of significant events in publishing].

Brooker, Peter and Andrew Thacker, eds. *Britain and Ireland 1880–1955.* Vol. 1 of *The Oxford Critical and Cultural History of Modernist Magazines.* Oxford: Oxford UP, 2009.

Brooker, Peter and Andrew Thacker, eds. *North America 1894–1960.* Vol. 2 of *The Oxford Critical and Cultural History of Modernist Magazines.* Oxford: Oxford UP, 2012.

Brooker, Peter, Sascha Bru, Andrew Thacker and Christian Weikop, eds. *Europe 1880–1940.* Vol. 3 of *The Oxford Cultural and Critical History of Modernist Magazines.* Oxford: Oxford UP, 2013.

Chielens, Edward E. *American Literary Magazines.* 2 vols. Westport, CT: Greenwood, 1986–92.

Churchill, Suzanne W. and Adam McKible, eds. *Little Magazines and Modernism: New Approaches*. Aldershot: Ashgate, 2007. This includes:
'Books and Articles on Little Magazines from 1890 to 1950' (Appendix B)
'Print Indexes to Little Magazines' (Appendix C)
'Electronic Indexes and Web Resources for Little Magazines' (Appendix D)
'Library Holdings of Little Magazines' (Appendix E)
Colclough, Stephen and Alexis Weedon, eds. *The History of the Book in the West. Vol. 4: 1800–1914*. Farnham: Ashgate, 2010.
Finkelstein, David and Alistair McCleery, eds. *Professionalism and Diversity, 1880–2000*. Vol. 4 of *The Edinburgh History of the Book in Scotland*. Edinburgh: Edinburgh UP, 2007.
Gerson, Carole and Jacques Michon, eds. *History of the Book in Canada. Vol. 3: 1918–1980*. Toronto, ON: U of Toronto P, 2007.
Hoffman, Frederick J., Charles Allen and Carolyn F. Ulrich. *The Little Magazine: A History and a Bibliography*. Princeton, NJ: Princeton UP, 1946.
Kaestle, Carl F. and Janice A. Radway. *Print in Motion: The Expansion of Publishing and Reading in the United States, 1880–1940*. Vol. 4 of *A History of the Book in America*, ed. David D. Hall. Chapel Hill: U of North Carolina P, 2014.
Miller, David and Richard Price, comp. *British Poetry Magazines 1914–2000: A History and Bibliography of 'Little Magazines'*. London: British Library and Oak Knoll P, 2006.
Mott, Frank Luther. *A History of American Magazines* 5 vols. Cambridge: Harvard UP, 1938–1968.
Peterson, Theodore. *Magazines in the Twentieth Century*. 2nd ed. Urbana: U of Illinois P, 1964. Digital version available at www.modjourn.org
Reed, David. *The Popular Magazine in Britain and the United States 1880–1960*. Toronto, ON: U of Toronto P, 1997 [includes content analysis tables].
Sullivan, Alvin, ed. *British Literary Magazines*. 4 vols. Westport, CT: Greenwood, 1984–86.
Weedon, Alexis, ed. *The History of the Book in the West, vol. 5: 1914–2000*. Farnham: Ashgate, 2010.

# Book series

Anthem Studies in Book History, Publishing and Print Culture.
Ashgate Studies in Publishing History: Manuscript, Print, Digital.
History of Print and Digital Culture (U of Wisconsin P).

Print Culture History in Modern America (U of Wisconsin P) [series concluded].
Studies in Book and Print Culture (U of Toronto P).
Studies in Print Culture and the History of the Book (U of Massachusetts P).

# Online resources

## Digital archives and digital editions

*Blue Mountain Project: Historical Avant-Garde Periodicals for Digital Research* (full runs of rare journals of international provenance and multilingual scope, with detailed metadata)
http://bluemountain.princeton.edu/index.html
*Canadian Magazines* (selected images from magazines printed in Canada 1873–1977)
http://www.crcstudio.org/canadianmagazines/index.php
*Chinese Women's Magazines in the Late Qing and Early Republican Period* (concerns the popular press in China 1904–1937)
http://www.womag.uni-hd.de/
*Modernist Journals Project* (full-text scans of culturally significant modernist periodicals up to 1922; teaching pages; full-text monographs)
www.modjourn.org
*Modernist Magazines Project* (research site from which the *Oxford Cultural and Critical History of Modernist Magazines* derives; includes over 4500 page scans of nearly 70 periodicals, indexed by author and article title)
http://modmags.dmu.ac.uk/home.html
*Modern Magazines Project Canada* (brings together scholars, magazine professionals, and digitization specialists, and centres on digitization of the full run of *Western Home Monthly* from 1899 to 1932)
http://modmag.ca/
*Modernist Versions Project* (makes available digitized versions of modernist texts that can be studied, searched, and compared in a collaborative environment)
http://web.uvic.ca/~mvp1922/
*Modernist Web* (includes digital facsimiles of modernist editions in a variety of genres, annotated texts for study, and some searchable little magazines)
https://www.modernistweb.com/
*Newsstand: 1925* (a virtual American newsstand from the summer of 1925, curated by David Earle)

https://secure.uwf.edu/dearle/enewsstand/enewsstand.htm
*Poetry* magazine (full-text archive from 1912 – present)
http://www.poetryfoundation.org/poetrymagazine/archive
*Print Culture and Urban Visuality* (images of twentieth-century publications produced in cities such as Toronto, Montreal, and New York City that contribute to the sense of the metropolis as a space of secrets)
http://strawresearch.mcgill.ca/streetprint/index.php?c=1
*Pulp Magazines Project* (archive of all-fiction pulpwood magazines 1896–1946)
http://www.pulpmags.org/default.htm
*Red Flags* (a resource site to further knowledge of the early labour press in Canada, c1840–1920)
https://prolitca.wordpress.com/
*UNZ.org* (massive database of periodicals from 1880s-2000)
http://www.unz.org/Pub/
*Woolf Online:* To the Lighthouse (digital archive of materials related to the composition, production and publication of Virginia Woolf's 1927 novel)
www.WoolfOnline.com
*Yellow Nineties Online* (facsimile editions of avant-garde aesthetic periodicals including *The Yellow Book* and *Evergreen*, marked up using TEI)
http://www.1890s.ca/

## Databases and research projects

*Australian Common Reader* (database of fiction reading experience in Australian since the 19th century)
http://www.australiancommonreader.com/
*Collecting the Modern Library* (collectors' site with a database searchable by author, designer, and title; also displays promotional material for the series)
http://www.modernlib.com/
*Modernist Archives Publishing Project* or MAPP (an aggregated collection of twentieth-century publishing histories, beginning with the Hogarth Press. Scheduled to launch in 2017)
http://www.modernistarchives.com/
*Pages Project* (archive of book pages bearing marks, notations and other marginalia)
http://thepagesproject.com/
*Penguin Checklist Project* (ongoing project to compile and sort every book published by Penguin Books)

https://penguinchecklist.wordpress.com/
*Reading Experience Database* (database of records of the reading experience of British subjects between 1450 and 1945; also provides a bibliography on 'Reading: History, Practice and Theory')
http://www.open.ac.uk/Arts/RED/
*Reading: Harvard Views of Readers, Readership, and Reading History* (the intellectual, cultural, and political history of reading reflected in historical holdings of the Harvard Libraries) http://ocp.hul.harvard.edu/reading/
*What Middletown Read Project* (database and search engine built upon Muncie Public Library circulation records from 1891–1902)
http://www.bsu.edu/libraries/wmr/index.php

## Catalogues

*British Library Periodicals Reference Sources* http://www.bl.uk/reshelp/findhelprestype/journals/persrc/reference.html
*Bruce Peel Special Collections Library* (U of Alberta, Canada, includes images from many modernist small presses)
https://bpsc.library.ualberta.ca/collections
*Index of Modernist Little Magazines* (A quick reference guide to selected titles)
http://sites.davidson.edu/littlemagazines/
*John Johnson Collection of Printed Ephemera* (a special collection of the Bodleian Library, of primary, uninterpreted printed documents produced for short-term use)
http://www.bodleian.ox.ac.uk/johnson
*Merrill C. Berman Collection* (extensive selection of images from a private collection of international modernist graphic art, including many periodicals and posters)
http://mcbcollection.com/

## Exhibitions

*Artist/Novelist* (exhibition of artists' books from collection of NY Museum of Modern Art)
http://www.moma.org/interactives/exhibitions/2014/artistnovelist/
*Greenwich Village Bookshop Door: A Portal to Bohemia, 1920–1925* (online exhibition of materials from the Harry Ransom Center related to Frank Shay's Bookshop in New York)

http://norman.hrc.utexas.edu/bookshopdoor/#1
*Magazines and War 1936–1939* (based on a 2007 exhibition in Madrid on Spanish Civil War Print Culture)
http://www.magazinesandwar.com/en.html
*Making Modernism: Literature and Culture in 20th-Century Chicago* (based on a 2013 exhibit at the Newberry Library)
http://publications.newberry.org/makingmodernism/exhibits/show/exhibit

## Associations and networks

*Association of Print Scholars* (brings together curators, collectors, academics, graduate students, artists, paper conservators, critics, independent scholars, and dealers)
http://printscholars.org/
*Editing Modernism in Canada* (EMiC facilitates collaborative editing projects in both print and digital formats, and provides a focus for discussion of editing theory and techniques)
http://editingmodernism.ca/
*European Society for Periodical Research*
http://www.espr-it.eu/
*Magazine Modernisms* (blogs, announcements, and forum for debate on modern periodical studies 1880 – present)
https://magmods.wordpress.com/
*Middlebrow Network* (provides a focus for research on 'middlebrow', offering bibliographies, resource guides, definitions and a researcher database)
http://www.middlebrow-network.com/Home.aspx
*Modernism Lab* (a virtual space dedicated to collaborative research into the roots of literary modernism)
http://modernism.research.yale.edu/
*Newspaper and Periodical History Forum of Ireland*
http://newspapersperiodicals.org/
*Projectgroep Tijdschriftstudies* (Magazine Studies group of the Huizinga Instituut, the national Dutch research network for Cultural History)
http://www.huizingainstituut.nl/projectgroep-tijdschriftstudies/
*Research Society for American Periodicals*
http://www.periodicalresearch.org/
*Research Society for Victorian Periodicals*
http://rs4vp.org/
*SHARP (Society for the History of Authorship, Reading and Publishing*
http://www.sharpweb.org/main/

## Presentations, conference papers

'American Little Magazines of the 1890s' (curator's talk by Kirsten McLeod at the Grolier Club in New York, 2013)
https://www.youtube.com/watch?v=t9wjkn_KdGE
*What is a journal?* (Papers from the 2013 MLA special session, 'What is A Journal? Towards a Theory of Periodical Studies')
http://tinyurl.com/novo42z

# Key texts

## Chapter 1: Sensuous print

Binckes, Faith. *Modernism, Magazines, and the British Avant-garde: Reading* Rhythm, *1910–1914* (2010).
Bornstein, George. *Material Modernism: The Politics of the Page* (2001).
Drucker, Johanna. *The Visible Word: Experimental Typography and Modern Art, 1909–1923* (1994).
Goeser, Caroline. *Picturing the New Negro: Harlem Renaissance Print Culture and Modern Black Identity* (2007).
MacLeod, Kirsten. *American Little Magazines of the 1890s: A Revolution in Print* (2013).
McGann, Jerome. *Black Riders: The Visible Language of Modernism* (1993) and *The Textual Condition* (1991).
Murphet, Julian. *Multimedia Modernism: Literature and the Anglo-American Avant-garde* (2009).
Saler, Michael T. *The Avant-Garde in Interwar England: Medieval Modernism and the London Underground* (1999).
Selborne, Joanna. *British Wood-Engraved Book Illustration 1904–1940: A Break with Tradition* (1998).
Turner, Catherine. *Marketing Modernism Between the Two World Wars* (2003).

## Chapter 2: Print in circulation

Churchill, Suzanne. *The Little Magazine* Others *and the Renovation of Modern American Poetry* (2006).
Churchill, Suzanne and Adam McKible, eds. *Little Magazines and Modernism: New Approaches* (2007).
Dettmar, Kevin and Stephen Watt. *Marketing Modernisms: Self-Promotion, Canonization, Rereading* (1996).

Earle, David M. *Re-Covering Modernism: Pulps, Paperbacks and the Prejudice of Form* (2009).
Marek, Jayne. *Women Editing Modernism: 'Little' Magazines and Literary History* (1995).
McKible, Adam. *The Space and Place of Modernism: The Russian Revolution, Little Magazines and New York* (2002).
Morrisson, Mark S. *The Public Face of Modernism: Little Magazines, Audiences and Reception, 1905–1920* (2001).
Rainey, Lawrence S. *Institutions of Modernism* (1998).
Southworth, Helen, ed. *Leonard and Virginia Woolf, The Hogarth Press and the Networks of Modernism* (2010).
White, Eric. *Transatlantic Avant-Gardes: Little Magazines and Localist Modernism* (2013).

## Chapter 3: Purposeful print

Ardis, Ann L. and Patrick Collier, eds. *Transatlantic Print Culture, 1880–1940: Emerging Media, Emerging Modernisms* (2008).
Chapman, Mary. *Making Noise, Making News: Suffrage Print Culture and US Modernism* (2015).
DiCenzo, Maria, Lucy Delap and Leila Ryan. *Feminist Media History: Suffrage, Periodicals and the Public Sphere* (2011).
Hammond, Mary. *Reading, Publishing and the Formation of Literary Taste in England, 1880–1914* (2006).
Hutchinson, George M. *The Harlem Renaissance in Black and White* (1995).
Marshik, Celia. *British Modernism and Censorship* (2006).
Nelson, Cary. *Repression and Recovery: Modern American Poetry and the Politics of Cultural Memory, 1910–1945* (1989).
Radway, Janice A. *A Feeling for Books. The Book-of-the-Month Club, Literary Taste, and Middle-Class Desire* (1997).
Schreiber, Rachel, ed. *Modern Print Activism in the United States* (2013).
Spoo, Robert. *Without Copyrights: Piracy, Publishing, and the Public Domain* (2013).

# WORKS CITED

Albertine, Susan. Introduction. Albertine xi–xxi.
Albertine, Susan, ed. *A Living of Words: American Women in Print Culture*. Knoxville: U of Tennessee P, 1995.
Altick, Richard D. *The Presence of the Past: Topics of the Day in the Victorian Novel*. Columbus: Ohio State UP, 1991.
Anderson, Elliott and Mary Kinzie. Prefatory Note. Anderson and Kinzie 3–5.
Anderson, Elliott and Mary Kinzie, eds. *The Little Magazine in America: A Modern Documentary History*. Yonkers, New York: Pushcart, 1978.
Ardis, Ann L. 'Making Middlebrow Culture, Making Middlebrow Literary Texts *Matter*: The *Crisis*, Easter 1912'. *Modernist Cultures* 6.1 (2011): 18–40.
Ardis, Ann L. 'Mediamorphosis: Print Culture and Transatlantic/Transnational Public Sphere(s)'. *Modernism/Modernity* 19.3 (2012): v–vii.
Ardis, Ann L. *Modernism and Cultural Conflict, 1880–1922*. Cambridge: Cambridge UP, 2002.
Ardis, Ann L. 'Staging the Public Sphere: Magazine Dialogism and the Prosthetics of Authorship at the Turn of the Twentieth Century'. Ardis and Collier 30–47.
Ardis, Ann L. and Patrick Collier. Introduction. Ardis and Collier 1–12.
Ardis, Ann L. and Patrick Collier, eds. *Transatlantic Print Culture, 1880–1940: Emerging Media, Emerging Modernisms*. Houndmills: Palgrave, 2008.
'Artist/Novelist'. *Moma.org*. Museum of Modern Art, New York, 2014. Web.
Artmonsky, Ruth and Brian Webb. *Enid Marx Design*. Woodbridge, Suffolk: Antique Collectors' Society, 2013.
Avery, Todd and Patrick Brantlinger. 'Reading and Modernism'. Bradshaw and Dettmar 243–61.
Aynsley, Jeremy. 'Fashioning Graphics in the 1920s: Typefaces, Magazines and Fashion'. Aynsley and Forde 37–55.
Aynsley, Jeremy and Kate Forde. Introduction. Aynsley and Forde 1–16.

Aynsley, Jeremy and Kate Forde, eds. *Design and the Modern Magazine*. Manchester: Manchester UP, 2007.

Baggett, Holly. 'The Trials of Margaret Anderson and Jane Heap'. Albertine 169–88.

Baines, Phil. *Penguin By Design. A Cover Story 1935–2005*. London: Penguin, 2005.

Banham, Rob. 'The Industrialization of the Book 1800–1970'. Eliot and Rose 273–90.

Barnes, James. *Free Trade in Books: A Study of the London Book Trade since 1800*. Oxford: Clarendon P, 1964.

Becnel, Kim. *The Rise of Corporate Publishing and Its Effects on Authorship in Early Twentieth-Century America*. New York: Routledge, 2008.

Bennett, David. 'Periodical Fragments and Organic Culture: Modernism, the Avant-Garde, and the Little Magazine'. *Contemporary Literature* 30.4 (Winter 1989): 480–502.

Benstock, Shari. *Women of the Left Bank: Paris 1900–1940*. Austin: U of Texas P, 1986.

Benton, Megan. '"Too Many Books": Book Ownership and Cultural Identity in the 1920s'. *American Quarterly* 49.2 (1997): 268–97.

Bergel, Giles. '*The Chap-Book* (1894–8)'. Brooker and Thacker 2: 154–75.

Berkey, James. 'Splendid Little Papers from the "Splendid Little War": Mapping Empire in the Soldier Newspapers of the Spanish-American War'. *Journal of Modern Periodical Studies* 3.2 (2012): 158–74.

Bibby, Michael. 'The Disinterested and Fine: New Negro Renaissance Poetry and the Racial Formation of Modernist Studies'. *Modernism/Modernity* 20.3 (2013): 485–501.

Biers, Kathleen. 'Djuna Barnes Makes a Specialty of Crime: Violence and the Visual in Her Early Journalism'. *Women's Experience of Modernity 1875–1945*. Ed. Ann L. Ardis and Leslie W. Lewis. Baltimore, MD: Johns Hopkins UP, 2003: 236–53.

Bilski, Emily D. *Berlin Metropolis: Jews and the New Culture, 1890–1918*. Berkeley: U of California P, 1999.

Binckes, Faith. *Modernism, Magazines, and the British Avant-garde: Reading* Rhythm, *1910–1914*. Oxford: Oxford UP, 2010.

Bingham, Adrian. *Family Newspapers? Sex, Private Life and the British Popular Press 1918–1978*. Oxford: Oxford UP, 2009.

Bingham, Adrian. *Gender, Modernity, and the Popular Press in Inter-War Britain*. Oxford: Clarendon, 2004.

Bingham, Adrian. '"Putting Literature out of Reach"? Reading Popular Newspapers in Mid-twentieth Century Britain'. *Evidence from the British Isles, c.1750–1950*. Vol. 2 of *The History of Reading*. Ed. Katie Halsey and W. R. Owens. London: Palgrave Macmillan, 2011.

Bishop, Edward. 'The "Garbled History" of the First Edition *Ulysses*'. *Joyce Studies Annual* 1998: 3–36.
Bishop, Edward. 'Re-covering *Ulysses*'. *Joyce Studies Annual* (1994): 22–55.
Bishop, Edward. 'The Sunwise Turn and the Social Space of the Bookshop'. Osborne 31–64.
Bixler, Paul. 'Little Magazine, What Now?' Kurowski 145–58.
Blair, Sara. 'Local Modernity, Global Modernism: Bloomsbury and the Places of the Literary'. *ELH* 71.3 (2004): 813–38.
Bluemel, Kristin. '"A Happy Heritage": Children's Poetry Books and the Twentieth-Century Wood Engraving Revival'. *The Lion and the Unicorn* 37.3 (2013). N. pag. Web.
Bluemel, Kristin. 'Rural Modernity and the Wood Engraving Revival in Interwar England'. *Modernist Cultures* 9.2 (2014): 233–59.
Bold, Christine, ed. *US Popular Print Culture 1860–1920*. Vol. 6 of *The Oxford History of Popular Print Culture*. Oxford: Oxford UP, 2012.
Bornstein, George. *Material Modernism: The Politics of the Page*. Cambridge: Cambridge UP, 2001.
Bornstein, George. 'What is the Text of a Poem by Yeats?' Bornstein and Williams 167–94.
Bornstein, George and Ralph G. Williams, eds. *Palimpsest: Editorial Theory in the Humanities*. Ann Arbor: U of Michigan P, 1993.
Bornstein, George and Theresa Tinkle, eds. *The Iconic Page in Manuscript, Print, and Digital Culture*. Ann Arbor: U of Michigan P, 1998.
Boyer, Paul S. *Purity in Print: Book Censorship in America from the Gilded Age to the Computer Age*. 2nd ed. Madison: U of Wisconsin P, 2002.
Bradley, Matthew and Juliet, eds. *Reading and the Victorians*. Farnham: Ashgate, 2015.
Bradshaw, David and Kevin J. H. Dettmar, eds. *A Companion to Modernist Literature and Culture*. Malden, MA: Blackwell, 2006.
Bradshaw, David and Rachel Potter, eds. *Prudes on the Prowl: Fiction and Obscenity in England, 1850 to the Present Day*. Oxford: Oxford UP, 2013.
Bradshaw, Tony. *The Bloomsbury Artists: Prints and Book Design*. Aldershot: Scolar P, 1999.
Bradshaw, Tony. 'Virginia Woolf and Book Design'. *The Edinburgh Companion to Virginia Woolf and the Arts*. Ed. Maggie Humm. Edinburgh: Edinburgh UP, 2010. 280–97.
Brake, Laurel. 'On Print Culture: The State We're In'. *Journal of Victorian Culture* 6 (2001): 125–36.
Brake, Laurel. *Print in Transition 1850–1910*. New York: Palgrave, 2001.

Brannon, Barbara A. 'Building a Database of American Women Booksellers'. *SHARP News* 7.4 (1998): 4–5.
Brannon, Barbara A. '"We Have Come to Stay": The Hampshire Bookshop and the Twentieth-Century Personal Bookshop'. Osborne 15–30.
Briggs, Julia. *Reading Virginia Woolf*. Edinburgh: Edinburgh UP, 2006.
Brinkman, Bartholomew. 'Making Modern *Poetry*: Format, Genre and the Invention of Imagism(e)'. *Journal of Modern Literature* 33.2 (Winter 2009): 20–40.
Brockington, Grace. *Above the Battlefield: Modernism and the Peace Movement in Britain, 1900–1918*. New Haven: Yale UP, 2010.
Brockington, Grace. 'The Omega and the End of Civilisation: Pacifism, Publishing, and Performance in the First World War'. Gerstein 60–69.
Broe, Mary Lynn. '"Yes, no, peut-être": Caresse Crosby after the Black Sun Set'. Albertine 207–27.
Brooker, Peter. General Introduction. Brooker et al. 1–21.
Brooker, Peter and Andrew Thacker. General Introduction. Brooker and Thacker 1: 1–26.
Brooker, Peter and Andrew Thacker, eds. *Britain and Ireland 1880–1955*. Vol. 1 of *The Oxford Critical and Cultural History of Modernist Magazines*. Oxford: Oxford UP, 2009.
Brooker, Peter and Andrew Thacker, eds. *North America 1894–1960*. Vol. 2 of *The Oxford Critical and Cultural History of Modernist Magazines*. Oxford: Oxford UP, 2012.
Brooker, Peter, Sascha Bru, Andrew Thacker and Christian Weikop, eds. *Europe 1880–1940*. Vol. 3 of *The Oxford Critical and Cultural History of Modernist Magazines*. Oxford: Oxford UP, 2013.
Brown, Bill. 'Introduction: Textual Materialism'. *PMLA* 125.1 (2010): 24–28.
Brown, Bill. 'Materialities of Modernism: Objects, Matter, Things'. *A Handbook of Modernism Studies*. Ed. Jean-Michel Rabaté. Chichester: Wiley-Blackwell, 2013: 281–95.
Brown, Kathryn. Introduction. *The Art Book Tradition in Twentieth-Century Europe*. Ed. Brown. Farnham: Ashgate 2013: 1–15.
Bru, Sascha. '"The Will to Style": The Dutch Contribution to the Avant-Garde: Leiden: *De Stijl* (1917–32), *Mécano* (1922–3); Amsterdam: *Wendingen* (1918–32), *iIo* (1927–9); and Groningen: *The Next Call* (1923–6)'. Brooker et al. 293–312.
Bryant, John. *The Fluid Text: A Theory of Revision and Editing for Book and Screen*. Ann Arbor: U of Michigan P, 2002.
Buck, Louisa. 'John Banting's Designs for the Hogarth Press'. *The Burlington Magazine* Feb. 1985: 88+.
Camboni, Marina, ed. *Networking Women: Subjects, Places, Links, Europe-America. Towards a Rewriting of Cultural History, 1890–1939*. Rome: Edizioni di Storia e Letteratura, 2004.

Cannadine, David. 'Growing Up with Penguin Books'. *Reading Penguin: A Critical Anthology*, Ed. William Wootten and George Donaldson. Newcastle: Cambridge Scholars, 2013: 91–110.
Carroll, Anne Elizabeth. *Word, Image, and the New Negro: Race and Identity in the Harlem Renaissance*. Bloomington: Indiana UP, 2005.
Carter, David. *Always Almost Modern: Australian Print Cultures and Modernity*. Melbourne: Australian Scholarly Publishing, 2013.
Carter, David. 'Modernity and the Gendering of Middlebrow Book Culture in Australia'. Macdonald 135–49.
Cave, Roderick. *The Private Press*. 1971. New York: Bowker, 1983.
Cendrars, Blaise. *Blaise Cendrars: Complete Poems*. Trans. Ron Padgett. Berkeley: U of California P, 1992.
Chambers, Matthew. *Modernism, Periodicals, and Cultural Poetics*. Houndmills: Palgrave, 2015.
Chapman, Mary. *Making Noise, Making News: Suffrage Print Culture and US Modernism*. New York: Oxford UP, 2015.
Christie, Alex, Andrew Pilsch, Shawna Ross and Katie Tanigawa. 'Manifesto of Modernist Digital Humanities'. *Shawnaross.com*, n.d. Web.
Churchill, Suzanne. *The Little Magazine* Others *and the Renovation of Modern American Poetry*. Farnham: Ashgate, 2006.
Churchill, Suzanne and Adam McKible, eds. *Little Magazines and Modernism: New Approaches*. Farnham: Ashgate, 2007.
Cianci, Giovannni. 'The New Critical Demotion of the Visual in Modernism'. *Modernism*. Ed. Astradur Eysteinsson and Vivian Liska. Vol. 1. Philadelphia: John Benjamins, 2007: 451–67.
Clarke, Bruce. 'Suffragism, Imagism, and the "Cosmic Poet": Scientism and Spirituality in *The Freewoman* and *The Egoist*'. Churchill and McKible 119–31.
Clay, Catherine. 'On not Forgetting "The Importance of Everything Else": Feminism, Modernism and *Time and Tide* (1920–1939)'. *Key Words* 8 (2009): 20–37.
Clay, Catherine. '"What we Might Expect – if the Highbrow Weeklies Advertized like the Patent Foods": *Time and Tide*, Advertising, and the "Battle of the Brows"'. *Modernist Cultures* 6.1 (2011): 60–95.
Clifford, John. *Graphic Icons: Visionaries Who Shaped Modern Graphic Design*. San Francisco: Peachpit, 2014.
Cohen, Debra Rae. 'Intermediality and the Problem of the *Listener*'. *Modernism/Modernity* 19.3 (2012): 569–92.
Cohen, Philip. *Devils and Angels: Textual Editing and Literary Theory*. Charlottesville: UP of Virginia, 1991.
Collier, Patrick. '*John O'London's Weekly* and the Modern Author'. Ardis and Collier 98–113.

Collier, Patrick. *Modern Print Artifacts: Textual Materiality and Literary Value in British Print Culture, 1890–1930s*. Edinburgh: Edinburgh UP. Forthcoming, 2016.

Collier, Patrick. *Modernism on Fleet Street*. Burlington: Ashgate, 2006.

Collier, Patrick. 'Virginia Woolf in the Pay of Booksellers: Commerce, Privacy, Professionalism, *Orlando*'. *Twentieth-Century Literature* 48.4 (Winter 2002): 363–92.

Collier, Patrick. 'What is Modern Periodical Studies?' *Journal of Modern Periodical Studies* 6.2 (2015): 92–111.

Collier, Patrick. 'Woolf Studies and Periodical Studies'. Dubino 151–65.

Collini, Stefan. '"The Chatto List": Publishing Literary Criticism In Mid-Twentieth-Century Britain'. *Review of English Studies* 63.261 (2012): 634–63.

Crosby, Caresse. *The Passionate Years*. Carbondale: Southern Illinois UP, 1953.

Cuddy-Keane, Melba. 'From Fan-Mail to Readers' Letters: Locating John Farrelly'. *Woolf Studies Annual* 11 (2005): 3–32.

Cuddy-Keane, Melba. *Virginia Woolf, the Intellectual, and the Public Sphere*. Cambridge: Cambridge UP, 2003.

Cullen, Darcy. 'Introduction: The Social Dynamics of Scholarly Editing'. *Editors, Scholars, and the Social Text*. Ed. Cullen. Toronto, ON: U of Toronto P, 2012. 3–32.

Cunard, Nancy. *These Were the Hours*. Carbondale: Southern Illinois UP, 1969.

Dane, Joseph A. *Blind Impressions: Methods and Mythologies in Book History*. Philadelphia: U of Pennsylvania P, 2013.

Dane, Joseph A. *The Myth of Print Culture: Essays on Evidence, Textuality, and Bibliographical Method*. Toronto, ON: U of Toronto P, 2003.

Dane, Joseph A. *Out of Sorts. On Typography and Print Culture*. Philadelphia: U of Pennsylvania P, 2011.

Danky, James P. and Wayne A. Wiegand, eds. *Print Culture in a Diverse America*. Champaign: U of Illinois P, 1998.

Darnton, Robert. *The Kiss of Lamourette: Reflections in Cultural History*. New York: Norton, 1990.

Daugherty, Beth Rigel. '"You See You Kind of Belong to Us, and What You Do Matters Enormously": Letters from Readers to Virginia Woolf'. *Woolf Studies Annual* 12 (2006): 1–12.

Davidson, Cathy N. 'Introduction: Toward a History of Books and Readers'. *Reading in America: Literature and Social History*. Ed. Davidson. Baltimore, MD: Johns Hopkins UP, 1989. 1–26.

Davidson, Michael. *Ghostlier Demarcations: Poetry and the Material Word*. Berkeley: U of California P, 1997.

Davis, Robert H., Jr. and Edward Kasinec. 'From Shelf to Spotlight: Rediscovering Modernist Books from Eastern Europe at the New York Public Library'. *Graphic Modernism from the Baltic to the Balkans, 1910–1935*. Ed. S. A. Mansbach and Wojciech Jan Siemaskiewicz. New York: New York Public Library, 2007. 52–69.

de Grazia, Edward. *Girls Lean Back Everywhere. The Law of Obscenity And the Assault on Genius*. New York: Random House, 1992.

Dean, Gabrielle. 'Cover Story: *The Smart Set*'s Clever Packaging, 1908–1923'. *Journal of Modern Periodical Studies* 4.1 (2013): 1–29.

Delap, Lucy and Maria DiCenzo. 'Transatlantic Print Culture: The Anglo-American Feminist Press and Emerging "Modernities"'. Ardis and Collier 48–65.

Dennison, Sally. *Alternative Literary Publishing: Five Modern Histories*. Iowa City: U of Iowa P, 1984.

Derrida, Jacques. *Of Grammatology*. Trans. Gayatri Chakravorty Spivak. Baltimore, MD: Johns Hopkins UP, 1976.

Dettmar, Kevin and Stephen Watt. *Marketing Modernisms: Self-Promotion, Canonization, Rereading*. Ann Arbor: U of Michigan P, 1996.

DiCenzo, Maria, Lucy Delap and Leila Ryan. *Feminist Media History: Suffrage, Periodicals and the Public Sphere*. London: Palgrave Macmillan, 2011.

Drew, Ned and Paul Sternberger. *By Its Cover: Modern American Book Cover Design*. New York: Princeton Architectural P, 2005.

Drucker, Johanna. 'Performative Materiality and Theoretical Approaches to Interface'. *Digital Humanities Quarterly* 7.1 (2013): n. pag. Web.

Drucker, Johanna. *The Visible Word: Experimental Typography and Modern Art, 1909–1923*. Chicago: U of Chicago P, 1994.

Dubino, Jeanne, ed. *Virginia Woolf and the Literary Marketplace*. New York: Palgrave, 2010.

Duffy, Maureen. *A Thousand Capricious Chances: A History of the Methuen List 1889–1989*. London: Methuen, 1989.

Earle, David M. *Re-Covering Modernism: Pulps, Paperbacks and the Prejudice of Form*. Burlington: Ashgate, 2009.

Edwards, Brent Hayes. *The Practice of Diaspora: Literature, Translation, and the Rise of Black Internationalism*. Cambridge: Harvard UP, 2003.

Eliot, Simon. 'A Prehistory for Penguin Books'. *Reading Penguin: A Critical Anthology*. Ed. William Wootten and George Donaldson. Newcastle: Cambridge Scholars, 2013. 1–26.

Eliot, Simon. *Some Patterns and Trends in British Publishing, 1800–1919*. London: Bibliographical Society, 1993.

Eliot, Simon and Jonathan Rose, eds. *A Companion to the History of the Book*. Oxford: Blackwell, 2007.

Eliot, Simon, Andrew Nash and Ian Willison. Introduction. Eliot, Nash and Willison 1–30.

Eliot, Simon, Andrew Nash and Ian Willison, eds. *Literary Cultures and the Material Book*. London: British Library, 2007.

Eliot, T. S. 'The Idea of a Literary Review'. *The New Criterion* 4.1 (1926): 1–6.

Eliot, T. S. 'Last Words'. *Criterion* 18 January 1939: 271.

Eliot, T. S. *The Letters of T. S. Eliot Vol. 1: 1898–1922*. Ed. Valerie Eliot. San Diego: Harcourt Brace, 1988.

Eliot, T. S. *The Letters of T. S. Eliot Vol. 2: 1923–1925*. Ed. Valerie Eliot and Hugh Haughton. London: Faber and Faber, 2009.

Epp, Michael. 'Full Contact: Robert McAlmon, Gertrude Stein, and Modernist Book Making'. *Papers of the Bibliographical Society of America* 99.2 (2005): 265–93.

Farebrother, Rachel. '*The Crisis* (1910–34)'. Brooker and Thacker 2: 103–24.

Felsenstein, Frank and James J. Connolly. *What Middletown Read: Print Culture in a Small American City*. Amherst: U of Massachusetts P, 2015.

Finkelstein, David. 'The Globalization of the Book 1800–1970'. Eliot and Rose 329–40.

Finkelstein, David and Alistair McCleery, eds. *Professionalism and Diversity, 1880–2000*. Vol. 4 of *The Edinburgh History of the Book in Scotland*. Edinburgh: Edinburgh UP, 2007.

Fitch, Noel Riley. 'Sylvia Beach: Commerce, Sanctification, and Art on the Left Bank'. Albertine 189–206.

Flam, Jack. 'Menu du Jour: Word and Image in Cubist Painting'. *Cubism: The Leonard A. Lauder Collection*. Ed. Emily Braun and Rebecca Rabinow. New York: Metropolitan Museum of Art, 2014. 136–46.

Fleischer, Georgette. 'Djuna Barnes and T. S. Eliot: The Politics and Poetics of *Nightwood*'. *Studies in the Novel* 30.3 (1998): 405–37.

Foley, Barbara. 'Questionnaire Responses'. *Modernism/modernity* 20.3 (2013): 439–41.

Ford, Hugh. *Published in Paris*. New York: Pushcart, 1975.

Ford, Karen Jackson. 'Making Poetry Pay: The Commodification of Langston Hughes'. Dettmar and Watt 275–96.

Fraser, Robert and Mary Hammond, eds. *The Cross-National Dimension in Print Culture*. Vol. 1 of *Books Without Borders*. Houndmills: Palgrave Macmillan, 2008.

Fry, Roger. 'Book Illustration and a Modern Example'. *Transformations: Critical and Speculative Essays on Art*. New York: Brentano's, 1927. 157–72.

Garber, Marjorie. *Patronizing the Arts*. Princeton: Princeton UP, 2008.
Garcia, Claire Oberon. 'Black Women Writers, Modernism, and Paris'. *International Journal of Francophone Studies* 14.1/2 (2011): 27–42.
Garrity, Jane. 'Selling Culture to the "Civilized": Bloomsbury, British *Vogue* and the Marketing of National Identity'. *Modernism/Modernity* 6.2 (1999): 29–58.
Gerstein, Alexandra, ed. *Beyond Bloomsbury: Designs of the Omega Workshops 1913–19*. London: Courtauld Gallery/Fontanka, 2009.
Gertzman, Jay A. *Bookleggers and Smuthhounds: The Trade in Erotica, 1920–1940*. Philadelphia: U of Pennsylvania P, 1999.
Gertzman, Jay A. *Samuel Roth, Infamous Modernist*. Gainesville: UP of Florida, 2013.
Gifford, James. *Personal Modernisms: Anarchist Networks and the Later Avant-gardes*. Edmonton: U of Alberta P, 2014.
Gillespie, Diane F. ' "Woolfs" in Sheep's Clothing: The Hogarth Press and "Religion" '. Southworth 74–99.
Gillespie, Diane F. *The Sisters' Arts: The Writing and Painting of Virginia Woolf and Vanessa Bell*. Syracuse: Syracuse UP, 1988.
Glass, Loren. *Authors Inc.: Literary Celebrity in the Modern United States, 1880–1980*. New York: New York UP, 2004.
Glass, Loren. 'Redeeming Value: Obscenity and Anglo-American Modernism'. *Critical Inquiry* 32.2 (2006): 341–61.
Gluck, Mary. *Popular Bohemia: Modernism and Urban Culture in Nineteenth-Century Paris*. Cambridge, MA: Harvard UP, 2005.
Goeser, Caroline. *Picturing the New Negro: Harlem Renaissance Print Culture and Modern Black Identity*. Lawrence: UP of Kansas, 2007.
Golden, Amanda. *Annotating Modernism: Marginalia and Pedagogy from Virginia Woolf to the Confessional Poets*. New York: Routledge. Forthcoming.
Golding, Alan C. 'The *Dial*, The *Little Review* and the Dialogics of Modernism'. *American Periodicals* 15.1 (2005): 42–55.
Goldman, Jonathan. *Modernism is the Literature of Celebrity*. Austin: U of Texas P, 2011.
Gordon, Elizabeth Willson. 'How Should One Sell a Book? Production Methods, Material Objects and Marketing at the Hogarth Press.' *International Influence and Politics*. Vol. 2 of *Virginia Woolf's Bloomsbury*. Ed. Lisa Shahriari and Gina Potts. Houndmills: Palgrave Macmillan, 2010: 107–23.
Gordon, Elizabeth Willson. 'On or About December 1928 the Hogarth Press Changed: E. McKnight Kauffer, Art, Markets and the Hogarth Press 1928–39'. Southworth 179–205.
Grant, Joy. *Harold Monro and the Poetry Bookshop*. Berkeley: U of California P, 1967.

Green, Barbara. 'Complaints of Everyday Life: Feminist Periodical Culture and Correspondence Columns in the *Woman Worker*, *Women Folk*, and the *Freewoman*'. *Modernism/Modernity* 19.3 (2012): 461–85.
Green, Barbara. 'Feminist Things'. Ardis and Collier 66–79.
Green, Fiona, ed. *Writing for* The New Yorker: *Critical Essays on an American Periodical*. Edinburgh: Edinburgh UP, 2015.
Groden, Michael. 'James Joyce's *Ulysses* on the Page and on the Screen'. Stoicheff and Taylor 159–75.
Gupta, Suman. 'In Search of Genius: T. S. Eliot as Publisher'. *Journal of Modern Literature* 27.1/2 (2003): 26–35.
Hage, Emily. 'The Magazine as Readymade: *New York Dada* and the Transgression of Genre and Gender Boundaries'. *Journal of Modern Periodical Studies* 3.2 (2012): 175–97.
Hamilton, Sharon. 'American Manners: *The Smart Set* (1900–29); *American Parade* (1926)'. Brooker and Thacker 2: 224–48.
Hamilton, Sharon. 'The *PMLA* and the Backstory to Making Poetry New'. *Journal of Modern Periodical Studies* 2.1 (2011): 54–85.
Hamilton, Susan. '"[T]o bind together in mutual helpfulness": Genre and/as Social Action in the Victorian Anti-Vivisection Press'. *Journal of Modern Periodical Studies* 6.2 (2015): 134–60.
Hammill, Faye. *Women, Celebrity, and Literary Culture Between the Wars*. Austin: U of Texas P, 2007.
Hammill, Faye and Michelle Smith. *Magazines, Travel, and Middlebrow Culture: Canadian Periodicals 1925–1960*. Liverpool: Liverpool UP, 2015.
Hammond, Mary. *Reading, Publishing and the Formation of Literary Taste in England, 1880–1914*. Farnham: Ashgate, 2006.
Harding, Jason. *The Criterion: Cultural Politics and Periodical Networks in Inter-War Britain*. Oxford: Oxford UP, 2002.
Harding, Jason, ed. *T. S. Eliot in Context*. Cambridge: Cambridge UP, 2011.
Harrison, Brian. 'Press and Pressure Group in Modern Britain'. *The Victorian Periodical Press: Samplings and Soundings*. Ed. Joanne Shattock and Michael Wolff. Toronto, ON: U of Toronto P, 1982. 261–95.
Harvey, Benjamin. 'Lightness Visible: An Appreciation of Bloomsbury's Books and Blocks'. *A Room of Their Own: The Bloomsbury Artists in American Collections*. Ed. Nancy E. Green and Christopher Reed. Ithaca: Herbert F. Johnson Museum of Art, 2008. 88–117.
Hasenbank, Andrea. 'Assembly Lines: Researching Radical Print Networks'. *English Studies in Canada* 41.2 (2015). Forthcoming.
Hayden, Sarah, Kerstin Fest, James Cummins, and Rachel Warriner. 'CFP: Etant-donnés: Questioning the Material and Marginal Givens

of Modernisms Scholarship'. Modernisms Research Centre, University College Cork, 2 January 2013. Web.
Heller, Steve. 'E. McKnight Kauffer'. *Aiga.org.* American Institute of Graphic Arts, 1992. Web.
Heller, Steven and Seymour Chwast. *Graphic Style. From Victorian to Post-Modern.* 1988. London: Thames and Hudson, 1994.
Henderson, Alice Corbin. 'A New School of Poetry'. *Poetry* (May 1916): 103–05. *MJP.*
Hewison, Robert. *Under Siege: Literary Life in London, 1939–1945.* Oxford: Oxford UP, 1977.
Hewitt, Martin. *The Dawn of the Cheap Press in Victorian Britain: The End of the 'Taxes on Knowledge', 1849–1869.* London: Bloomsbury Academic, 2013.
Hoffman, Frederick J., Charles Allen and Carolyn F. Ulrich. *The Little Magazine: A History and a Bibliography.* Princeton, NJ: Princeton UP, 1946.
Hogarth Press Catalogue, 1925. E. J. Pratt Memorial Library, Toronto. N. pag.
Hollis, Catherine W. 'Virginia Woolf's Double Signature'. *Woolf in the Real World: Selected Papers from the Thirteenth International Conference on Virginia Woolf.* Ed. Karen V. Kukil. Clemson: Clemson U Digital P, 2005. 18–23.
Honey, Maureen. 'Questionnaire Responses'. *Modernism/modernity* 20.3 (2013): 441–43.
Howarth, Peter. 'Georgian Poetry'. Harding 221–30.
Howsam, Leslie. *Old Books and New Histories: An Orientation to Studies in Book and Print Culture.* Toronto, ON: U of Toronto P, 2006.
Hubert, Renée and Judd D. Hubert. 'Reading Gertrude Stein in the Light of the Book Artists'. *Modernism/modernity* 10.4 (2003): 677–704.
Huculak, J. Matthew. 'Reading Forensically: Modernist Paper, Newfoundland, and Trans-Atlantic Materiality'. *Journal of Modern Periodical Studies* 6.2 (2015): 161–90.
Humble, Nicola. 'Sitting Forward or Sitting Back: Highbrow v. Middlebrow Reading'. *Modernist Cultures* 6.1 (2011): 41–59.
Hussey, Mark. 'How Should One Read a Screen?' *Virginia Woolf in the Age of Mechanical Reproduction.* Ed. Pamela L. Caughie. New York: Garland, 2000. 249–65.
Hutchinson, George M. *The Harlem Renaissance in Black and White.* Cambridge, MA: Harvard UP, 1995.
Hutchinson, George M. Introduction. *The Cambridge Companion to the Harlem Renaissance.* Ed. Hutchinson. Cambridge: Cambridge UP, 2007. 1–10.

Huyssen, Andreas. *After the Great Divide: Modernism, Mass Culture, Postmodernism*. Bloomington: Indiana UP, 1986.

Irvine, Dean. *Editing Modernity: Women and Little-Magazine Cultures in Canada, 1916–1956*. Toronto, ON: U of Toronto P, 2007.

Jackson, H. J. *Marginalia: Readers Writing in Books*. New Haven, CT: Yale UP, 2001.

Jackson, H. J. *Romantic Readers: Evidence from Marginalia*. New Haven, CT: Yale UP, 2005.

Jaffe, Aaron. *Modernism and the Culture of Celebrity*. Cambridge: Cambridge UP, 2005.

Jaffe, Aaron and Jonathan Goldman, eds. *Modernist Star Maps: Celebrity, Modernity, Culture*. Farnham: Ashgate, 2010.

Jaillant, Lise. *Modernism, Middlebrow and the Literary Canon in the Modern Library Series, 1917–1955*. London: Pickering & Chatto, 2014.

Jaillant, Lise. 'Sapper, Hodder & Stoughton and the Popular Literature of the Great War'. *Book History* 14 (2011): 137–66.

Johanningsmeier, Charles. 'Understanding Readers of Fiction in American Periodicals, 1880–1914'. Bold 591–609.

Johnson, Abby Arthur and Ronald Maberry Johnson. *Propaganda and Aesthetics: The Literary Politics of African-American Magazines in the Twentieth Century*. Amherst: U of Massachusetts P, 1991.

Joost, Nicholas. *Schofield Thayer and "The Dial": An Illustrated History*. Carbondale: Southern Illinois UP, 1964.

Jupp, James. *The Radical Left in Britain 1931–1941*. 1982. London: Taylor and Francis e-library, 2005. Web.

Keating, Peter. *The Haunted Study: A Social History of the English Novel 1875–1914*. London: Secker & Warburg, 1989.

Kenner, Hugh. *The Mechanic Muse*. New York: Oxford UP, 1987.

Keyser, Catherine. 'The Butter Printer: U.S. Middlebrow Periodicals, Mass Production, and Taste Anxiety'. *Journal of Modern Periodical Studies* 3.2 (2012): 136–57.

Keyser, Catherine. *Playing Smart: New York Women Writers and Modern Magazine Culture*. New Brunswick: Rutgers UP, 2010.

Kirschenbaum, Matthew G. *Mechanisms: New Media and the Forensic Imagination*. Boston, MA: MIT P, 2008.

Kurowski, Travis, ed. *Paper Dreams. Writers and Editors on the American Literary Magazine*. Madison, NJ: Atticus, 2013.

Lang, Anouk. 'TEI and the Bigger Picture: An Interview with Julia Flanders'. Blog. 23 August 2010. Web.

Latham, Sean. *The Art of Scandal: Modernism, Libel Law, and the Roman à Clef*. New York: Oxford UP, 2009.

Latham, Sean. 'The Mess and Muddle of Modernism: The Modernist Journals Project and Modern Periodical Studies'. *Tulsa Studies in Women's Literature* 30.2 (2011): 407–28.

Latham, Sean. '"*New Age*" Scholarship: The Work of Criticism in the Age of Digital Reproduction'. *New Literary History* 35.3 (2004): 411–26.
Latham, Sean and Gayle Rogers. *Modernism: History of an Idea*. London: Bloomsbury Academic. Forthcoming.
Latham, Sean and Robert Scholes. 'The Rise of Periodical Studies'. *PMLA* 121.2 (2006): 517–31.
Leavis, Q. D. *Fiction and the Reading Public*. 1932. New York: Russell & Russell, 1965.
Leick, Karen. 'Popular Modernism: Little Magazines and the American Daily Press'. *PMLA* 123.1 (2008): 125–39.
Lerer, Seth. 'Epilogue: Falling Asleep Over the History of the Book'. *PMLA* 121.1 (2006): 229–34.
Lowell, Amy. 'The Poetry Bookshop'. *The Little Review* May 1915: 19–22. *MJP*.
Luckhurst, Nicola. *Bloomsbury in Vogue*. London: Cecil Woolf, 1998.
Lupack, Barbara Tepa, with Alan Lupack. *Illustrating Camelot*. Cambridge: D. S. Brewer, 2008.
Lupton, Ellen and Elaine Lustig Cohen. *Letters from the Avant-Garde: Modern Graphic Design*. New York: Princeton Architectural P, 1996.
Lutes, Jean M. 'Newspapers'. Bold 97–112.
Lutz, Tom. *Cosmopolitan Vistas: American Regionalism and Literary Value*. Ithaca, NY: Cornell UP, 2004.
Lyall, Mary Mills and Earl Harvey Lyall. *The Cubies' ABC*. New York: G. P. Putnam's Sons, 1913. N. pag. Web.
Macdonald, Kate, ed. *The Masculine Middlebrow, 1880–1950: What Mr Miniver Read*. Houndmills: Palgrave, 2011.
MacLeod, Kirsten. *American Little Magazines of the 1890s: A Revolution in Print*. Sunderland: Bibelot P, 2013.
MacLeod, Kirsten. 'The Fine Art of Cheap Print: Turn-of-the-Century American Little Magazines'. Ardis and Collier 182–98.
Mahood, Aurelea. 'Fashioning Readers: The *Avant Garde* and British *Vogue*, 1920–9'. *Women: A Cultural Review* 13.1 (2002). Web.
Mao, Douglas. *Solid Objects. Modernism and the Test of Production*. Princeton, NJ: Princeton UP, 1998.
Mao, Douglas and Rebecca Walkowitz. 'The New Modernist Studies'. *PMLA* 123.3 (2008): 737–48.
MAPP. *Modernist Archives Publishing Project*, n.d. Web.
Mapp, Rennie. 'Olive Beaupré Miller's *My Book House*: From William Morris to Modernism Under One Roof'. *Modernism/Modernity* 19.3 (2012): 543–67.
Marcus, Laura. 'Virginia Woolf and the Hogarth Press'. Willison et al. 124–50.

Marcus, Laura. 'Virginia Woolf as Publisher and Editor'. *The Edinburgh Companion to Virginia Woolf and the Arts*. Ed. Maggie Humm. Edinburgh UP, 2010. 263–79.
Marek, Jayne. *Women Editing Modernism: 'Little' Magazines and Literary History*. Lexington: UP of Kentucky, 1995.
Marcus, Laura. 'Women Editors and Little Magazines in the Harlem Renaissance'. Churchill and McKible 105–18.
Marshik, Celia. *British Modernism and Censorship*. Cambridge: Cambridge UP, 2006.
Marshik, Celia. 'Thinking Back Through Copyright: Individual Rights and Collective Life in Virginia Woolf's Nonfiction' Saint-Amour 65–86.
McAleer, Joseph. *Popular Reading and Publishing in Britain 1914–1950*. Oxford: Clarendon P, 1992.
McDonald, Gail. *Learning to be Modern: Pound, Eliot, and the American University*. Oxford: Clarendon, 1993.
McDonald, Peter D. 'Ideas of the Book and Histories of Literature: After Theory?' *PMLA* 121.1 (2006): 214–28.
McDonald, Peter D. 'Modernist Publishing: "Nomads and Mapmakers"'. *A Concise Companion to Modernism*. Ed. David Bradshaw. Malden, MA: Blackwell, 2003. 221–42.
McGann, Jerome. *Black Riders: The Visible Language of Modernism*. Princeton, NJ: Princeton UP, 1993.
McGann, Jerome. *The Textual Condition*. Princeton, NJ: Princeton UP, 1991.
McGill, Meredith. 'Copyright and Intellectual Property: The State of the Discipline'. *Book History* 16 (2013): 387–427.
McGinn, Emily, Amy Leggette, Matthew Hannah and Paul Bellew. 'Comparing Marks: A Versioning Edition of Virginia Woolf's "The Mark on the Wall."' *Scholarly Editing* 35 (2014). Web.
McGregor, Hannah. 'Remediation as Reading: Digitising *The Western Home Monthly*'. *Archives and Manuscripts* 20.10 (2014): 1–10.
McKible, Adam. 'Our (?) Country: Mapping "These 'Colored' United States" in *The Messenger*'. Vogel 123–39.
McKible, Adam. *The Space and Place of Modernism: The Russian Revolution, Little Magazines and New York*. New York: Routledge, 2002.
McKible, Adam and Suzanne W. Churchill. 'Introduction. In Conversation: The Harlem Renaissance and the New Modernist Studies'. *Modernism/modernity* 20.3 (2013): 427–31.
McLean, Ruari. *Jan Tschichold: Typographer*. New York: David R. Godine, 1975.
McTaggart, Ursula. 'Opening the Door: The Hogarth Press as Virginia Woolf's Outsiders' Society'. *Tulsa Studies in Women's Literature*. 29.1 (Spring 2010): 63–81.

Menkes, Richard. *Telegraphic Realism: Victorian Fiction and Other Information Systems*. Stanford, CA: Stanford UP, 2008.
Miller, Cristanne. *Cultures of Modernism: Marianne Moore, Mina Loy, and Else Lasker-Schüler*. Ann Arbor: U of Michigan P, 2005.
Miller, Elizabeth Carolyn. *Slow Print: Literary Radicalism and Late Victorian Print Culture*. Stanford, CA: Stanford UP, 2013.
Miller, Elizabeth Carolyn. 'William Morris, Print Culture, and the Politics of Aestheticism'. *Modernism /Modernity* 15.3 (2008). 477–502.
Miller, Nina. *Making Love Modern: The Intimate Public Worlds of New York's Literary Women*. Oxford: Oxford UP, 1998.
Monroe, Harriet. 'The Motive of the Magazine'. *Poetry* 1.1 (1912): 26–28. *MJP*.
Moody, A. David. *Ezra Pound: Poet. Vol. 1: The Young Genius, 1885–1920*. Oxford: Oxford UP, 2009.
Morrisson, Mark S. *The Public Face of Modernism: Little Magazines, Audiences and Reception, 1905–1920*. Madison: U of Wisconsin P, 2001.
Morrisson, Mark S. 'Publishing'. Bradshaw and Dettmar 133–42.
Munson, Gorham. *The Awakening Twenties: A Memoir-History of a Literary Period*. Baton Rouge: Louisiana State UP, 1985.
Murphet, Julian. *Multimedia Modernism: Literature and the Anglo-American Avant-garde*. Cambridge: Cambridge UP, 2009.
Murphy, J. Stephen. 'Introduction: Visualizing Periodical Networks'. *Journal of Modern Periodical Studies* 5.1 (2014): iii–xv.
Murphy, Michael. '"One Hundred per Cent Bohemia": Pop Decadence and the Aestheticization of Commodity in the Rise of the Slicks'. Dettmar and Watt 61–89.
Murray, Simone. 'The Cuala Press: Women, Publishing, and the Conflicted Genealogies of "Feminist Publishing"'. *Women's Studies International Forum* 27.5/6 (2004): 489–506.
Mussell, James. 'In Our Last'. *Victorian Periodicals Review*. 'Repetition: Or, "In Our Last"'. *Victorian Periodicals Review* 48.3 (2015): 343–58.
Mussell, James. 'The Matter with Media'. What is a Journal? Towards a Theory of Periodical Studies. MLA Annual Convention. Westin, Boston. 4 January 2013. Web.
Nadell, Martha Jane. '"Devoted to Younger Negro Artists": *Fire!!* (1926) and *Harlem* (1928)'. Brooker and Thacker 2: 801–24.
Nadell, Martha Jane. *Enter the New Negroes: Images of Race in American Culture*. Cambridge: Harvard UP, 2004.
Nash, Andrew. 'Literary Culture and Literary Publishing in Inter-War Britain'. Eliot, Nash and Willison 323–42.
Nelson, Cary. 'Politics and Labor in the Poetry of the Fin de Siècle and Beyond: Fragments of an Unwritable History'. *Modernism Inc.* Ed.

Jani Scandura and Michael Thurston. New York: New York UP, 2001. 269–88.

Nelson, Cary. *Repression and Recovery: Modern American Poetry and the Politics of Cultural Memory, 1910–1945*. Madison: U of Wisconsin P, 1989.

Newcomb, John Timberman. '*Poetry*'s Opening Door: Harriet Monroe and American Modernism'. Churchill and McKible 85–103.

Nin, Anais. *The Journals of Anais Nin. Vol. 3 1939–1944*. London: Quartet, 1974.

Noland, Carrie. *Voices of Negritude in Modernist Print: Aesthetic Subjectivity, Diaspora, and the Lyric Regime*. New York: Columbia UP, 2015.

North, Michael. *Reading 1922: A Return to the Scene of the Modern*. Oxford: Oxford UP, 1999.

Ohmann, Richard. *Selling Culture: Magazines, Markets, and Class at the Turn of the Century*. New York: Verso, 1996.

Osborne, Huw, ed. *The Rise of the Modernist Bookshop: Books and the Commerce of Culture in the Twentieth Century*. Farnham: Ashgate, 2015.

Paley, Nicholas. 'Experiments in Picture Book Design: Modern Artists Who Made Books for Children 1900–1985'. *Children's Literature Association Quarterly* 16.4 (Winter 1991): 264–69.

Pankow, David. *Tempting the Palette: A Survey of Color Printing Processes*. 1997. Rochester: Rochester Institute of Technology, 2005.

Parisi, Joseph. 'The Care and Funding of Pegasus'. Anderson and Kinzie 216–35.

Porter, David. *Virginia Woolf and the Hogarth Press: Riding a Great Horse*. London: Cecil Woolf, 2004.

Porter, David. ' "We All Sit on the Edge of Stools and Crack Jokes": Virginia Woolf and the Hogarth Press'. *Book Illustrated: Text, Image, and Culture 1770–1930*. Ed. Catherine J. Golden. New Castle, DE: Oak Knoll, 2001. 277–311.

Potter, Rachel. *Obscene Modernism: Literary Censorship and Experiment 1900–1940*. Oxford: Oxford UP, 2013.

Pound, Ezra. 'The Classics "Escape"'. *The Little Review* Mar. 1918: 32–34. *MJP*.

Pound, Ezra. 'Small Magazines'. *The English Journal* 19.9 (1930): 689–704.

Pound, Ezra. ' "The Sphere" and Reflections on Letter Press'. *New Age* 20 September 1917. *MJP*.

Pound, Ezra. ' "The Strand," or How the Thing May Be Done'. *New Age* 9 September 1917. *MJP*.

Pound, Ezra. '—? Versus Camouflage'. *New Age* 10 January 1918. *MJP*.

Powers, Alan. *Front Cover: Great Book Jackets and Cover Design*. London: Mitchell Beazley, 2001.

Price, Leah. *How To Do Things With Books in Victorian England.* Princeton, NJ: Princeton UP, 2013.
Price, Leah. 'Introduction: Reading Matter'. *PMLA* 121.1 (2006): 9–16.
Putnam, Lara. 'Provincializing Harlem: The "Negro Metropolis" as Northern Frontier of a Connected Caribbean'. *Modernism/Modernity* 20.3 (2013): 469–84.
Rabaté, Jean-Michel. *1913: The Cradle of Modernism.* Oxford: Blackwell, 2007.
Rabinowitz, Paula. *American Pulp: How Paperbacks Brought Modernism to Main Street.* Princeton, NJ: Princeton UP, 2014.
Radway, Janice A. *A Feeling for Books. The Book-of-the-Month Club, Literary Taste, and Middle-Class Desire.* Chapel Hill: U of N Carolina P, 1997.
Rainey, Lawrence S. *Institutions of Modernism: Literary Elites and Public Culture.* New Haven, CT: Yale UP, 1998.
Raizman, David. *History of Modern Design: Graphics and Products Since the Industrial Revolution.* London: Laurence King, 2003.
Ransom, Will. *Private Presses and their Books.* New York: Bowker, 1929.
Reed, Christopher. 'Design for (Queer) Living: Sexual Identity, Performance and Décor in British *Vogue*, 1922–26'. *GLQ* 12.3 (2006): 377–404.
Reed, Christopher, ed. *A Roger Fry Reader.* Chicago: U of Chicago P, 1996.
Reed, Christopher. 'A *Vogue* That Dare Not Speak its Name: Sexual Subculture during the Editorship of Dorothy Todd, 1922–26'. *Fashion Theory* 10.1–2 (2006): 39–72.
Reed, David. *The Popular Magazines in Britain and the United States of America 1880–1960.* Toronto, ON: U of Toronto P, 1997.
Reiman, Donald H. *Romantic Texts and Contexts.* Columbia: U of Missouri P, 1997.
Reiman, Donald H. 'Textual Criticism in Nineteenth-Century Studies'. *Nineteenth-Century Contexts* 11 (1987): 9–21.
Rhein, Donna E. *The Handprinted Books of Leonard and Virginia Woolf at the Hogarth Press, 1917–1932.* Ann Arbor: UMI Research Press, 1985.
Rifkind, Candida. 'Too Close to Home: Middlebrow Anti-Modernism and the Poetry of Edna Jaques'. *Journal of Canadian Studies* 39.1 (2005). 90–114.
Rittner, Leona, W. Scott Haine and Jeffrey H. Jackson, eds. *The Thinking Space: The Café as a Cultural Institution in Paris, Italy and Vienna.* Farnham: Ashgate, 2013.
Rodgers, Terence. 'The Right Book Club: Text Wars, Modernity and Cultural Politics in the Late Thirties'. *Literature and History* 12.2 (2003 Autumn): 1–15.

Rogers, Gayle. *Modernism and the New Spain: Britain, Cosmopolitan Europe, and Literary History*. New York: Oxford UP, 2012.

Rogers, Stephen. 'Bruno's Bohemia: *Greenwich Village* (1915); *Bruno's Chap Books* (1915–16); *Bruno's Weekly* (1915–16); *Bruno's* (1917); *Bruno's Bohemia* (1918); *Bruno's Review* (1919); *Bruno's Review of Two Worlds* (1920–2)'. Brooker and Thacker 2: 445–64.

Rose, Jonathan. 'The Horizon of a New Discipline: Inventing Book Studies'. *Publishing Research Quarterly* (2003): 11–19.

Rose, Jonathan. 'Marx, Jane Eyre, Tarzan: Miners' Libraries in South Wales 1923–52'. *Leipziger Jahrbuch zur Buchgeschichte* 4 (1994): 187–207. Rpt in *The History of the Book in the West: 1914–2000*. Ed. Alexis Weedon. Farnham: Ashgate, 2010. 331–51.

Rubery, Matthew. *The Novelty of Newspapers: Victorian Fiction After the Invention of the News*. Oxford: Oxford UP, 2009.

Rubin, Joan Shelley. *The Making of Middlebrow Culture*. Chapel Hill: U of North Carolina P, 1992.

Ryan, Barbara and Amy M. Thomas, eds. *Reading Acts: U. S. Readers' Interactions with Literature 1800–1950*. Knoxville: U of Tennessee P, 2002.

Saint-Amour, Paul K. *The Copywrights: Intellectual Property and the Literary Imagination*. Ithaca, NY: Cornell UP, 2003.

Saint-Amour, Paul K. ed. *Modernism and Copyright*. Oxford: Oxford UP, 2011.

Saler, Michael T. *The Avant-Garde in Interwar England: Medieval Modernism and the London Underground*. New York: Oxford UP, 1999.

Sangrey, Trevor Joy. 'Productive Fiction and Propaganda: The Development and Use of Communist Party Pamphlet Literature'. Schreiber 123–43.

Schaffner, Anna Katharina. 'How the Letters Learnt to Dance: On Language Dissection in Dadaist, Concrete and Digital Poetry'. *Avant-garde/Neo-avant-garde*. Ed. Dietrich Scheunemann. Amsterdam: Rodopi, 2005. 149–72.

Scholes, Robert and Clifford Wulfman. *Modernism in the Magazines: An Introduction*. New Haven, CT: Yale UP, 2010.

Schreiber, Rachel. Introduction. Schreiber 1–13.

Schreiber, Rachel, ed. *Modern Print Activism in the United States*. Burlington: Ashgate, 2013.

Schuchard, Ronald. 'American Publishers and the Transmission of T. S. Eliot's Prose: A Sociology of English and American Editions'. Willison, Gould and Chernaik 171–201.

Schwartzburg, Molly. 'The Door'. *The Greenwich Village Bookshop Door: A Portal to Bohemia 1920–1925*. Harry Ransom Center, University of Texas at Austin, 2007. Web.

Schwartzburg, Molly. 'Frank Shay's Greenwich Village: Reconstructing the Bookshop at 4 Christopher Street, 1920–1925'. Osborne 65–87.

Scott, Bonnie Kime. Introduction. *The Gender of Modernism*. Ed. Scott. 1–18.

Scott, Bonnie Kime, ed. *The Gender of Modernism. A Critical Anthology.* Bloomington: Indiana UP, 1990.

Scott, Bonnie Kime, ed. *Gender in Modernism: New Geographies, Complex Intersections.* Urbana: U of Illinois P, 2007.

Selborne, Joanna. *British Wood-Engraved Book Illustration 1904–1940: A Break with Tradition.* Oxford: Clarendon P, 1998.

Seshagiri, Urmila. 'Making It New: Persephone Books and the Modernist Project'. *Modern Fiction Studies* 59.2 (2013): 241–87.

Shloss, Carol Loeb. 'Privacy and the Misuse of Copyright: The Case of Shloss v. The Estate of James Joyce'. Saint-Amour 243–59.

Sigler, Amanda. 'Expanding Woolf's Gift Economy: Consumer Activity Meets Artistic Production in *The Dial*'. *Tulsa Studies in Women's Literature* 30.2 (2011): 317–42.

Silverman, Willa Z. *The New Bibliopolis: French Book Collectors and the Culture of Print, 1880–1914.* Toronto, ON: U of Toronto P, 2008.

Simpson, Lewis P. 'The *Southern Review* and a Post-Southern American Letters'. Anderson and Kinzie 78–99.

Snaith, Anna. 'The Hogarth Press and Networks of Anti-Colonialism'. Southworth 103–27.

Snaith, Anna. 'Wide Circles: The *Three Guineas* Letters'. *Woolf Studies Annual* 6 (2000): 1–10.

Sonstegard, Adam. ' "Singularly like a bad illustration": The Appearance of Henry James's "The Real Thing" in the Pot-Boiler Press'. *Texas Studies in Literature and Language.* 45.2 (2003): 173–200.

Sorensen, Jennifer J. *Modernist Experiments in Genre, Media, and Transatlantic Print Culture.* Farnham: Ashgate, 2016.

Southworth, Helen. 'The Bloomsbury Group and the Book Arts'. *The Cambridge Companion to the Bloomsbury Group.* Ed. Victoria Rosner. Cambridge: Cambridge UP, 2014. 144–61.

Southworth, Helen. Introduction. Southworth 1–27.

Southworth, Helen, ed. *Leonard and Virginia Woolf, The Hogarth Press and the Networks of Modernism.* Edinburgh: Edinburgh UP, 2010.

Spencer, Herbert. *Pioneers of Modern Typography.* London: Lund Humphries, 1969.

Sponenberg, Ashlie. 'Book Clubs'. *Encyclopedia of British Women's Writing, 1900–1950.* Ed. Faye Hammill, Esme Miskimmin, and Ashlie Sponenberg. 2006. Houndmills: Palgrave, 2009. 18–20.

Spoo, Robert. *Without Copyrights: Piracy, Publishing, and the Public Domain.* Oxford: Oxford UP, 2013.

Staveley, Alice. 'Marketing Virginia Woolf: Women, War and Public Relations in *Three Guineas*'. *Book History* 12 (2009): 295–339.
Steloff, Frances. 'In Touch with Genius'. *Journal of Modern Literature* 4.4 (1975): 749–827.
Stevenson, Iain. *Book Makers: British Publishing in the Twentieth Century*. London: British Library, 2010.
Stillinger, Jack. *Coleridge and Textual Instability: The Multiple Versions of the Major Poems*. New York: Oxford UP, 1994.
Stoicheff, Peter and Andrew Taylor. 'Introduction: Architectures, Ideologies, and Materials of the Page'. Stoicheff and Taylor 3–25.
Stoicheff, Peter and Andrew Taylor, eds. *The Future of the Page*. Toronto: U of Toronto P, 2004.
Straw, Will. 'Squawkies and Talkies'. *Parallax* 14.2 (2008): 20–30.
Tabatadze, Tea. 'The Kimerioni: A Modernist Café in Tbilisi (1919–1921)'. *Modernism/Modernity* 21.1 (2014): 307–17.
Thacker, Andrew. 'General Introduction: "Magazines, Magazines, Magazines!"' Brooker and Thacker 2: 1–39.
Thurston, Michael. '"Bombed in Spain": Langston Hughes, the Black Press, and the Spanish Civil War'. Vogel 140–58.
Tjora, Aksel and Graham Scambler, eds. *Café Society*. New York: Palgrave, 2013.
Towheed, Shafquat, Rosalind Crone and Katie Halsey. General Introduction. *The History of Reading: A Reader*. Ed. Towheed, Crone and Halsey. London: Routledge, 2011: 1–8.
Travis, Molly Abel. *Reading Cultures: The Construction of Readers in the Twentieth Century*. Carbondale: Southern Illinois UP, 1998.
Turner, Catherine. *Marketing Modernism Between the Two World Wars*. Amherst: U of Massachusetts P, 2003.
Turner, Mark. 'Periodical Time in the Nineteenth Century'. *Media History* 8 (2002): 183–96.
Twyman, Michael. *The British Library Guide to Printing: History and Techniques*. London: The British Library, 1998.
Twyman, Michael. *Printing: 1770–1970: An Illustrated History of its Development and Uses in England*. London: Eyre & Spottiswoode, 1970.
Unwin, Stanley. *The Truth About Publishing*. 1926. London: Allen & Unwin, 1960.
Viklund, Jon. 'Ambivalent Beginnings: Strindberg, the Artist's Book, and the Foundation of Swedish Material Modernism'. *Scandinavian Studies* 84.3 (2012): 299–322.
Vogel, Todd, ed. *The Black Press: New Literary and Historical Essays*. New Brunswick: Rutgers UP, 2001.
Vogel, Todd. Introduction. Vogel. 1–14.

Von Lintel, Amy M. 'Wood Engravings, the "Marvellous Spread of Illustrated Publications," and the History of Art'. *Modernism/Modernity* 19.3 (2012): 515–42.
Warren, Diana. *Djuna Barnes' Consuming Fictions*. Aldershot: Ashgate, 2008.
Welky, David. *Everything Was Better in America: Print Culture in the Great Depression*. Champaign: U of Illinois P, 2008.
Wellbery, David. Foreword. *Discourse Networks 1800/1900*. By Friedrich Kittler. Stanford, CA: Stanford UP, 1990.
West, M. Genevieve. *Zora Neale Hurston and American Literary Culture*. Gainesville: UP of Florida, 2005.
Westman, Karin E. 'Children's Literature and Modernism: The Space Between'. *Children's Literature Association Quarterly*. 32.4 (Winter 2007): 283–86.
Wetzsteon, Ross. *Republic of Dreams. Greenwich Village: The American Bohemia, 1910–1960*. New York: Simon & Schuster, 2002.
Wexler, Joyce Piell. *Who Paid for Modernism? Art, Money, and the Fiction of Conrad, Joyce, and Lawrence*. Fayetteville: U of Arkansas P, 1997.
White, Eric B. 'Continental Conjecture: Ephemera, Imitation and America's (late) Modernist Canons in the Three Mountains Press and Robert McAlmon's Contact Editions'. *European Journal of American Culture* 32.3 (2013): 285–306.
White, Eric B. *Transatlantic Avant-Gardes: Little Magazines and Localist Modernism*. Edinburgh: Edinburgh UP, 2013.
White, Peter. 'Literary Journalism'. Harding 93–104.
Whitworth, Michael H., ed. *Modernism*. Malden, MA: Blackwell, 2007.
Wicke, Jennifer. *Advertising Fictions: Literature, Advertisement, and Social Reading*. New York: Columbia UP, 1988.
Wild, Jonathan. '"Insects in Letters": *John O'London's Weekly* and the New Reading Public'. *Literature and History* 15.2 (2006): 50–62.
Wild, Jonathan. '"Watching the papers daily in fear and trembling": The Boer War and the Invention of Masculine Middlebrow Literary Culture'. Macdonald 56–72.
Willis, J. H. *Leonard and Virginia Woolf as Publishers*. Charlottesville: UP of Virginia, 1992.
Willison, Ian, Warwick Gould and Warren Chernaik, eds. *Modernist Writers and the Marketplace*. Houndmills: Macmillan, 1996.
Wilson, Nicola. '"Boots Book-lovers" Library and the Novel: The Impact of a Circulating Library Market on Twentieth-Century Fiction'. *Information and Culture: A Journal of History* 49.4 (2014): 427–49.
Wilson, Nicola. 'Circulating Morals (1900–1915)'. Bradshaw and Potter 52–70.

Wilson, Nicola. "Virginia Woolf, Hugh Walpole, the Hogarth Press and the Book Society." *English Literary History* 79.1 (2012): 237–60.

Wolff, Geoffrey. *Black Sun: The Brief Transit and Violent Eclipse of Harry Crosby*. New York: Random House, 1976.

Wollaeger, Mark. 'D. H. Lawrence and the Technological Image: Modernism, Reference and Abstraction in *Women in Love*'. *English Language Notes* 51.1 (2013): 75–92.

Wollaeger, Mark. *Modernism, Media, and Propaganda: British Narrative from 1900 to 1945*. Princeton, NJ: Princeton UP, 2006.

Woolf, Leonard. *An Autobiography Vol. 2: 1911–1969*. Oxford: Oxford UP, 1980.

Woolf, Leonard. 'On Advertising Books'. *Books and the Public*. London: Hogarth P, 1927. 48–52.

Woolf, Virginia. *The Diary of Virginia Woolf*. Vol. 2. Ed. Anne Olivier Bell. London: Hogarth P, 1978.

Woolf, Virginia. *The Letters of Virginia Woolf*. Vol. 2. Ed. Nigel Nicolson and Joanne Trautmann Banks. New York: Harcourt, 1976.

Wye, Deborah. *Artists and Prints: Masterworks from The Museum of Modern Art*. New York: The Museum of Modern Art, 2004. Web.

Young, John K. 'William Plomer, Transnational Modernism and the Hogarth Press'. Southworth 128–49.

Zackodnik, Teresa. 'Recirculation and Black Internationalism in Jessie Fauset's "The Looking Glass" and Amy Jacques Garvey's "Our Women and What They Think"'. *Modernism/modernity* 19.3 (2012): 437–59.

Zboray, Ronald J. and Mary Saracino Zboray. 'The Changing Face of Publishing'. Bold 23–42.

Zurier, Rebecca. *Art for* The Masses: *A Radical Magazine and Its Graphics, 1911–1917*. Philadelphia: Temple UP, 1988.

# INDEX

*Adelphi* 20, 100
advertising 70–1
  bibliophiles and 42
  competition between text and 81
  *The Crisis* and 158
  on dust jackets 10, 56
  as genre marker 28
  magazines and 20, 48, 78, 117–19, 121, 123, 173
  'Mrs Dalloway in Bond Street' and 174
  as new discursive practice 3
  role in modernist publishing 34, 83–4, 125
  typography and 73, 76
Albertine, Susan 88
Aldington, Richard 127, 167–8
Aldridge, John 55
Allen, Charles 18, 29–31, 88
Altick, Richard D. 115
Anderson, Benedict 137
Anderson, Elliott 8, 18–19, 116, 118
Anderson, Margaret 113, 165, 169
Anderson, Sherwood 84
annotations *see* marginalia
anthologies 58, 97–8, 123, 158, 176
  as 'annuals' 14
  magazine culture and 18
  modernist bookshops and 105
  recovery work and 135
  T. S. Eliot and 101–2
  version theory and 33, 46–7
anti-colonialism 131, 162
Apollinaire, Guillaume 60, 73–4
Aragon, Louis 55
Ardis, Ann 7–8, 21–2, 157–8, 171–2
  on print culture 5
Art Deco 56
*The Athenaeum* 20, 100–2
autonomy 54, 60, 134
avant-gardes 176
  in America 95–6
  commerce and 31, 34, 76, 129
  feminist press and 22
  as international movement 8–9
  modernist studies and 54
  *Poetry* and 93–4
  posters and 81–2
  as small press audience 110
  typography and 59, 73
  *see also* Constructivism; Cubism; Dada; Futurism; Vorticism
Avery, Todd 113
Aynsley, Jeremy 70–1, 77, 81

Baines, Phil 71, 125
Banting, John 64
Barnes, Djuna 13, 43, 100
  *Book of Repulsive Women* 55
  *Nightwood* 10

Beach, Sylvia 42, 109–10, 118, 165
Beardsley, Aubrey 79
Beaupré Miller, Olive 58
Becnel, Kim 141, 143
Bell, Vanessa 2, 54, 63–7
Benjamin, Walter,
 'The Work of Art in the Age of Mechanical Reproduction' 42, 51–2
Bennett, David 134
Benstock, Shari 88, 110
Benton, Megan 138–9
Bergel, Giles 14
Berkey, James 14
Berlant, Lauren 153
Bernard, Emile 58
Bewick, Thomas 61
Bibby, Michael 134, 154–5
bibliographic codes 32, 43–7, 53, 61–2, 94, 96
bibliography 4, 31, 89
Bilski, Emily 111
Binckes, Faith 79
Bingham, Adrian 13
Bird, William 43
Bishop, Edward (Ted) 42, 85, 104
Bixler, Paul 30
*Black and White* 80
Black Sun Press 27, 37, 55, 99–100, 118
Blair, Sara 88
*Blast* 14, 40, 96
Bloomsbury Group, the 64, 88, 113, 127
*Blue Mountain Project* 44
Bluemel, Kristen 61
Bonnard, Pierre 58
book clubs 11, 131, 134–5, 138–43, 149
book history 171, 173
 development of 3–4
 periodical studies and 12
print culture and 4–5, 24, 26, 31–3, 68
publishing and 89
readership profiles in 111, 115
theory and 38–9
*see also* advertising; bibliographic codes; censorship; circulation; copyright; design; fine printing; limited editions; marginalia; print culture studies; print technology; thing theory
bookshops 13, 48, 56, 90, 104–5, 107–11, 162
Bornstein, George 3, 28, 32, 46–7, 50–2, 67, 98–9
Bourdieu, Pierre 20
Bowen, Elizabeth 134
Bradshaw, Tony 64
Brake, Laurel 12–13
Brannon, Barbara A. 111
Brantlinger, Patrick 113
Braque, Georges 2
Breton, André,
 *Nadja* 55
Brinkman, Bartholomew 94
Brockington, Grace 63
Broe, Mary Lynn 99–100
Brooke, Rupert 111
Brooker, Peter 20, 48, 100, 120, 129
Brown, Bill 39
Brown, Kathryn 55–6
Bru, Sascha 9
Bruno, Guido 107
Buck, Louise 64
Bush, Ronald 34

cafés 110–11
Camboni, Maria 90
Carter, David 9, 148

Cendrars, Blaise 1–2, 176
  *La fin du monde* 55
censorship 162–4, 166–70
*Century Guild Hobby Horse* 20
Césaire, Aimé 40
Chagall, Marc 58
*The Chap-Book* 14–15
Chapman, Mary 151–3, 162
Chartier, Roger 41
children's literature 58–61, 67
Churchill, Suzanne W. 92–3, 95, 97, 100, 102, 154
Chwast, Seymour 71
Cianci, Giovanni 53
circulation 5, 10, 91, 119–20, 129
  *see also* bookshops; cafés; libraries
Clarke, Bruce 153
Clay, Catherine 22, 81
Clifford, John 77
*Close Up* 20
*Co. F. Enterprise* 14
Coady, Robert J. 97
Cohen, Debra Rae 139
collage 40, 43, 68, 76
Collier, Patrick 13, 22, 26, 31, 135, 147–8, 172–3
Collini, Stefan 146–7
Communist Party USA 132
Connolly, James J. 112–13
Constructivism 77
Contact 5, 10, 43, 118
contextual codes 47
copyright 11, 85, 131–2, 144, 164–6, 170
  The Chace International Copyright Act 163
  effect on publishing industry 7
  national frameworks of 8–9
*Cosmopolis* 2, 73
Crane, Hart 107
Crane, Stephen 13

Crevel, René,
  *Babylone* 55
*The Crisis* 56, 127, 154, 157–8
*The Criterion* 8, 20, 29, 91, 93, 100
Crosby, Caresse 27–8, 55, 99–100, 118
  *The Passionate Years* 37
Crosby, Harry 27–8, 55, 99
Cuala Press 10, 42, 47, 99, 117, 125–6
Cubism 40, 82, 173
Cuddy-Keane, Melba 113–14
Cullen, Darcy 89
cultural capital 18, 82–3, 103, 128–9
Cunard, Nancy 55, 88, 109, 118

Dada 14, 16, 28, 40, 59, 73, 76, 87, 97, 173
*Daily Herald* 82
Damas, Léon 40
Dane, Joseph 5, 50
Danky, James P. 135
Darnton, Robert 24
Daugherty, Beth Rigel 114
Davidson, Cathy N. 111–12
Davidson, Michael 40
Davis, Robert H. 54
De Stijl 59
Dean, Gabriella 85
deconstruction 40
Delap, Lucy 22, 137, 151, 173
Delaunay-Terk, Sonia 1–2, 67
Denis, Maurice 58
Derain, André 60
Derrida, Jacques 38–9
design 9–10
  history and theory of 70–1
*The Dial* 29, 87, 97, 117, 121–2, 174
DiCenzo, Maria 22, 137, 151, 173
Diepeveen, Leonard 60

digital humanities 44, 49, 170, 172, 175
'Manifesto of Modernist Digital Humanities' 40
digitization 53–4, 172
digital objects 44, 49–50
Douglas, Aaron 56, 159
Drew, Ned 71
Drucker, Johanna 49–50, 54, 62, 73, 76
Du Bois, W. E. B. 154
Duchamp, Marcel 55
Duffy, Maureen 144
Dufy, Raoul 58
dust jackets 54, 56, 64, 66, 68, 83–5, 125

Earle, David 18, 84–5, 123
Edwards, Brent Hayes 155–6
*The Egoist* 20, 29, 96–8, 113, 118
Eisenstein, Elizabeth 4
El Lissitzky,
*About Two Squares* 59
Eliot, Simon 3, 32, 125, 146
Eliot, T. S. 33, 91, 172
  book-copies and 50–1
  as editor 100–2, 113
  Harriet Monroe and 94, 97
  'Last Words' 29
  Marianne Moore and 46, 98–9
  masculinist modernism of 174
  New Criticism and 31
  on print culture 6
  role in institutionalizing modernist literature 24–5
  *The Waste Land* 10, 121
engraving 18, 60–3, 72
Epp, Michael 43–4
Ernst, Max 55
Erskine, John 140, 149

Faulkner, William 84
Felsenstein, Frank 112–13

feminism *see* women's movements
feminist criticism 27, 34, 38, 99, 101, 137, 149
  *see also* women's movements
fine printing 7, 10, 18, 43, 58, 60, 63
*Fire!!* 14, 155
First World War, the 30–1, 46, 53–4, 61, 95, 111, 156, 169
Fitzgerald, F. Scott 84
Flam, Jack 2
Fleischer, Georgette 101
Foley, Barbara 154
Ford, Hugh 88, 102, 117–18
Forde, Kate 70–1, 81
forensic materiality 49–50
formal materiality 49–50
Foucault, Michel 163–4
Fraser, Nancy 136
Fraser, Robert 9
*The Freewoman* 108, 151, 153
Fry, Roger 60–4
Futurism 40, 59, 73

Garber, Marjorie 117
Garland, Hamlin 6
Garrity, Jane 19, 127
Gertzman, Jay A. 164–6
Gill, Eric 60, 77
Gillespie, Diane 54, 64, 66–7, 162
Gluck, Mary 110
Goeser, Caroline 56, 158–9
Golden, Amanda 51
Golding, Alan 122
Goldman, Jonathan 128
*Good Housekeeping* 126, 133
Gordon, Elizabeth Willson 63, 68
Grant, Duncan 64
Grant, Joy 104
Green, Barbara 34, 37–8, 151–3
Green, Fiona 19
Gris, Juan 58

Gupta, Suman  101
Gutenberg, Johannes  5, 71

H. D.  33, 46, 97–8
Habermas, Jürgen  136, 158
Hage, Emily  16
Hamilton, Sharon  31, 122
Hammill, Faye  48–9, 128, 148
Hammond, Mary  9, 143–4
Harding, Jason  93, 100
Harlem Renaissance, the  136–7, 153–4, 156–9, 173, 175
  visual culture in  56
Harrison, Brian  135
Hartley, Marsden  16
Harvey, Benjamin  64, 67
Hasenbank, Andrea  160
Hassall, Joan  61
Haussman, Raoul  28
Heap, Jane  88, 113, 165, 169
Heller, Steven  71
Hemingway, Ernest  43
Henderson, Alice Corbin  94–6
Hewison, Robert  8
high modernism  7, 31, 43, 54, 85, 128
highbrow culture  12, 22, 112, 127, 138, 141, 146
Hoffman, Frederick J.  18, 29–31
Hogarth Press  10, 109, 142
  censorship and  167
  cover designs  2
  digital humanities approaches to  175
  in modernist publishing networks  88–90, 102–3, 115
  public political debate and  161–2
  scholarship on  33
  series published by  16–17
  typography and  28
  use by Leonard and Virginia Woolf  25
  visual artists and  55, 63–8
  *see also* Leonard Woolf; print culture studies; Virginia Woolf
Holliday, Robert Cortes  109
Hollis, Catherine  66
*Hound and Horn*  29
Hours Press  10, 55, 88, 109, 118
Howarth, Peter  101
Howsam, Leslie  4–5, 137
Hubert, Judd D.  58–9
Hubert, Renée Riese  58–9
Huculak, Matthew J.  49
Huebsch, B. W.  83–4, 164–5
Hughes, Langston  126, 156–7
Humble, Nicola  112, 146
Hurd, Clement  59
Hussey, Mark  42
Hutchinson, George  136, 154, 159
Huyssen, Andreas  31, 85

illustration  44, 55, 58–9, 78–80, 159, 175
Imagism  94–5
Irvine, Dean  9, 99

Jackson, H. J.  51
Jaffe, Aaron  128
Jaillant, Lise  85, 144–5
James, Henry  13, 27, 38
  'The Real Thing'  79–81
Jenison, Madge  104
Jepson, Edgar  96–7
Johanningsmeier, Charles  119
*John O'London's*  147–8
Johnson, Abby A.  155
Johnson, Ronald M.  155
Joyce, James  29, 34, 53, 83–4, 126, 168–70
  *Dubliners*  123, 167
  *A Portrait of the Artist as a Young Man*  6

*Ulysses* 26–7, 42–3, 85,
    109–10, 115, 163–6
Jupp, James 143

Kahnweiler, Daniel Henry 58, 60
Kasinec, Edward 54
Kauffer, E. McKnight
    68–70, 82–3
Kelmscott Press 28, 41, 61, 63,
    177 n.2
Kenner, Hugh 94
    *The Mechanic Muse* 26–7
Keynes, John Maynard 17
Keyser, Catherine 81, 127
Kimball, Hannibal 16
Kinzie, Mary 8, 18–19, 116, 118
Kirschenbaum, Matthew 49–50
Kittler, Friedrich 27
Kokoschka, Oskar 59
Kreymborg, Alfred 95–7, 105, 107
Kurowski, Travis 118

*Ladies' Home Journal* 133
Lascaux, Elie 58
Lasker-Schüler, Else 111
Latham, Sean 18, 23, 123, 136,
    167, 174
Lawrence, D. H. 29, 84, 168–9
    *Lady Chatterley's Lover* 163
    *Women in Love* 27
Leavis, Q. D. 26, 52, 108, 138
Léger, Fernand,
    *La fin du monde* 55
Leick, Karen 128
Lerer, Seth 32
Lewis, Wyndham 14, 26, 29
    'Cantleman's Spring-Mate' 169
*The Liberator* 87
libraries,
    in the 1890s 7
    book clubs and 142
    censorship and 168
    cloth binding and 64

as magazine archives 123
modernist networks
    and 103–4, 108
The New York Public
    Library 54
in print culture studies 32
readership research
    and 112, 114
serials preservation in 17
*Life and Letters* 20
limited editions 18, 37, 43, 59,
    98–9, 102
little magazines 116–17
    in the 1890s 7
    'American' literature and 95–7
    Ezra Pound on 29
    the Harlem Renaissance
        and 158
    international nature of 9
    in modernist studies 87
    network analysis and 88–9,
        92–3, 100
    and new verse 94
    online archives of 174
    political engagement
        of 133–4, 153–5
    popular audiences and 128
    in print culture studies 5
    resistance to consumer culture
        in 3, 8
    taxonomies of 19–23, 30–1
    *The Waste Land* and 121
    see also *Adelphi*; *The
        Athenaeum*; *Black and
        White*; *Century Guild Hobby
        Horse*; *The Chap-Book*;
        *Close Up*; *Cosmopolis*; *The
        Crisis*; *The Criterion*;
        *The Dial*; *The Egoist*;
        *Fire!!*; *Hound and Horn*;
        *John O'London's*; *The
        Liberator*; *Life and Letters*;
        *The London Mercury*; *The*

*Messenger; The New Age; The New Criterion; The New Freewoman; New York Dada; Others;* periodical studies; *This Quarter; Rhythm; S4N; The Seven Arts; The Smart Set; The Soil; Time and Tide; transition; Tyro; The Yellow Book*
*The Little Review* 5, 29, 87, 96–8, 121–2, 128, 169
Locke, Alain 154
*The London Mercury* 8
London Underground, the 67, 81–2, 176
Longus 58
Lowell, Amy 104
  *Some Imagist Poets* 14
Loy, Mina 102, 111
Luckhurst, Nicola 127
Lupton, Ellen 71
Lustig, Elaine 71
*Lustra* 41
Lutes, Jean M. 136
Lutz, Tom 9
Lyall, Earl Harvey 59
Lyall, Mary Mills 59

McAlmon, Robert 43
  *Contact* 97
McDonald, Gail 29, 31
McDonald, Peter M. 38–9, 41
McGann, Jerome 10, 47, 50, 53, 58
  *Black Riders* 40, 42–3, 45–6, 61–2
  *The Textual Condition* 32–3, 41, 45
  see also bibliographic codes
McGill, Meredith 131–2, 170
McKay, Claude,
  *Home to Harlem* 56–7
McKenzie, D. F. 41

McKible, Adam 87–8, 92–3, 154
MacLeod, Kirsten 24, 31, 71
Mallarmé, Stephane,
  *Un Coup de Dés Jamais N'Abolira Le Hasard* 2, 73
Mao, Douglas 27, 39
Mapp, Rennie 58
Marcus, Laura 27, 41
Marek, Jayne 29, 94–5, 113, 157
marginalia 32, 51, 101
Marinetti, Filippo Tommaso 73
Markham, Edwin 161
Marsden, Dora 97–8
Marshik, Celia 164, 166–7
Marx, Enid 67
Masereel, Frans 55
*The Mask* 20
mass-market publishing 16, 61, 113, 148–9
  as critical term 22–3
  limited editions as resistance to 18
  middlebrow publishers and 146
  as source of income 125–6
  as subsidy of art publishing 10–11
  see also popular print
*The Masses* 71, 105, 159
media history 137, 171–3
  see also book history; new media
'men of 1914' 27
*The Messenger* 87
middlebrow culture 11, 131–4, 139–41, 145–7
Miller, Cristanne 110–11
Miller, Elizabeth 168–9
Mirrlees, Hope,
  *Paris: A Poem* 28
Modern Library, the 85, 134, 145
Modernist Archives Publishing Project 103

*Modernist Journals Project* 14, 21, 44, 123, 174
modernist studies 7
  and book publishing 89
  expanding archives in 27, 68, 135
  materialist turn in 24, 28, 32, 37–9, 44, 172
  print culture in 5–6, 176
  racial formation of 134
  types of print culture in 11–24
Monro, Harold 104, 108
Monroe, Harriet 29, 93–5, 116, 118
Moore, Marianne 33, 46, 97–9, 102, 111
*Morada* 29
Moré, Gonzalo 28
Morris, William 28, 41, 58, 60–1, 63, 79
  'Some Thoughts on the Ornamented Manuscripts of the Middle Ages' 62
Morrisson, Mark 28, 42, 90, 102, 104, 108, 136
Mowbray-Clarke, Mary 105
Muir, Willa 17
Munson, Gorham 106–7
Murphet, Julian 39–40, 72, 76
Murphy, J. Stephen 92
Murray, Simone 99, 125–6
Murry, John Middleton 100
Mussell, James 11–12

Nadell, Martha 155
Nash, Andrew 26, 32
*The Nation* 100
Negritude 40, 156
Nelson, Cary 23, 150–1, 161
networks,
  in modernist print culture 5, 9–11, 33, 35, 88–9, 92, 114, 117
  of periodicals 93–7, 161
  of women 90, 98–100
  *see also* censorship; circulation; little magazines; small presses
*The New Age* 20–2, 25, 29, 166
*The New Criterion* 29
New Criticism 27, 31, 54, 98, 153–5, 174
*The New Freewoman* 41
new media 8, 27, 40, 139
New Negro, the 134, 156, 158
*New Numbers* 20
*New Verse* 8, 100
*New Writing* 8
*New York Dada* 14, 16
*New York Times Book Review* 128
*The New Yorker* 19, 81
Newcomb, John Timberman 92–3
Nicholls, Norah 115
Nin, Anaïs 28
Noland, Carrie 40, 156
North, Michael 78
Northcliffe, First Viscount 78

Ohmann, Richard 8, 78, 81, 125
Omega Workshops, the 62–3
Oppenheim, James 97
Ortega y Gasset, José 90–1
Osborne, Huw 105
*Others* 95–6, 100

page, history of 52
painting 2–3, 40, 55, 60–1, 72
Paley, Nicholas 59
Parisi, Joseph 116
pedagogy,
  cultural 145
  in the humanities 32, 174–5
Penguin Books 71, 77, 125, 145–6, 149
periodical codes 48–9
periodical studies 7, 12, 25, 33, 81, 92, 119–20, 157–8, 171–3

photography 40, 55, 72, 78–9
Picasso, Pablo 2, 58
Pick, Frank 81–2
Pinker, J. B. 120–1
Plomer, William 103
*Poetry* 29, 41, 93–6, 98, 116–17
popular print 13, 22, 37, 72–3, 78, 84, 108, 125, 128–9, 133
  *see also* mass-market publishing
Porter, David 64
Post-Impressionism 60–2, 105
posters 4, 11, 70
  archiving of 54
  *Blast* and 40
  as modernist print form 2–3, 38, 68, 81–3
  typography and 28, 73, 76
Potter, Rachel 169
Pound, Ezra 33, 43, 45–6, 92
  *The Cantos* 45
  *Catholic Poetry* 101
  as critic of American copyright laws 166
  Harriet Monroe and 93–4
  'In a Station of the Metro' 41, 94
  in magazines with large sales 126
  Marianne Moore and 98
  as masculinist modernist 34, 174
  on new American poetics 96
  New Criticism and 31
  the page and 40
  on print culture 6
  'Small Magazines' 29, 93
  'Studies in Contemporary Mentality' 25, 28–9
Powers, Alan 83
Price, Leah 38–9
print activism 132–3, 150–1
  aesthetic dimensions of 134–5
  black print culture and 153–60
  counterpublics and 135–8
  labour print culture and 161–2
  suffrage print culture and 151–3
print culture studies 17–18, 24–5, 37–9, 41, 44, 54, 68, 128–9, 171–4
  *see also* bibliography; book history; media history; periodical studies; version theory; visual culture studies
printing technology 9, 27, 42, 70–2
  modernist interest in 6
  nineteenth century innovations in 3
  printing manuals 76–7
  typewriters 27
propaganda 83, 132, 135, 154

*This Quarter* 29

Rabaté, Jean-Michel 2
Rabinowitz, Paula 18
Radway, Janice 112, 131, 135, 138–41, 146
Rainey, Lawrence 91
  *Institutions of Modernism* 3, 26–7, 34–5, 41–3, 92, 120–2, 127
Raverat, Gwen 61
Ray, Man 55, 107
readerships 8–9, 13, 20, 48, 97, 100, 112, 114–15, 147
Reed, Christopher 19, 127
Reiman, Donald H. 46
Renner, Paul 77
*Revista de Occidente* 89–90
Rhein, Donna E. 63
*Rhythm* 5, 79
Richards, I. A. 31
Riding, Laura,
  *The Life of the Dead* 55
Rodgers, Terence 143

Rodin, Auguste 58
Rogers, Gayle 90–1
Rose, Jonathan 3–4, 112
Roth, Samuel 164–6
Rouault, Georges 58
Rubin, Joan Shelley 135, 139–41, 146
Ryan, Barbara 112
Ryan, Leila 137

*S4N* 29
Saint-Amour, Paul 163–4
Saler, Michael T. 81–2
Sangrey, Trevor Joy 132
*Saturday Evening Post* 81, 106, 128
Scholes, Robert 21, 23, 25, 30–1, 48, 118–19, 126
Schreiber, Rachel 132–3
Schulze, Robin 97
Schwartzburg, Molly 106
Schwitters, Kurt 59
Scott, Bonnie Kime 34, 92
Second World War, the 7–8, 118
Selborne, Joanna 60–1, 63, 77
Seltzer, Thomas 84
Senghor, Léopold Sédar 40
Seshagiri, Urmila 149
*The Seven Arts* 97
Shakespeare & Company 109–10, 118
Shay, Frank 105–6
Silverman, Willa Z. 42
Simpson, Lewis P. 18
Simultanism 1–2
Sitwell, Edith 127
  *Wheels* 14–15
small presses 43, 102–3
  bookshops and 108
  critical interest in 10
  critical use of term 22–3
  development of movement 5, 8
  funding of 117
  international vision of modernism 9
  memoirs and 118
  networks among 88–9, 92–3
  political engagement of 133
  series and 16–17
  Sylvia Beach and 110
  transatlantic influences on 99
  *see also* circulation; Contact; Cuala Press; Black Sun Press; Hogarth Press; Hours Press; Three Mountains Press
*The Smart Set* 122–4, 126
Smith, Michelle 48–9, 148
Snaith, Anna 114, 162
socialism 22, 131, 136, 143, 156, 160
*The Soil* 97
Sonstegard, Adam 79–81
Sorensen, Jennifer 38, 64
Southworth, Helen 33, 66, 103, 175
Spanish Civil War, the 156–7
Spencer, Herbert 76
Staveley, Alice 115
Stein, Gertrude 2, 6, 29, 43, 45, 58–9, 127–8
Steinitz, Kate 59
Steloff, Frances 109
Sternberger, Paul 71
Stevens, Wallace 102
Stevenson, Iain 102
Stieglitz, Alfred 72
Stillinger, Jack 46
Stoicheff, Peter 52
Stone, Herbert 16
*The Strand* 28
Straw, Will 139
*Sun* 80

Tabatadze, Tea 110
Taylor, Andrew 52
textuality 4, 38, 45, 49–50

Thacker, Andrew  9, 20, 48, 91, 100, 106–7, 120, 126
thing theory  39
Thomas, Amy M.  112
Three Mountains Press  43, 118
Thurston, Michael  156–7
*Time and Tide*  22, 81
Tinkle, Teresa  47
*transition*  29, 134
Travis, Molly Abel  115
Tschichold, Jan  76–7
Turner, Catherine  83–4
Turner, Mark  17
Twyman, Michael  68
typography  44
*Tyro*  20
Tzara, Tristan  73
  'To Make a Dadaist Poem'  76

Ulrich, Carolyn F.  18, 29–31, 88

van Doesburg, Theo  59
van Rensselaer, Alexander  109
*Vanity Fair*  6, 121, 126–7, 176
Verlaine, Paul,
  *Parallèlement*  56
version theory  46
Victorian print culture  7, 12, 31, 115, 168, 172
Viklund, Jon  62
visual culture studies  31, 54, 173
Vogel, Todd  158
*Vogue*  19, 127
Vollard, Ambroise  58
Vorticism  40, 60–1

Walkowitz, Rebecca  27
Warner, Michael  136
Weaver, Harriet Shaw  98
Welky, David  149
Westman, Karin E.  58
Wexler, Joyce Piell  84, 120–1, 136

White, Eric B.  43, 95–7, 107
White, Walter,
  *Flight*  56
Whitworth, Michael H.  39
W. H. Smith's  143–4
Wicke, Jennifer  3
Wiegand, Wayne A.  135
Wild, Jonathan  147
Williams, Raymond  5
Williams, William Carlos  43, 96, 102
  *Contact*  97
Willis, J. H.  33, 68, 89
Willison, Ian  32
Wilson, Nicola  142, 168
Wollaeger, Mark  27, 83, 134–5
Woolf, Leonard  2, 63–4, 109
  on books as commodities  37
  censorship and  167
  involvement with periodical networks  161–2
  as publisher  16–17, 25, 33, 88–90, 102–3, 117
  *Quack, Quack!*  68
Woolf, Virginia  50–1, 63–4, 109
  aspirational periodicals and  148
  The Book Society and  142
  censorship and  167
  consumer culture and  174
  copyright and  164
  digital humanities approaches to  175
  in *Good Housekeeping*  126
  'The Patron and the Crocus'  113
  on print culture  6
  as publisher  16–17, 25, 33, 88–90, 102–3, 117
  readers' letters to  114
  'Reading'  41–2

as typographer 28
Vanessa Bell and 54, 64–7
women's movements 11, 34, 131,
  133, 136–7, 150–3
  black feminist modernism 156
Wright, Richard 134
Wulfman, Clifford 21, 23, 25,
  30–1, 48, 118–19, 126

Yeats, Elizabeth 99
Yeats, W. B. 33, 42, 45–7, 125–6
*The Yellow Book* 14
Young, Francis Brett 61
Young, John 103

Zdanevich, Ilia 73, 75–6
Zurier, Rebecca 71